"My mom made chicken soup for me to give me strength and encouragement to feel better. It made me feel warm inside. I know now that it was both the soup and my mom's love at work. And this is why *A 5th Portion of Chicken Soup for the Soul* will inspire every reader. Inside these pages, you will find strength, encouragement and love."

Jim Tunney
professional speaker and former NFL referee

"Another great batch of soul soup!"

Jeff Bridges
actor

"The *Chicken Soup for the Soul* series encourages us to create the best possible world imaginable."

LeVar Burton
actor/producer

"*A 5th Portion of Chicken Soup for the Soul* is a book the whole family can enjoy. The stories will challenge you, change you or just make you laugh. Read it all at once or a little at a time. It won't matter—it's good any way you can get it."

Porter Wagoner
Grand Ole Opry

"Time and time again *Chicken Soup* nourishes us with graceful accounts of the divine gift of love."

James Redfield
author of *The Celestine Prophecy* and *The Celestine Vision*

"There's always room for a little more *Chicken Soup*. On tour across America, I recently 'ate' my way through *A 3rd* and *4th Course of Chicken Soup.* They kept my heart on track every step of the way. Thank you for the soul food."

Kenny Loggins
singer, songwriter and coauthor of *The Unimaginable Life*

"The *Chicken Soup* series is so successful because every book gives us what we all want—happiness, hope, security, courage and inspiration. These books and stories touch our heart and bring out the very best of what it means to be a human being."

Dennis Wholey
host of the PBS series *This is America*
and author of *The Miracle of Change*

"The *Chicken Soup for the Soul* series will ignite your deepest passion for life in all its vibrant colors. The stories will touch your heart and fill your soul."

Cathy Lee Crosby
actress and author of *Let the Magic Begin*

"*Chicken Soup for the Soul* is a phenomenal series!"

Sidney Sheldon
bestselling author

"With great respect for all you have done to make America great Again! Thank you!"

Dick DeVos
president, Amway Corporation

"The *Chicken Soup for the Soul* series has been outstanding and an emotional lift for millions of people around the world causing us all to laugh and cry. Mark and Jack have also discovered the universal principle of sharing financial blessings with others by donating a portion of sales to worthy charities. I know you will enjoy these wonderful stories."

Barry Borthistle
president, Enrich North America
and International Ambassador

A 5th Portion of
CHICKEN SOUP
FOR THE SOUL®

101 *More* Stories to
Open the Heart and
Rekindle the Spirit

Jack Canfield
Mark Victor Hansen

Health Communications, Inc.
Deerfield Beach, Florida

www.hci-online.com

We would like to acknowledge the following publishers and individuals for permission to reprint the following material. (Note: The stories that are public domain, or that were written by Jack Canfield or Mark Victor Hansen are not included in this listing.)

The Seed Jar. Reprinted by permission of Dee Berry. ©1997 Dee Berry.

Mr. Gillespie. Reprinted by permission of Angela Sturgill. ©1997 Angela Sturgill.

Night Watch. Reprinted by permission of Roy Popkin. ©1964 Roy Popkin.

Turn Back. ©1992 Tom Clancy. Reprinted by agreement. Originally published in the *Baltimore Sun Magazine.* All rights reserved.

The Little Red Wagon. Reprinted by permission of Bonita L. Anticola. ©1997 Bonita L. Anticola.

John. Reprinted by permission of Terry O'Neal. ©1997 Terry O'Neal.

Does God Care About Lost Dogs? Reprinted by permission of Marion Bond West. ©1997 Marion Bond West.

(Continued on page 385)

Library of Congress Cataloging-in-Publication Data

A 5th portion of chicken soup for the soul : 101 more stories to open the heart and rekindle the spirit / [compiled by] Jack Canfield, Mark Victor Hansen.
    p.   cm.
   ISBN 1-55874-544-0 (hardcover). — ISBN 1-55874-543-2 (pbk.). —
ISBN 1-55874-545-9 (audio CD). — ISBN 1-55874-546-7 (audio tape)
    1. Spiritual life.   I. Canfield, Jack, date.   II. Hansen, Mark Victor.
III. Title: Fifth serving of chicken soup for the soul.
BL624.A15   1998   97-46612
158.1'28—dc21   CIP

Publisher: Health Communications, Inc.
              3201 S.W. 15th Street
              Deerfield Beach, FL 33442-8190

Cover re-design by Andrea Perrine Brower

We tell ourselves stories in order to live.

Joan Didion

With love and appreciation we dedicate
this book to the more than 20 million people who
have purchased, read and shared the fourteen
Chicken Soup for the Soul books with their families,
friends, business partners, employees, students and
congregations, and to the over five thousand readers
who have sent us stories, poems, cartoons and
quotes for possible inclusion in
A 5th Portion of Chicken Soup for the Soul.
Although we couldn't use everything you sent in,
we were deeply touched by your heartfelt
intention to share yourselves and
your stories with us and our readers.
Love to you!

SHOE

JEFF MACNELLY

Contents

4. ON DEATH AND DYING

5. A MATTER OF PERSPECTIVE

6. OVERCOMING OBSTACLES

7. ECLECTIC WISDOM

Acknowledgments

This fifth volume of *Chicken Soup for the Soul* took over a year to write, compile and edit. It has been a joyous though often difficult task, and we wish to thank the following people whose contributions have made it possible.

Our wives, Georgia and Patty, and our children—Christopher, Oran, Kyle, Elisabeth and Melanie—who once again have given us up for months to the process of writing this book.

Patty Aubery, who worked closely with us in all aspects of the book, oversaw every aspect of the production, managed the staff of The Canfield Training Group and Self-Esteem Seminars—all while moving into her new house and being four months pregnant!

Nancy Mitchell, who managed to continually find the gold nuggets among the thousands of stories we sifted through, found cartoons and quotes, and started on this project while Jack and Heather were busy completing *Chicken Soup for the Mother's Soul*. We also thank her for her incredible effectiveness and perseverance at getting all the permissions we needed.

Heather McNamara, our senior editor, who was the project coordinator for this book. She was instrumental at every stage—compiling, editing, sequencing, choosing quotes and cartoons, and keeping the whole thing on track in the midst of constant chaos.

Kimberly Kirberger, our managing editor, who read and commented on the manuscript during its various incarnations, and helped immensely in getting more stories when we needed them at the end.

Leslie Forbes, for spending weeks reading and evaluating hundreds of stories.

Ro Miller, our exceptional assistant, for handling much of our correspondence and phone communications with our many contributors.

Veronica Romero, Teresa Esparza, Lisa Williams and Laurie Hartman, for holding down the fort while the rest of us wrote and edited.

Rochelle M. Pennington, for sending us so many stories, poems and quotes for our consideration.

Mark Colucci, Sharon Linnéa, Patricia Lorenz, Penny Porter and Stephanie Sneddon for the excellent editing help they provided—often with little advance warning.

Larry and Linda Price, who, in addition to keeping Jack's Foundation for Self-Esteem operating smoothly, continue to administer the Soup Kitchens for the Soul project, which distributes thousands of *Chicken Soup for the Soul* books free each year to prisoners, halfway houses, homeless shelters, battered women's shelters and inner city schools.

Peter Vegso and Gary Seidler at Health Communications, Inc., for their continuing vision when it comes to the direction and value of these books, and for their unflagging support in getting these stories out to people all over the world.

Christine Belleris, Matthew Diener, Allison Janse and Lisa Drucker, our editors at Health Communications, Inc., who skillfully take our work to the highest level possible before it is published.

Randee Goldsmith, the *Chicken Soup for the Soul* product manager at Health Communications, Inc., who is always there to support us and give us words of encouragement along the way.

Lisa Aurello, for typing the manuscript and giving us valuable feedback for each story.

Trudy Klefstad at OfficeWorks, for her skillful and quick typing whenever we needed it.

Anna Kanson at *Guideposts*, who continually goes out of her way to help us.

Katherine Burns at *Reader's Digest*, who generously gives us her time and provides us with the information needed to locate hard-to-find authors.

Steve Parker and Patrick D'Acre, for their knowledge on the Internet, giving us the assistance that we so badly need.

Arielle Ford, Kim Weiss and Ronni O'Brien, our incredibly creative and effective publicists, who continue to help us keep our books on the bestseller lists.

Terry Burke, Irene Xanthos, Jane Barone, Lori Golden, Kelly Johnson Maragni, Karen Bailiff Ornstein and Yvonne zum Tobel, the people at Health Communications who are responsible for selling and marketing our *Chicken Soup* books.

Claude Choquette, who manages year after year to get each of our books translated into over twenty languages around the world.

John and Shannon Tullius, John Saul, Mike Sacks, Bud Gardner, Dan Poynter, Bryce Courtney, Terry Brooks and all our other friends at the Maui Writers Conference and Retreat who inspire and encourage us every year.

The following people who sent us cartoons we used: Peggy Gorton, Christine Scholl, Pam Schwerthy, Gary Pinder and Louise K. Priest.

The following people who found time in the midst of

their very busy schedules to read the 250-plus stories that were the finalists for inclusion in this book and to give us their invaluable evaluations, comments and suggestions for improvement. We could never even come close to creating such a high quality book without all of them. They include: Terri Altwies, Sandra Anderson, Rosa Arlington, Chell and Lisa Atchley, Sheri Austin, Pamela Bice, Liz Brendel, Julie Brookhart, Sandy Brooks, Harrah Brown, Dave and Marsha Carruthers, Diana Chapman, Nance Cheifetz, Svea and Maja Christensen, Caryn Colgan, Patrick Collins, Patrick D'Acre, Helen Dannatt, Joyce Davis, Lisa Drucker, Honora Evans, Mary Factor, Frank Fedak, Randee Goldsmith, Sherry Grimes, Gail Harris, Allison Janse, Richard Kraemer, Robert Lackamayer, Robert MacPhee, Karen Matz and Annie Slawik.

We also wish to thank the more than five thousand people who took the time to submit stories, poems and other pieces for consideration. You all know who you are. While many of the stories submitted were wonderful, not all of them fit into the overall structure of the book. However, many will be used in future volumes of the *Chicken Soup for the Soul* series, which includes *Chicken Soup for the Parent's Soul, Loving Couple's Soul, Kid's Soul, Divorced Soul, Laughing Soul, Jewish Soul, Man's Soul, Teacher's Soul, Writer's Soul* and *Sports Fan's Soul,* just to name a few.

Because of the immensity of this project, we may have left out names of some people who helped us along the way. If so, we are sorry. Please know that we really do appreciate all of you.

We are truly grateful for the many hands and hearts that made this book possible. We love you all!

Share with Us

We would love to hear what you think. Please let us know how these stories affected you and which ones were your favorites.

Also, please send us any stories you would like to submit for consideration in our upcoming *6th Serving of Chicken Soup for the Soul.* You can send us either stories and poems that you have written or ones that you have read and liked.

We hope you enjoy reading this book as much as we enjoyed compiling, editing and writing it. Making this *Chicken Soup* has truly been a labor of love.

Send these stories to:

P.O. Box 30880
Santa Barbara, CA 93130
e-mail: Soup4Soul@aol.com
Web site: http://www.chickensoup.com

Introduction

Without the stories we are nothing.

Bryce Courtney

From our hearts to yours, we are delighted to offer you *A 5th Portion of Chicken Soup for the Soul.* This book contains 101 more stories that we know will inspire and motivate you to love more fully and unconditionally, live with more passion and compassion, and pursue your heartfelt dreams with more conviction, action and perseverance. We believe that this book will sustain you in times of challenge, frustration and failure, and comfort you in times of confusion, pain and loss. We hope it will truly become a lifelong companion, offering continual insight and wisdom in many areas of your life.

How to Read This Book

We have been blessed with readers from all over the world who have given us feedback. Some read our books from cover to cover; others pick out a particular chapter that interests them. Some simply can't put our books down from beginning to end, going through a big box of tissues en route. We've been particularly touched by those readers who have reconnected to loved ones or old friends as a result of being inspired by one of the stories.

Many times we have been approached by readers—at a speech or public appearance—who told us how one or more stories were of inestimable value during a period of trial and testing, such as the death of a loved one or a serious illness. We are grateful for having had the opportunity to be of help to so many in this way. Some have told us they keep their *Chicken Soup* book at bedside, reading one story each night, often rereading favorites. Many use these books as a family gathering experience, reading a story aloud with parents and children gathered together in the evening.

You may choose the path of readers who have gone before you, or simply enjoy reading this book with no particular pattern in mind, letting each story guide your thoughts in new directions. Find the path that's best for you, and most of all, enjoy!

From a Previous Reader

[EDITORS' NOTE: *We received the following poem from Karen Taylor, who wrote this after she finished reading* A 3rd Serving of Chicken Soup for the Soul.]

CHICKEN SOUP

A wintry day once found me
home in bed and feeling bad . . .
sneezing, wheezing, coughing
with the worst cold I'd yet had.
I heard my mother's footsteps
and tried to fake a sleep
so she wouldn't try to feed me
when I didn't want to eat.
"I was going to fix some ice cream,
but couldn't find the scoop.
So I guess you'll have to settle
for a bowl of chicken soup."
I sat up. She fluffed the pillows,
put her cool hand on my brow . . .
then set the tray upon my lap.
"You eat this all up now."

Though my joints were stiff and achy
and my body felt like wood,
I have to say that chicken soup
sure tasted mighty good.
Now that I've grown older,
there's a different sort of pain.
When I'm tired and discouraged
and the loss outweighs the gain,
I curl up on the sofa
with a book and not a bowl
and enjoy another helping
of *Chicken Soup for the Soul.*

Karen Taylor

1

ON LOVE

The greatest disease is not TB or leprosy; it is being unwanted, unloved, and uncared for.
We can cure physical diseases with medicine, but the only cure for loneliness, despair and hopelessness is love. There are many in the world who are dying for a piece of bread, but there are many more dying for a little love.

Mother Teresa

The Seed Jar

Look around for a place to sow a few seeds.

Henry Van Dyke

Being the youngest of four girls, I usually saw to Grandma Lou's needs at family gatherings. Lucinda Mae Hamish—Grandma Lou for short—was a tall twig of a woman, with a long gray braid and sharp features. She was the undisputed Master Gardener in our family, for she had come of age in the Depression, where she learned to use every old thing twice. And when it was worn out, she'd use it again—in her garden.

When Grandma Lou visited, she brought packets of her own seeds, folded in scraps of envelopes and labeled with instructions. Her handwriting was precise and square. She gave each of us a particular plant; usually tomatoes and carrots and marigolds for my sisters—foolproof sorts of seeds, for my sisters were impatient and neglectful gardeners. But for me, she saved the more fragile varieties.

At the time of my next oldest sister's wedding, Grandma Lou was eighty-four and living alone, still weeding her large beds herself. And as she had for my older sisters' weddings, Grandma Lou gave Jenny a Mason jar layered with seeds from her garden.

Round and round the colorful spiral of seeds curled in the fat-mouthed jar. Heavy beans in rich, deep earth tones held the bottom steady. Next came corn kernels, polished in cheesecloth until they gleamed like gold. Flat seeds of cucumber, squash and watermelon filled the upper reaches, interspersed with the feathery dots of marigolds. At the very top, separated with cheesecloth, were the finer herb seeds of mint and basil. The jar was crowned with a gleaming brass lid and a cheerful ribbon. There was a lifetime supply of seeds pressed into the jar; a whole garden's worth of food for the new couple.

Two years later, Grandma Lou suffered a stroke, which forced her into an assisted-living apartment. And though she was unable to attend my own wedding that year, I was delighted to see a Mason jar among the brightly wrapped gifts at my reception.

But unlike its predecessors, my jar held no graceful pattern of seeds. Instead, it was a haphazard blend, as if all the seeds had been dumped into a pillowcase and then poured into the jar. Even the lid seemed like an afterthought, for it was rusty and well used. But considering Grandma Lou's state of health, I felt blessed that she remembered the gentle tradition at all.

My groom, Mark, found work in the city, and we moved into a small apartment. A garden was all but impossible, so I consoled myself by placing the seed jar in our living room. There it stood as a promise to return to the garden.

Grandma Lou died the year our twins were born. By the time our sons were toddlers, I had moved the seed jar to the top of the refrigerator, where their curious little hands couldn't tip over my treasure.

Eventually we moved to a house, but there still wasn't enough sun in our yard to plant a proper garden. Struggling yet courageous fescue grass vied for what little space there was between the dandelions, and it was all I could do to keep it mowed and occasionally watered.

The boys grew up overnight, much like the weeds I continuously pulled. Soon they were out on their own, and Mark was looking at retirement. We spent our quiet evenings planning for a little place in the country, where Mark could fish and I could have a proper garden.

A year later, Mark was hit by a drunk driver, paralyzing him from the neck down. Our savings went to physical therapy, and Mark gained some weak mobility in his arms and hands. But the simple day-to-day necessities still required a nurse.

Between the hospital visits and the financial worries, I was exhausted. Soon Mark would be released to my care, and at half his size, I knew I wouldn't even be able to lift him into our bed. I didn't know what I would do. We couldn't afford a day nurse, let alone full-time help, and assisted-care apartments were way out of our range.

Left to myself, I was so tired I wouldn't even bother to eat. But Jenny, my sister who lived nearby, visited me daily, forcing me to take a few bites of this or that. One night she arrived with a pan of lasagna, and she chatted cheerfully as we set our places. When she asked about Mark, I broke down in tears, explaining how he'd be home soon and how tight our money was running. She offered her own modest savings—even offered to move in and help take care of him—but I knew Mark's pride wouldn't allow it.

I stared down at my plate, my appetite all but gone. In the quiet that fell between us, despair settled down to dinner like an old friend. Finally I pulled myself together and asked her to help me with the dishes. Jenny nodded and rose to put the leftover lasagna away. As the refrigerator door flopped to a close, the seed jar on top rattled against the wall. Jenny turned at the sound. "What's this?" she asked, and reached for the jar.

Looking up from the sink, I said, "Oh, that's just Grandma Lou's seed jar. We each got one for a wedding present, remember?" Jenny looked at me, then studied the jar.

"You mean you never opened it?" she asked.

"Never had a patch of soil good enough for a garden, I guess."

Jenny tucked the jar in one arm and grabbed my sudsy hand in her other. "Come on!" she said excitedly.

Half dragging me, she went back to the dinner table. It took three tries, but she finally got the lid loose and overturned the jar upon the table. Seeds went bouncing everywhere! "What are you doing?!" I cried, scrambling to catch them. A pile of faded brown and tan seeds slid out around an old, yellow envelope. Jenny plucked it from the pile and handed it to me.

"Open it," she said, with a smile. Inside I found five stock certificates, each for one hundred shares. Reading the company names, our eyes widened in recognition. "Do you have any idea what these are worth by now?" she asked.

I gathered a handful of seeds to my lips and said a silent prayer of thanks to Grandma Lou. She had been tending a garden for me all these years and had pressed a lifetime supply of love into that old Mason jar.

Dee Berry

Mr. Gillespie

When I was in seventh grade, I was a candy striper at a local hospital in my town. I volunteered about thirty to forty hours a week during the summer. Most of the time I spent there was with Mr. Gillespie. He never had any visitors, and nobody seemed to care about his condition. I spent many days there holding his hand and talking to him, helping with anything that needed to be done. He became a close friend of mine, even though he responded with only an occasional squeeze of my hand. Mr. Gillespie was in a coma.

I left for a week to vacation with my parents, and when I came back, Mr. Gillespie was gone. I didn't have the nerve to ask any of the nurses where he was, for fear they might tell me he had died. So with many questions unanswered, I continued to volunteer there through my eighth-grade year.

Several years later, when I was a junior in high school, I was at the gas station when I noticed a familiar face. When I realized who it was, my eyes filled with tears. He was alive! I got up the nerve to ask him if his name was Mr. Gillespie, and if he had been in a coma about five years ago. With an uncertain look on his face, he replied yes. I explained how I knew, and that I had spent many hours talking with him in the hospital. His eyes welled up with tears, and he gave me the warmest hug I had ever received.

He began to tell me how, as he lay there comatose, he could hear me talking to him and could feel me holding his hand the whole time. He thought it was an angel, not a person, who was there with him. Mr. Gillespie firmly believed that it was my voice and touch that had kept him alive.

Then he told me about his life and what happened to him to put him in the coma. We both cried for a while and exchanged a hug, said our good-byes and went our separate ways.

Although I haven't seen him since, he fills my heart with joy every day. I know that I made a difference between his life and his death. More important, he has made a tremendous difference in my life. I will never forget him and what he did for me: he made me an angel.

Angela Sturgill

Night Watch

Not he who has much is rich, but he who gives much.

Erich Fromm

"Your son is here," the nurse said to the old man. She had to repeat the words several times before the man's eyes opened. He was heavily sedated and only partially conscious after a massive heart attack he had suffered the night before. He could see the dim outline of a young man in a Marine Corps uniform, standing alongside his bed.

The old man reached out his hand. The Marine wrapped his toughened fingers around the old man's limp hand and squeezed gently. The nurse brought a chair, and the tired serviceman sat down at the bedside.

All through the night, the young Marine sat in the poorly lighted ward, holding the old man's hand and offering words of encouragement. The dying man said nothing, but kept a feeble grip on the young man's hand. Oblivious to the noise of the oxygen tank, the moans of the other patients, and the bustle of the night staff coming in and out of the ward, the Marine remained at the old man's side.

Every now and then, when she stopped by to check on her patients, the nurse heard the young Marine whisper a few comforting words to the old man. Several times in the course of that long night, she returned and suggested that the Marine leave to rest for a while. But every time, the young man refused.

Near dawn the old man died. The Marine placed the old man's lifeless hand on the bed and left to find the nurse. While the nurse took the old man away and attended to the necessary duties, the young man waited. When the nurse returned, she began to offer words of sympathy, but the Marine interrupted her.

"Who was that man?" he asked.

Startled, the nurse replied, "He was your father."

"No, he wasn't," the young man said. "I've never seen him before in my life."

"Then why didn't you say something when I took you to him?"

"I knew there had been a mistake by the people who sent me home on an emergency furlough. What happened was, there were two of us with the same name, from the same town and we had similar serial numbers. They sent me by mistake," the young man explained. "But I also knew he needed his son, and his son wasn't there. I could tell he was too sick to know whether I was his son or not. When I realized how much he needed to have someone there, I just decided to stay."

Roy Popkin

Turn Back

Each friend represents a world in us, a world
possibly not born until they arrive, and it is only
by this meeting that a new world is born.

Anäis Nin

How do you talk about the death of a little boy? In April of 1990, I received a piece of fan mail. There was a little boy from Long Island who was a patient at Memorial Cancer Center in New York, his name was Kyle, and at the time he was six. His grandfather, I learned, had read one of my books to the little guy, and Kyle enjoyed it. There was more to the letter, some subtextual things, and this one grabbed me rather hard. It gave me an address, from which I got a phone number. So I called, and asked what I might do for Kyle. At the time I had a box full of poster-size aircraft photos—gifts from McDonnell–Douglas, the defense contractor—and since little boys usually like pictures of fighter planes, I sent a bunch.

Chemotherapy, a form of treatment as thoroughly vile as it is vitally necessary, typically causes a child's hair to fall out. This does give the excuse to wear hats, however, and I sent a few of those as well.

Kyle suffered from Ewing's sarcoma, a fast-growing cancer that afflicts young people, starting in a bone and moving, in time, to the lungs. There are no good forms of cancer, and this sort is worse than most. I'd later learn that Kyle's personal version of cancer was mobile, virulent and unusually resistant to medical science. The odds never looked good, but this little guy was a fighter. He was also unusually bright, possessed of an active, questioning mind. It's a fact that children stricken with serious disease are kicked way up the learning curve. They somehow become adults very quickly, though they never quite lose a child's innocence. The result of this is both immensely sad and wonderfully charming. In any case, keeping the little guy entertained and distracted became a major diversion for me. It was like a little flag on the Rolodex. Whenever I happened to visit a new place I wondered if Kyle would like a souvenir, which would necessitate a letter explaining where I'd picked up the new gewgaw. Even so, sooner or later you run out of fresh ideas.

At that point I started calling in markers. It has been my privilege to make numerous friends in the U.S. Military. These men and women have daily access to the most intricate bits of hardware known to civilized man, and kids invariably find them as interesting as I do.

The first such unit I "pinged" was the 37th Tactical Fighter Wing, the people who own and operate the F-117A stealth fighter. Little prompting was needed. People in uniform live by the warrior's code. Rule No. 1: The first duty of the strong is to protect the weak. Our people understand that. The first packet of material was followed by letters of encouragement even after the 37th deployed to fight in the Persian Gulf War.

Kyle got one of the first videos of "my" movie—*The Hunt for Red October*—and just about memorized it. He wanted to see the USS *Dallas*, the submarine depicted in the story. It couldn't be just any submarine—it had to be *Dallas*, but it was away on deployment, the Pentagon told me.

On the Friday before the shooting started in the Persian Gulf, a little light bulb went off in my head, the one you get that says, "Why don't you call." And so I phoned up to Long Island, and learned that Kyle had just spent his first day in school in a year and a half.

Ewing's was gone, his parents told me. It was over. The little guy had lucked out and slain his particular dragon. That was some feeling. I got the word out as quickly as I could, especially to the 37th TFW in Saudi Arabia, and then I got back to work on my new book, secure in the knowledge that the good guys had won a small but important battle. Getting up to see Kyle became a matter of lower priority. Kids have more fun with other kids than they do with stuffy adults.

On a business trip in March, I called home, as usual, for messages and the news was bad: Mr. Ewing was back. The early return after surgery, CAT scans and abusive chemotherapy was a particularly evil omen, but the people at Sloan-Kettering did not want to give up on my little friend. He was being blasted with hard gamma radiation, and if the new growth in his leg was killed, and if the CAT scan showed no additional activity elsewhere, then Kyle would be lucky enough merely to have his left leg surgically removed, followed by another bout of chemotherapy. Otherwise . . . The family hadn't wanted to bother me with the news for fear of interfering with my new book, and Kyle didn't want me to know because, his dad explained, I might stop liking him if I discovered he was losing a leg. Kids think that way, of course. The emotional impact of this was horrific, but there was work to be done.

The next day I established that the USS *Dallas* was finally back in its home port of Groton, Connecticut, and it seemed a good idea to get the little guy aboard while he was still largely intact. The Navy fast-tracked a visit for him. On the day after Kyle's CAT scan, the crew of the *Dallas* gave my little buddy what was probably the best day of his life. He bubbled about it. "I got to shoot a torpedo and look out of the periscope, and I ate everything they served for me!" he told me that night. They made him a member of the crew, and presented him with gold dolphins that he still wears. Five days later, his left leg was taken off.

The resilience of these kids is something that confounds reason. Kyle was at this point only seven and had already been through an experience to crush the soul of any adult. He sat up on the gurney and steered himself into the operating room. Then began yet another bout of chemotherapy. When "phantom pain" from his amputated leg caused him discomfort, Kyle would say out loud, "I'm sorry, the leg you have reached is no longer in service. Please contact the right leg for further information."

Kyle's parents. It requires no great insight to note that they were living through the ultimate nightmare. Set aside the fact that they faced the death of a child. Consider for the moment only the day-to-day routine. When the child is in the hospital, you live there with him, sleeping in a chair of dubious comfort, eating whatever you might warm in the nearby microwave. Forget your job. Forget your spouse. Forget the rest of your family. Forget sleeping more than four hours at a stretch. You learn a lot of what the medics have to know, and end up as a highly skilled nurse's aide. You get to sit there and watch poisons drip into your child's bloodstream. You are the one who has to be strong for a child who occasionally gets discouraged.

Every time you return to the hospital, you learn about another child—oh, God, not her, she has the same disease that . . . You learn to decode what the doctors and nurses tell you, searching for hope among the circumlocutions. And there's always the lingering fear that someday you will leave this place for the last time, and the wrong reason.

Oh, yeah, all this goes on for months—if you're lucky.

But, perversely, the parents *are* lucky. Consider the doctors, nurses and technicians. They are bright, sharp, dedicated, and so fiercely competitive as to make an NFL coach look mellow. Their personal enemy is Death himself, and they fight their nasty little war on many fronts, each one of which is the body of a human child, hairless, pale as parchment, with sunken but twinkling eyes. And these health professionals lose the battle a lot. We award medals and honors to professional soldiers who risk their lives in battle, typically in a brief span of hours. These medics put their souls at risk, and do it every day, and do you wonder then who are the most courageous people in the world?

Kyle's principal physician was Norma Wollner, director of the Pediatric Day Hospital at Sloan-Kettering. She is a woman of sixty years and pixieish proportions who started treating kids with cancer when hope was a lie. Professional soldiers would say that she has a clear sense of mission and tenacity of purpose, with few parallels except in her own elite community. Norma was the blue-force commander in the war, and she fought valiantly, with consummate skill and obstinate determination.

Unfortunately, the red-force won.

I got a call one afternoon in May from Kyle's dad. The little guy was terminal. Make-A-Wish, an organization that grants wishes to dying children, was sending him to Disney World. I was unprepared for this. Probably I am too optimistic, and perhaps the family was overly careful in what they had told me. That night I had to travel to Baltimore for a college trustees meeting. I checked myself into a nice place with a nice bar and proceeded to consume a great deal of alcohol in a puerile and pointless exercise. I had to see Kyle, of course, and I cursed myself for not having taken the time sooner. Since I am something of an expert on Disney World (seven trips), I offered my services as tour guide.

Why did I go? Fear. Everything about this frightened me. I was afraid that I would lose control of myself while with my little buddy. I was afraid that we'd be alone and he would turn to me and ask the question he'd not asked his mom and dad: When am I going to die? But most of all I was afraid of living the rest of my life as someone who failed to stand up for a sick little boy.

We met in the lobby of the Contemporary Resort. Rick and Eileen hadn't told their son that I'd be there. Kyle was easy to spot, the pale little one-legged guy in the wheelchair. I strolled over and dropped my cap on Kyle's head. Rick handled the introduction, and Kyle was incredulous for an instant—and then, his eyes lit the room like a strobe. I lifted him up for a rather ferocious hug, my heart already broken. It got immediately worse. His grandfather took me aside a moment later to say that you couldn't hug him like that. "He has a tumor in his chest, Mr. Clancy, and it hurts him when you do that." I'd never known such horror and shame in my life.

Strangely, that didn't matter to Kyle at all. Kyle, by God, wanted to have fun, and didn't want anything as trivial as cancer to stand in his way. It was an admirable clear mission statement, and with that fixed in my mind I led the family into the Magic Kingdom.

It is good to report that the Disney people have paid systematic and expert attention to their "special" guests. We were fast-tracked into every attraction. The costumed characters, Mickey and the rest, singled the group out for priority attention.

The family stayed at Kids' Village in Kissimmee, where Make-A-Wish houses its guests. It's superbly designed and well executed for its purpose, and wonderfully supported by local businesses. Disney (and other) characters come there—the lovely young lady who plays Snow White was particularly angelic in her attention to my little buddy—and they often come on their own time and out of uniform to spell the parents in their duties. Walt Disney would be proud of them.

Rick and Eileen allowed me to spell them too. I most often drew the duty of wheeling my little buddy around. It was a joy beyond words. I quickly learned that my fears on the trip down were even dumber than my usual mistakes. Kids like Kyle, sick as they may be, are more intensely alive than anything on earth. Their eyes glow brightly indeed, and when you see them smile and drink in the wonder of such a place as Disney World, you realize that what you are really seeing is life itself, the entire miracle of existence in one brilliant moment.

My little buddy was having a hard time. Every moment drugs were going into his system through a useful obscenity called a Broviac, which had been inserted in his jugular vein. His thin, abused body was often weak. Eating came hard to him. But he fought back in a way that makes "courage" all too small a word, visibly pushing the discomfort aside and concentrating on the mission at hand, which was having fun.

We were already friends from our letters and conversations, but at this time and in this place, something unexpected happened. Suddenly we were not just friends anymore. As though through some form of divine magic, we were closer still. Kyle trusted me, loved me. He was my son, too.

It wasn't all easy. Every so often reality crashes back into your consciousness. This little boy is dying, Clancy. I suppose the one really surprising thing was the rage. You become ferociously protective of a stricken child. Something was killing my little buddy; even as I watched, those misbegotten cells were dividing and spreading. I'm a person who's played with the best killing machines known to man. I've driven and fired tanks, scored a "possible" with a handmade sniper rifle on a 1,000-yard range, shot pistol with the FBI.

You wish cancer really were a dragon, because if it were, you could go after it, hunt the bastard down. You lust for that chance. I know how, and what I cannot do, others of my acquaintance would leap at. All the people in uniform who'd stood up for my little buddy, the world's most effective warriors, and Clancy, the minstrel who writes about them, any of us would have risked it all for Kyle. But cancer is not that kind of enemy. You look around at the passing crowd and start hoping that someone will attack your little buddy so that you might do something to protect him. That's how crazy you get, and when you face the fact that there is not a single thing you can do to save him, all you have left is an undirected killing rage that feeds on itself. And then you step away for a moment, and swallow, and take a deep breath, staring off above the heads of a passing crowd as though looking for something. In such moments you understand what it's like to be the parent of a critically ill child.

So, you turn back, smile and ask your little buddy where he wants to go next. Because even if fate and science have failed him, you can't, not now you can't. And you put it all aside until you get back to your room, because you know when you get there you're going to come apart again.

It was only four days. I was trying to squeeze a lifetime of friendship in a brief span of hours, doing so with a child whose frail body often twisted with pain. But we did have fun. At the "Indiana Jones Thrill Show," Kyle hopped off his wheelchair and stood on his one leg to get a better view—swallow, deep breath, set it aside! We discussed things mundane and profound. His child's mind wanted to learn, and I dealt with his numerous questions. We talked about the future, what Kyle would do on growing up.

A few moments stand out. Holding Kyle in my lap—this required subterfuge since he didn't like that sissy stuff—during the ride through Spaceship Earth. Explaining to him that the hard part about the magic fountains at "Journey Through Imagination" was training the water to jump repeatedly on command (I almost had him going on that). Having a few pictures taken together. The feel of his arm around my shoulder.

And then it was over. When he hugged me, he must have hurt himself. He went his way. I went mine. From there on we spoke on the phone almost every day.

I saw him again four times, all of them at Sloan-Kettering. The medics gave him one more shot of chemotherapy. What Rick and Eileen didn't tell me was that nobody had ever survived this treatment, and the last time I saw my little buddy, I drew the duty of persuading him to take on one last medication. That wasn't easy. Kyle knew how to resist argumentation, but my last card was to ask him what he would tell me if the situation were reversed. Kyle saw the logic, and took it like a man.

All it did was hurt him. It's not the sort of thing you want on your conscience. Sooner or later, "right" and "wrong" get muddled, the knowledge of the intellect isn't quite the same as the knowledge of the heart, and you wish that there were some agency to tell you that you did the right thing.

Kyle made it to his eighth birthday, had his party, and then Mr. Ewing came back to stay. His last ten days were lost in a cloud of narcotics. In our last conversation, Kyle told me, "When I grow up, I'd like to be like you, but a doctor instead of a writer." I think I left fingerprints on the telephone.

And then he was gone, buried in his treasured USS *Dallas* T-shirt, a custom-made U.S. Air Force flight suit, with Navy wings of gold, and dolphins and the unit patch of the 37th TFW. His parents spent much of their time comforting me. They'd essentially given over their son to a stranger for four days, and they actually thanked me for it. Rick and Eileen had made me a part of their family, promoted me to be Kyle's backup dad, and graced me with their friendship. Most of all, I'd received the love of their son. Of all the things I've earned in life, that's the one I'll take beyond the grave.

Life offers few opportunities to do something for which you can be unequivocally proud. It's not very often you can see the person in the mirror and whisper, "Yeah, you really did that one right, pal." Maybe the price of that is the pain that defines it. What did I learn? I'm no different from the next person, certainly no more courageous, no more decent. In the 1960s, when a cousin died of cancer in his teens, I wasn't there. I've always avoided funerals, as though doing so causes their reality to vanish. Kyle's death forced me to face things I'd managed to avoid all my life, and to see things that I'd never before cared to look at.

Perhaps the worst thing that happens to the parents of such a child is that others turn away from them. The unspeakable agony this inflicts can scarcely be described, and the parents view it as a lack of feeling, a lack of caring. I think not. What happens, I think, is denial and rage. When you watch a child suffer, you must accept the fact that it could easily be your own. When you watch a child suffer, every cell of your being wants to do something to fix things, and in the understanding that all your money and skills and contacts cannot extend his life a single day, you feel singularly useless. Turning away is a defense mechanism, to protect your own feelings, to distance yourself from the rage of the parents that you have no wish to share, and from a personal impotence you have no wish to acknowledge.

My own involvement began with the arrogant certainty that luck was transferable: My just being involved with him could change things. Tom Clancy won't let a little boy die. I can put him in touch with others. I can push buttons. I can make things happen. In my blindness I failed to see that I was right after all. In this kind of war the big victories depend on physicians and their skills, but big victories are not the only sort. By turning back, you can give friendship and get friendship in return.

Kyle passed by far too quickly, but he was here, for some part of which time he was my friend. That was a victory for both of us. When you see a stricken child having fun, you are watching Death being defeated, and seeing that is a godlike feeling. When he leaves, your heart will be more broken than you ever thought possible. Mine surely was. But even that is a victory, because Kyle might have died without my knowing who and what he was. And then how poorer would I have been.

Medicine has advanced remarkably in the past century. Louis Pasteur buried half of his children, and it's too easy to forget that there are places still in the world where watching your child die is an all too normal part of life. The very success of medicine has removed from us the understanding that some of the dragons have not yet been defeated. But until they are, more kids like Kyle will suffer all the pains of hell, and some of them will not survive.

When I went up for the funeral, I took a walk with one of Kyle's nurses. I was in a wretched state. I told her that I was glad for having met and befriended the little guy, but that I'd never be able to do the same thing again. It just hurt too much. I was begging for sympathy, but instead got what I really deserved. She stopped dead in the street and looked up at me: "What about all the other kids?" Her words had the force of a blow. What would Kyle think? You're a coward after all, aren't you?

There are other kids. Each of them, however ill, is alive and needful of the same things that we all need: love, friendship, conversation. Their parents need to know that they are not alone in their personal hell. Be there for them. Will it hurt? Worse than anything one can imagine. But there are compensations. You will come to know people ennobled by their suffering, and children whose sheer force of being will teach you lessons you never dreamed about. You'll learn that Death is ever out there, waiting for his shot, sometimes patiently, sometimes not. But you'll also learn that life is here and now, that every moment has meaning, and that even Death cannot take from you the things that others give. You'll rediscover the truth that the love of a child is the truest gift from God, and while the price may be high, the value is higher still.

It's easy to turn away. It's even safe, because doing so is soon forgotten. Turn back anyway. There are children who need us. And along the way, you'll see what life really is.

Tom Clancy

The Little Red Wagon

My friend Gayle has been "living" with cancer for four years and it is progressively getting worse. During a conversation with another friend, Gayle expressed that one of her childhood wishes was to have a red Radio Flyer wagon. As a child she never received one because she believed that if you told your birthday wish it wouldn't come true. I was at an ice cream stand one day and in the window was a miniature red Radio Flyer wagon that could be won in a weekly drawing. Every time you made a purchase you could fill out a ticket for a chance to win. After several weeks and many ice cream cones, I didn't win. I got up the courage to ask the person in charge if I could buy one. I went to the window and as I began to tell my story, I could feel my throat tighten and my eyes overflowed with tears. Somehow I managed to explain my reason for wanting to purchase the wagon, and after writing a check, I left carrying it. The wagon was delivered the next day, and for Gayle it was a dream come true. The following day I received a letter that read:

Dear Bonnie,

Every once in a while there is an opportunity to pass on a kindness—no questions asked. I lost my parents to cancer six months apart from each other. I cared for both of them but could not have done it without the love and generosity of friends—friends who care.

The best to you,
Norma

It was from the owner of the ice cream stand. Enclosed was my uncashed check.

Bonita L. Anticola

John

Charity sees the need, not the cause.

German Proverb

For many years now I've struggled with my purpose, working in what is a very high-crime area. I've encountered prostitutes performing sex acts on clients in the alley as I took out the trash. I've had heated discussions with the City to enforce health laws with other business owners, as transients would leave behind feces in and around trash areas. I've picketed and even faced the City Council, pleading that they close down adult bookstores in the neighborhood. I've seen the corruption and the destruction pornography can do to people's lives, especially to the children in our neighborhood. I've found myself on several occasions driving to work in tears, asking God, "What is it that I'm supposed to be doing here?"

About a year ago I met John. He's what many people might call a street person, or a panhandler. Most might even call him crazy.

When I first met John, he came by my office selling cigarette lighters, two for a dollar. I'd probably never have thought much more about him, but a few days later he stopped in again just to ask if I minded if he drank water from our water fountain. We talked for a while. As he left he apologized for taking up so much of my time.

John came from a wealthy family. At one time he had it all by today's standards: a home, a boat, a business, and he even flew a plane. He stood to inherit enough money to live his retirement years comfortably anywhere in the world he would have liked to. The very sad thing about John is that he has never felt loved. Certainly he has never experienced unconditional love before. As an adult he suffered from post-traumatic stress syndrome (stemming from service in Vietnam) and depression (because of a few sad events that drew his beloved little girl away from him). John decided to walk away from his life as he had known it.

Looking at John today, you might think I am crazy to believe in him, and that he does not have much to offer this world anymore. You would be very sadly mistaken. Besides offering me practical advice on how not to go crazy in life, when he visits he pumps me with self-esteem and pride as a person. He is one of the kindest people I know. He's borrowed money to buy milk for a lady and her children that he had met on the street, and we've shared stories of how we have both helped the same elderly man that stands on a nearby corner with a sign that says, "Will work for food." (The poor soul can hardly stand with the help of his cane, much less work.)

John tells me how sad it is that people go without lunch, when he gets a free lunch every day at the park. After the school bus leaves with the children on their field trips, he pulls their unopened milk cartons and uneaten lunches out of the trash can. He helped get a prostitute into a home for abused women and has written a letter of recommendation to help her get her daughter back.

I can always tell when John has had a hard time fighting his depression, as I won't see him for a few days. Then he shows up looking a little tired from the wear on his body, but with a story to share about a book he has read, a new person he has met on the street, or possibly even about being beaten up by someone.

On June fifteenth the apple of his eye will graduate with honors from California State University at Santa Barbara. He has hired a taxi to drive him there. The taxi driver (who knows him) will take his own private vehicle, so that John will not embarrass his daughter in any way. John will bathe, shave and put on an old suit to go and watch his little girl receive her degree. My heart is happy yet broken for him, as I've mentally thought of what he will be going through when he sees her walk up on stage to receive her degree. I can feel the love and pride that he feels collide with the hurt and regret. I pray that when the time comes, God will sustain him and help him get through it. I will hold my friend up in thought and spirit and once again, my heart will break with his.

"Do you know they say I'm crazy?"

I smile. "I don't think you're crazy, John."

There are times I envy a part of John's life. There are no earthly things he is attached to—only the desire to love others and to be loved. Maybe someday, even unconditionally.

Tomorrow, on my way to work once again, I will struggle and ask God, "What was it I'm supposed to be doing down here, Lord?" And probably he will send another person, from whose shoes I am not worthy of wiping the dirt, and I'll do my best to love him.

Terry O'Neal

"We can't have any children."

Does God Care About Lost Dogs?

The bitter cold weather had forced the large red dog to curl into a tighter ball, tucking his nose under his big, muddy feet. Old Red lived outside Larry's Barber Shop, sleeping on a small scrap of carpeting. The mongrel dog had panted through a hot summer, watching hopefully as the children came out of the small grocery store that adjoined the barber shop. Many shared their treats with him. On Valentine's Day, someone left a handful of candy hearts on Old Red's carpet.

Old Red once had a buddy—a scrawny black dog. Constant companions, they slept curled together. During a cold spell the smaller dog disappeared. Old Red mourned his friend by keeping his usually wagging tail motionless. As friends stooped to pat him, Old Red wouldn't even look up.

Someone dumped a puppy out one day, and Old Red immediately adopted him. He followed the puppy around like a mother hen. During the cold nights, Old Red shared his carpet with the frisky puppy, letting him sleep against the wall. Old Red slept on the cold outside.

Soon that puppy disappeared too, and the old dog was alone again.

I would have taken him home in a minute. Any homeless dog or cat could win my instant friendship—all it took was one hopeful look. But my husband had explained time and again that we simply could not take in stray animals. I knew he was right, but sometimes my heart forgot. With great determination I tried to steel myself against looking into the eyes of any stray, hungry dog or cat. Old Red never looked hungry, though, so I decided it was all right to form a relationship with him.

One day I found out by accident from the barber's wife that her husband was feeding the dog daily. "He won't even buy cheap food," she laughed. "He buys the most expensive there is."

I stopped by the barber shop to tell Larry how grateful I was that he was feeding the dog. He brushed aside my thanks and insisted the dog meant nothing to him. "I'm thinking of having him taken off," Larry mumbled gruffly.

He didn't fool me a bit.

During a snowstorm Old Red disappeared. I haunted the barber shop. "Larry, where can he be?" I'd ask.

"I'm glad he's gone. He was a bother, and it was getting expensive feeding him." Larry continued to cut a customer's hair, not looking at me.

Later, his wife told me that Larry had driven for miles looking for the dog.

On the third day the dog reappeared. I ran to him and patted his head. The big, dirty tail didn't flop once. He didn't even raise his head. I felt his nose: hot and dry. Bursting into the barber shop, I hollered, "Larry, Old Red's sick!"

Larry continued cutting a customer's hair. "I know. Won't eat."

"Where do you think he's been?"

"I can't prove it, but I think someone at the shopping center complained and he was hauled off. Did you see his feet? Looks like he's been walking for days to get back."

I lowered my voice. "Let him inside, Larry."

The customers seemed to be enjoying our conversation.

"I can't do that. This is a place of business."

I left the shop, and for hours I tried to get someone involved in helping Old Red. The Humane Society said they'd take the dog, but they were an hour's drive across Atlanta, and I had no idea how to get there. Anyway, no one would adopt a sick dog, and they'd put him to sleep. A vet I phoned said right away that he didn't take charity cases. The police, fire department, and manager of the shopping center could offer no help. None of my friends were interested.

I knew I was about to bring Old Red home despite my husband's rules about strays. I hadn't brought an animal home in a long time.

As I fixed supper that night I said very little. My husband finally asked grimly, "Do you want me to go look at that dog with you?" Translated, this meant: "I'll get involved a little bit. But we cannot keep the dog."

I ran to the attic and got a large box and a blanket. Grabbing some aspirin and an antibiotic one of the children had been taking, then warming some milk, I finally announced, "I'm ready." We piled our four children in the car and started for the shopping center. Snow covered the ground. *Hold on, Old Red. We're coming.*

As we entered the shopping center, all my hopes faded. He was gone. "Oh, he's gone off to die," I moaned. We drove around and looked and called, but the dog didn't come.

The next day I took the boys in for a haircut. Old Red was back! But he looked worse than ever. After feeling his hot nose, I ran into the barber shop. "Larry, the dog is going to die right in front of your shop."

Larry liked to tease me—even about this. He didn't look up. "Think he's already dead. Haven't seen him move all morning."

"Larry," I screamed, "you've got to do something!"

I left the barber shop with a heavy heart. It took all my willpower not to put Old Red in our car. He seemed resigned to his fate. I was almost in tears. One of my twins kept asking me something as we sat in our car. He repeated his question for the third time.

"Does God care about lost dogs, Mama?"

I knew I had to answer Jeremy even though God seemed far away. I felt a little guilty, too, because I never thought about bothering God with this. "Yes, Jeremy, God cares about all his creatures." I was afraid of his next question.

"Then let's ask him to make Old Red well. Can we do that, Mama?"

"Of course, Jeremy," I answered, somewhat exasperated. What else could I say to a five-year-old?

Jeremy bowed his head, folded his hands, shut his eyes and said, "God, I want to ask you to make Old Red well again. And please . . . send a little boy to love him. Amen."

Jeremy waited patiently for my prayer. I felt like explaining to him that animals were suffering everywhere. But I prayed, "Dear Lord, thank you for caring about all your creatures. Please send someone to care about Old Red. Please hurry."

Jon added his prayer to ours, and I backed out of the parking place. I was crying now, but Jeremy and Jon didn't seem to notice. Jeremy let down the window and called out cheerfully, "Bye, Old Red. You're gonna be okay. Someone's coming to get you."

The tired old dog raised his head slightly as we drove off.

Two days later Larry called. "Guess what?" he said.

I was afraid to ask.

"Your dog's well."

"What . . . how . . ."

There was unmistakable excitement in Larry's voice. "Yesterday a vet came in to have his hair cut, and I asked him to take a look at the dog—'cause you were about to drive me crazy. He gave Old Red a shot, and he's all well."

Weeks passed, and Old Red continued to live outside the barber shop. I sometimes wondered if he ever noticed the dogs that came to the stores with families. Dogs often leaned out of car windows and barked at Old Red, or just looked at him. Old Red didn't pay any attention.

Jeremy continued to talk about the someone whom God would send to love Old Red.

One day we rode by the barber shop and Old Red was gone. I went in and asked Larry where he was.

Larry started grinning as soon as I came in. "Strangest thing happened yesterday. This lady brought her little boy in for a haircut. I didn't know them. New in this area. She asked about the dog. Her little boy had a fit over him. When I told her he didn't belong to anyone, she took him home with her."

"Larry, don't tease me."

"I'm not teasing. I'll give you her telephone number. I got it. She was going to take the dog to the vet for shots and a bath. Man, you should have seen Old Red sitting up in the front seat of that Buick. If I didn't know better, I'd say he was grinning. Happiest dog I've ever seen."

I walked out of the barber shop quickly. I didn't want Larry to see me crying.

Marion Bond West

Rufus

We had a basset hound named Rufus. We called him the "ding dong boy" but I don't know why. He was a very, very sweet soul. He never bit man nor beast. When the vet would cut his toenails too short, making them bleed, he would cry and lick the vet. Mean dogs befriended Rufus and turned nice in his presence.

Rufus died yesterday. He was fourteen.

I went for a walk in the park today. The world felt different. Changed. There was one less sweet soul. There was a missing piece of the puzzle. It wasn't just *my* world that was different. It was the whole world . . . everyone's world. People I passed were unaware of the change. They looked so . . . centered, so normal. They didn't know the world was different. I felt so small and alone in the knowing.

I know that when I tell clients that I wasn't in yesterday because my dog died that it will sound small; insignificant. Everyone has a dog die at some point. But somehow it feels like no one has ever . . . or will ever . . . feel like I do today.

Someone said once that love feels like that same kind of . . . exclusivity. Maybe it's the same. Maybe what I'm feeling is love.

It feels as if I have an aura. And, if that aura is radiating shades of blue there's a red lightning bolt running through the light blue part . . . clear to the center of my being.

I love you Rufus and bless you. And send you somewhat reluctantly to your new adventure.

Hoping it is filled with fields of green grass, chew bones, all the treats you can eat and strong legs without arthritis to run in the green fields.

Carmen Rutlen

One Wing and a Prayer

Jouncing down a twisty trail on our Arizona cattle ranch one morning, we suddenly came across thousands of mourning doves. They were lined up like clothespins along miles of telephone wires, their bead-bright eyes riveted on our pickup loaded with grain.

"Dumbest birds on earth," Bill grumbled as he pulled up beside a cattle-feed trough.

"Daddy, why do you always call them dumb?" asked Jaymee, our eight-year-old daughter.

"Because they're always out to kill themselves," Bill said. "They fly into windowpanes and break their necks. They lean over too far and drown in stock tanks. And they build nests with holes so big they wouldn't hold a Ping-Pong ball, let alone an egg."

"Then how come there are so many?" Jaymee asked as Bill ripped open a sack and began to pour. He never had time to answer.

Alerted by the clatter of grain, scores of doves swooped down in a frenzied quest. Some lit on the cows' horns, others blanketed their backs. But most settled around the stomping hooves of our cattle.

"Daddy!" Jaymee screamed. "That cow's standing on a dove's wing!"

Bill hurried toward the cow and twisted her tail until she shifted her weight. "Dumb bird," he muttered. The dove was free, but one wing lay on the ground, severed at the shoulder.

The pathetic creature flapped its remaining wing and spun in circles until it mercifully lay still. *Thank God*, I thought with relief. *It's dead.* After all, there was nothing we could do for a bird with one wing.

Then Bill nudged the dove with the toe of his boot, and it flipped onto its back, wild-eyed with pain. "It's alive, Daddy!" Jaymee cried. "Do something!" Bill leaned down, wrapped the tiny broken creature in his red handkerchief and handed it to Jaymee.

"What are we going to do, Mama?" she asked, her brow creased with worry. She was forever rescuing kittens, rabbits and squirrels. But this was different: This was a grotesquely wounded bird.

"We'll put it in a box and give it water and grain," I said. The rest would be up to God.

When we got home, Jaymee put the bird into a shoe box filled with dried grass, and set the box near the wood stove for warmth.

"What are you going to name it?" asked her ten-year-old sister, Becky.

"Olive," Jaymee answered.

"Why Olive?"

"Because Noah's dove flew all the way back to the ark with an olive branch—and that wasn't so dumb."

While the girls were in school that day, I lathered the hideous wound with antibiotic salve. *Poor thing,* I thought, looking at the small, ghost-like creature. Certain it would die, I closed the lid. We'd done everything we could.

The next morning we heard a stirring in the box.

"Olive's eating!" Jaymee shouted. "And she's a girl. I can tell because she's just plain gray—and sometimes pink."

We put the bird in a wire-mesh cage filled with leaves and twigs. In the sudden shock of light and space, Olive sensed freedom and flapped her wing, repeatedly hurling herself against the mesh screen. Finally she stopped and wandered around off balance, like half a bird, yet taking the time to rearrange her feathers as though trying to draw a cape over the gaping hole. When evening came, she curled her pink claws around a small manzanita branch we'd wedged in a corner. She perched there in a trancelike state—dreaming, I supposed, of life in the sky.

Early one morning a few days later, Jaymee squealed, "Olive laid an egg! Come look!"

Resembling an elliptical, oversized pearl, the egg rolled around between a few twigs in the dove's favorite corner. "But why didn't she build a nest?" Jaymee asked.

"Too lazy," Bill said. "They slap three twigs together and call it home."

He was right. Doves' nests are flimsy little platforms that appear to be tossed at random among the bushes. I'd often discovered at my feet the empty broken shells of eggs that had fallen through. Yet these birds kept right on laying in the same miserable nests.

Now here was Olive, piteously wounded, soon laying an egg almost daily. Since she had no mate, the eggs would be infertile. But for Jaymee, it was magic. She began collecting the eggs in a teacup.

At first Bill didn't pay much attention to the dove. Then one day he noticed Jaymee's teacup was full, and he disappeared into his workshop. When he emerged he handed her a wooden egg-box he'd made. It had forty two-inch compartments that were padded with black velvet. "It's a treasure chest," he told her, "with a special place for each egg."

"Oh, Daddy, thank you!" Jaymee said, hugging him. "Maybe I can show Olive and her eggs for a 4-H project." At the Cochise County Fair that year, there was a special 4-H competition built around Arizona's wildlife. Kids' projects would be judged for originality, effort and record-keeping. "Maybe I could even win a blue ribbon!" Jaymee said. It was her big dream.

By this point, Olive was becoming tame. At the sight of Jaymee she cooed softly, pecking seeds and morsels of apple from her palm. When Jaymee took her out of the cage, the dove perched contentedly on her finger and shared an ice cream cone. She especially enjoyed her shower, a gentle misting from a spray bottle.

We liked to think she was happy. But when we moved her cage to the glassed-in porch where she could see other birds sail by, Olive's wing would quiver and her little gray head would bob anxiously.

Incredibly, the egg-laying continued: sixteen, seventeen, eighteen. *How much longer can this go on?* I wondered.

Around that time a fierce storm pounded our ranch. Fearsome winds ripped nests from trees, dashing eggs and newly hatched birds to the ground. Jaymee gathered many different kinds of eggs, miraculously unbroken, and put them in her treasure chest. Then she ran into the kitchen cupping a pink, open-beaked baby bird in her hands. "Maybe Olive can be its mama!" she cried.

Well, why not? I thought. My broody hen had raised ducks, pheasants and quail. Besides, if it worked, Olive wouldn't be so lonesome.

"We'll fix up a nice nest first," I said, "a sturdy one like a dove should make, soft and deep so the baby won't fall out." The girls found a storm-damaged nest and lined it with horsehair and chicken feathers. We laid the newborn in the nest and placed it inside the cage. "Maybe Olive will think the baby is really hers," Jaymee said.

During the night I awoke to strange sounds, reminders that wild birds belong outdoors—not in my kitchen. Expecting the worst, I hurried to the scene. The nest was destroyed. But huddled in one corner on three small twigs, Olive nested, bright eyes aglow, with the newborn cradled under her wing.

The egg-laying ceased, and Olive became a proud and protective mother. She chirped anxiously when we took the baby out for feeding and examined him thoroughly when we put him back. It was clear she loved him.

The fledgling thrived, and silver-white and black feathers soon appeared first on stubby wings and then everywhere. The short hooked beak was soon topped by a tiny black bandit mask. Our bird book dubbed him a loggerhead shrike; Jaymee named him Bandit. Soon he was perching on Jaymee's finger, gobbling down spaghetti, bologna and pepperoni strips. His passion was live flies, which Jaymee fed to him with tweezers.

The morning we'd been dreading came when Bandit discovered he had wings. We found him clinging upside down to the top of the cage, fluttering his wings eagerly. Olive cringed in her corner, feathers frazzled. "You'll have to let him go," Bill told Jaymee. "He's scaring the dove."

When Jaymee removed Bandit from the cage, the young shrike instantly shot up to the chandelier. "Take him outside," Bill said. "I don't want feathers in my coffee." By now Olive was chirping with alarm.

I placed Bandit in a cottonwood tree so he could practice flying. We watched him flit from branch to branch, and grabbed him when he landed on the ground. But the moment we tried to step inside, he zipped through the doorway and landed on the chandelier again. Hearing Olive, he dove back to the cage.

Bandit grew increasingly adept at flying and darting in and out of the door at will. Soon he was flitting between

barn roofs, trees and barbed-wire fences. Our little shrike
had grown up, and gradually he flew farther away. One
day we watched him head for the river. That was the last
we saw of him.

Shortly after Bandit's departure, Olive began sleeping
most of the day, perched unnaturally fluffed on her manzanita limb. In the early dawn she uttered a plaintive
"oooh-ah-hoo-hoo-hoo," like the sorrowful cry of a lost
soul seeking comfort. Then she started molting.

We added sugar to her water and a night light to her
cage. I played happy songs on the radio. Nothing seemed
to work.

Then Bill returned from the feed store with a small box
of "special diet for indisposed canaries." Looking sheep-
ish, he said, "I thought maybe a couple of vitamins might
help Olive." To our surprise, she seemed to perk up.

In her 4-H journal, Jaymee entered a paragraph about
Olive's baby, listed miscellaneous dove-project expenses
and wrote facts about doves. Meanwhile, Becky counted
the eggs. "You have only thirty-one," she said. "That
leaves nine empty holes." Unless Jaymee filled the box
with forty eggs, Becky feared the judges might consider
the project incomplete.

Despite the vitamins, Olive had never fully recovered
from her sadness. She'd become frail, almost spectral. Yet
the following morning, she laid another egg. Hope lit
Jaymee's eyes. "Only eight more to go," she murmured,
dashing off to catch every live fly she could find.

Olive rallied with six more eggs. Then, three days
before the fair and two more eggs to go, our weary little
dove huddled on her manzanita limb for the last time. We
found her in the morning, motionless, like a tiny piece of
driftwood washed up on the sand.

"Do you think Olive was happy in a cage?" Jaymee asked
Bill as he wrapped the dove in his old red handkerchief.

"Why, of course she was," he answered awkwardly, trying to make sense out of the bird's life. Then, in a blur of words that a man could only say to a child, he stumbled ahead. "You took care of her, fed her and gave her showers and a baby. And you told her how smart she was." He paused. "And she was smart because she knew you loved her."

"And she gave me her eggs because she loved me, too?"

"Her treasures," he said. "All that she had."

He watched Jaymee gather two handfuls of pale pink and gray feathers and fill the two empty velvet nests. "Even though Olive died," she murmured, "I'm going to show my egg collection anyway."

He smiled and hugged her. "I'll bet you win the blue ribbon."

And she did.

Penny Porter

Nonny

A single grateful thought raised to Heaven is the most perfect prayer.

Gotthold Ephraim Lessing

Johnny was three years older than me, almost to the day. I was born on August 28, and he on August 29. "You were my birthday present, Sal!" he used to say. Only my brother could get away with calling me Sal.

Since both our parents worked, Johnny took care of me after school. In the winter he made sure I was dressed warmly. On rainy days, he played records and we danced around the house.

When Johnny was a high school senior, he asked me to be his prom date. We danced the night away! Though it would be years before he would tell me, I knew he was gay. All I wanted was for Johnny to be happy and loved.

And he got plenty of love from my kids. The twins, Nicholas and Matthew, couldn't get enough of him. In their tiny voices, they called him "Nonny," and the nickname stuck.

My husband, Howard, and I loved our house so full of

laughter, and we wanted to fill all five bedrooms with kids. The trouble was, by the time we were ready for more, I couldn't get pregnant. At thirty-two, I was going through early menopause.

So we put our name on the long adoption waiting lists. Sometimes in the middle of the night, unable to sleep, I'd call Johnny. "I'll never have another baby," I'd sob. Johnny's gentle voice soothed me. "Yes, you will," he said. "Never give up, Sal."

Then in 1990, my world came crashing down. Johnny told me he had AIDS. "No!" I cried, tears streaming down my face. I refused to believe that my dear brother would die. I took him in my arms and we rocked and cried. If only I could hold on to him forever and protect him. . . .

Johnny lived only a few blocks away, and I was there all the time helping out when the disease started to claim him. There were times when, with a sparkle in his eye, he'd take me in his arms and dance me around the room. But those days were fleeting.

By the fall of 1992, we knew the end was near. On a September afternoon, Mom, Dad and I gathered around his bed. "I'll miss you most of all," I whispered, bending to kiss him. "When you see the bright light, you can go. It's okay." And with a last, shallow breath, he was gone.

Numb with grief, I picked up the small religious medallion that Johnny had kept at his side throughout his illness. I pressed it to my heart and cried. When I got home, I placed the medallion on a shelf.

How would I get through the rest of my life without him? I would weep and hold the medallion, praying. My big brother was gone. No more dancing. No more "Sal!"

Then one morning a few weeks later, Nicholas and Matthew ran into the kitchen, crying "Nonny is here."

I felt my legs tremble. "What?" I stammered.

"He came to us," they said. "He was wearing a red shirt."

How I wanted to believe! But I knew the boys missed him and that this was their way of expressing it.

The "visits" continued for months until one day the boys just stopped mentioning them. *They're okay now,* I thought. Life was going on, but it was a sadder life. "We've got to have a baby," I cried to Howard one night. "We need hope in our lives."

So we stepped up our search, this time with an international adoption agency. The weeks turned into months without any word, while my heart grew eager to give a child the love I could no longer give to Johnny. In dark moments when my hope started to turn to despair, I heard Johnny's words: *Never give up, Sal.*

I didn't. After two years we got the call. A two-year-old Russian girl named Anna needed a family. Before I knew it, I was on a plane. Though her life had been hard, Anna was healthy, and she thrived with us. She didn't know English, but she communicated through smiles and kisses.

She'd been with us a few months, when one afternoon I came home from shopping to find Howard anxiously waiting at the door. Taking my arm, he led me over to Anna. In her hand was the religious medallion I had taken from Johnny's deathbed. Looking up at me, Anna held out the medal and said, "Nonny," then laid it down at my feet. "She's been saying his name all afternoon," Howard said.

My eyes filled with tears and my mind was wild with wonder. Shakily, I put down my packages. "We've never talked to her about him. She barely understands what we say!" I cried. And even if she'd heard the boys talk about Johnny, how did she know the medallion had been his?

Had Johnny visited her, too? Here in our home? Maybe back in Russia, keeping her safe until we could take her in our arms? Perhaps Johnny was Anna's guardian angel, and she'd seen him. That's why she called out his name. I thought I'd lost Johnny forever, but now it seemed I was wrong.

Last night, Anna stopped playing with her toys and ran up to hug me. I looked down at her sweet face and for a moment I saw Johnny in her joyful nature. The bonds of love never die. Johnny will always be with us—if only in Anna's beautiful smile.

Eva Unga
Excerpted from Woman's World Magazine

The Light Was On

The love of our neighbor in all its fullness sim-ply means being able to say to him, "What are you going through?"

Simone Weil

When I was in private practice as a pediatrician, life was always busy, and the days and nights often ran together. I usually found myself in the office late at night, just catching up on paperwork. I found this time alone very peaceful. It allowed me to think about my patients and their problems without distractions. It also allowed for clear thinking about my own life.

One evening, after putting my own family to bed, I was back at the office, going through stacks of charts. As I sat studying a patient's chart, I heard a knock at the door. I assumed it was my partner, since he was on call at the time.

I opened the door to find Brian, a sixteen-year-old patient of mine. I had seen Brian enough times over the past few years to know him by name. I asked him why he was wandering around at two o'clock in the morning. "I was just out taking a walk and thinking," he replied. I invited him in to have some hot chocolate and "talk and think together."

I put the water on to boil, and we began to chat. As the conversation progressed, we both began to share a little bit about ourselves, our worries and our frustrations. It was obvious Brian was full of fears and anxieties that he definitely needed to express.

Brian told me about his girlfriend, who had just broken up with him, and about his grades, which weren't as good as he would have liked. He wanted to be an architect, but he worried that it would be impossible with his grades. He told me that his parents fought a lot and that he felt it was his fault. He said that he didn't know whether there was a God and, if there was, whether God loved him.

I tried just to listen and offer encouragement where I could. I had some contacts among architects, so I told Brian I wanted him to meet them and learn more about the profession. Brian and I also talked about positive things we planned to do to address some of our worries and fears. Our conversation lasted two hours. Finally I drove Brian home, where I saw him sneak in through a first-story window.

After that night, Brian frequently stopped by my office (at more reasonable hours) to give me an update on his progress in various areas of his life. He was a very pleasant, outgoing young man who soon became good friends with my staff.

About six months after my first conversation with Brian, I moved my practice to a different location. A year after the move, I received a graduation announcement from Brian. Folded inside the formal invitation was a handwritten note.

Dear Dr. Brown,

    I wanted to thank you for caring about me that night.
I don't think you ever knew, but I felt so bad that night,
I planned to kill myself. Everything in my life seemed
so bad, and I didn't know what to do next. As I was
walking down the street, I saw your office and noticed
the light was on. Then, for some reason, I decided to talk
to you. All that talking, and your listening, made me
realize a lot of things about my life that were good. Some
of the options and ideas you mentioned to me really
helped. I am graduating from high school, and I've been
accepted to the university's architecture school. I couldn't
be happier. I know I'll have hard times, but I also know
I'll get through the hard times. I'm very, very thankful
that your light was on that night.

Sincerely,
Brian

I don't believe this note was the result of anything extraordinary I did with Brian; our conversations had been very ordinary. But reflecting on my acquaintance with Brian makes me think there was something quite exceptional at work.

One might say it was fortuitous that I was in the office and that the light was on, that night when Brian was contemplating suicide. I believe the world works in a different way.

There is a light, or energy, that shines in and through each of us, to provide guidance and support for ourselves and our fellow human beings. And it was that light that shone brightest on the night when Brian knocked at my office door.

James C. Brown, M.D.

We cannot hold a torch to another man's path without brightening our own.

Ben Sweetland

Scarecrow

"Hey, 'Bones,'" my brother, Parker, asked me, "what are you going to be for Halloween?"

The elementary school party started at 7:00 P.M. The winner of the prize for the most original costume got two free tickets for the Sunday matinee. Parker was dressed and ready to go.

I watched him parade in front of the mirror in his pirate costume. *He's so handsome,* I thought. All the girls in the fifth and sixth grades were madly in love with him. I'd spent the afternoon defending myself from his rubber dagger.

"I'm not going!" I replied.

"Why not?"

"No costume."

"That's dumb," he said. "You hardly need a costume. You're already a perfect scarecrow!"

I was used to these observations. Furthermore, he spoke the truth. At twelve, I was already six feet tall and weighed eighty-nine pounds. Tack on red hair and freckles and it added up to one thing: I was a scarecrow.

School days were charged with searing taunts. "Down

in front." "How's the weather up there?" "Are those skis or shoes?" It was hard to smile back, and even harder to make friends.

I tried plastering my hair down flat on the top of my head and prying the heels off my shoes. I took scalding hot baths, hoping I'd shrink. In bed at night, I put my feet against the footboard, hands against the headboard and pushed, hoping to press myself back together. Nothing worked. So I saved nickels and dimes in a cider jug to pay the future surgeon who would find fame in *Ripley's Believe It or Not* by cutting six inches of bone from the legs of the tallest girl in the world and making her the same height as everybody else.

"When I grow up," I told Parker, as he brandished his cutlass in front of the mirror, "I'm going to live on an island where there's no one to stare."

My brother raised his eye patch and looked at me hard. "Sounds awful," he said, and left for the party.

Alone, I listened to the cheerless night and pictured the costumes my classmates had bought. I had tried on a few, too, but nothing fit.

I could picture my classmates in their costumes, having a wonderful time. As I wandered about the house, I remembered happier days—before Mommy and Daddy were separated. When Daddy lived with us, he always made me feel loved and wanted. Seeing him now for short visits wasn't the same.

The more I brooded, the more my self-pity grew. Then I spotted a broomstick standing in the kitchen corner. Maybe I could make a costume, I thought. Outside, a sheet and pillowcase billowed on the clothesline. I could be a witch or a ghost. Then my gaze fell on the back of the cellar door. My father's old plaid work shirt, faded overalls, jacket and cap were hanging right where he had left them.

"I could be a hobo," I murmured as I buried my face in the dusty clothes. But Parker's taunt kept coming back at me. "You're a scarecrow." As much as I hated to admit it, he was right. Well then, a scarecrow was what I'd be.

The closer I got to the school, the louder the cheers and clapping became, and the more my fears grew. What if they laughed at me? Worse still, what if they didn't do anything?

Hiding behind the tool shed next to the gym, I pulled everything out of the pillowcase and started to dress. Because I was so tall, I could peek through the high window and see everybody taking turns on the stage in quest of the coveted prize. Ghosts, princesses, monsters, cowboys, soldiers and brides—they were all there, clad in store-bought costumes, fragile dreams for one night. My teeth were chattering. Would they clap for me? Would they whistle and cheer? My stomach ached from anticipation.

I'll run home! I decided. No one would know I had been there. But Parker came on stage and glanced at the window. It was too late. He had seen me. If I left now, he'd call me chicken.

I watched him bow to the audience and listened to the squeals from the girls as he leaped on chairs and tables and parried with his sword. Next, a small gorilla climbed on top of a ladder and ate a banana. Lincoln gave a brief address. Cleopatra danced with a rubber snake in her hands, and a soldier marched and twirled his gun. Only Tarzan remained.

Maneuvering carefully through the entrance, I went in, held my breath and prayed, *Please, God, don't let me make a fool of myself.*

The applause was so loud for the King of the Jungle when he gave his call and swung on a curtain rope that no one seemed to notice me walk slowly to the center of the stage. A pillowcase covered my head. With arms out-stretched and hands clutching the broomstick inserted through the sleeves of an old plaid shirt, I wore a felt hat and faded overalls stuffed with straw. The room was suddenly still.

Nobody clapped. Nobody cheered. The only sound I heard was the hammering of my own heart. *I'm going to die,* I thought, *right here in front of everybody.* The world was tilting, and my ears were ringing when the hood slid down my nose, just enough so I could peer through the eyeholes.

And that's when I saw my classmates for the first time, as they really were. Petite blonde fairies with golden wands—and steel braces on their teeth. A baseball hero with a bat and mitt—and bottle-thick eyeglasses. A boxer with fighting gloves—sitting in a wheelchair.

Someone asked, "Hey, who is that?"

"Parker's sister!"

They looked at one another, surprise brightening their faces. Clapping and cheering filled the room.

The principal came up on stage. "The first prize for the most original costume goes to . . ." I never heard my name, only Parker, fear in his voice, saying, "I'll hold those tickets for her. She can't let go of that broomstick or her shirt will fall off."

Later, classmates came over to talk with me. "How'd you ever get such a good idea?"

"Parker," I said.

"Where did you get the costume?"

"My daddy." And in that single moment, I recaptured a memory that had almost slipped away. I was sitting on Daddy's lap and I heard him say, "I love you, sweetheart, just the way God made you." I felt his fingers riffling my hair, and I smiled inside, glad that God had made me a scarecrow.

I left the party early, but not before Nancy had said, "You'll come over to my house sometime, won't you?" and Elaine had confided, "I get goosebumps every time Mr. Allen is our substitute teacher. Don't you?"

I didn't want to stay and dance—the boys' heads came only to the middle of my chest. But on my way home, I decided that Parker was right. A deserted island would be pretty awful.

I waited up for Parker that night. I wanted to hear about the fun I'd missed. "Did you dance a lot?" I asked.

"Sort of," he said. "If you think it's any fun for a fifth-grade guy to dance with a bunch of puny third- and fourth-graders!" He kicked at the fringe on the rug and started up the stairs.

"Oh, I almost forgot," he said. "Here's your two tickets."

"Thanks."

"It's going to be a double feature. One's *The Wizard of Oz*. Ray Bolger plays a scarecrow." He had reached the fourth step. We stood eye to eye.

"And the other's *The Sea Hawk*," I said. "Can you believe it? Errol Flynn plays a pirate!"

"Are you taking anyone special?" Parker asked.

"Yes," I said. "Wanna go?"

Penny Porter

Best Friends Forever

When I said good-bye to my best friend, Opal, we promised to write and vowed that we'd see each other again. At fourteen, our futures seemed full of possibilities, despite our coming separation. It was June 1957, and we had spent two and a half of the happiest years of our lives on Chitose Air Force base in Japan. Now her family was being transferred to England, mine to Florida. What hurt most about leaving each other was that she was not only my first, but my best, best friend.

Growing up with a father in the military meant moving often. The two-room schoolhouse on the northern island of Hokkaido was my ninth school—and I was only in sixth grade when I arrived. Opal's roving childhood was similar to mine, except that I was terribly, horribly, painfully, miserably shy. I loathed always being "the new girl." Once or twice I'd managed to make a friend, but before we could get to know each other well, I'd moved on to a different school.

Then one January day in 1955, when the snowdrifts were ten feet high and the wind howled around the chimney of the coal stove, I stood in the doorway of my newest classroom. As always, my stomach ached with dread, and shivers of fear ran through me like tiny sharp arrows. I hoped no one could tell I was trying to hold back tears. Twenty kids silently stared at me, and I turned red from my ears down to my toes. I kept my eyes on the floor, sneaking only quick peeks at the strange faces. Then I saw a girl beaming, her smile like warm sunshine flooding my shaking soul. She actually seemed to welcome me! When the teacher told me to take the desk next to Opal's, some of my frozen terror began to melt slightly.

"Hi, I'm Opal." Her voice carried the twang of the Midwest, her face was round, her eyes soft behind her thick glasses, her hair long and brown. And as I quickly learned, her heart was crafted of twenty-four-karat gold.

That first day, as we moved from history to math to English, she helped me find the right place in the books and filled me in on the other kids. It appeared they were all terrific, even the class pains. "Don't mind about him. He likes to tease, but he sure can be funny." Or, "She acts a little snobby sometimes, but she's a real nice girl."

Because we had fourth, fifth and sixth grades in the same room, the teacher would take small groups up front while the rest of us worked at our desks, very much like the school in *Little House on the Prairie*. With only five of us in sixth grade, the angels were working overtime when they made sure one of them was Opal.

By the end of that first day, an unspoken promise had been made. Opal and I knew we would be best friends, the first either of us had found. During the next months, more and more new kids moved to the base and Opal welcomed everyone—teaching me by example to do the same. Red-haired Maureen arrived and became an especially close friend. But we all hung out together, both boys and girls, playing kickball and Red Rover, skiing on the snowy mound behind my house, exploring the woods where we were officially forbidden to go, swimming in the frigid pool when the short summers arrived, camping on what we hoped was an extinct volcano, attending the Japanese Cherry Blossom and Snow festivals.

In that large group, Opal and I were rock-solid best friends, a true Mutt and Jeff duo. She was tall and slim, I was short and plump; she was good in math, I loved reading; she wasn't athletic, but cheerfully joined the games and sports I dragged her into. Her father was a master sergeant (the fire chief! So romantic!), mine a lieutenant colonel. She admired my get-up-and-go; I admired her gentleness with young children, the way she always gave of herself, her ability to see the smallest rose in a thicket of thorns. Our differences meshed and never clashed.

Two years flew by—miracle years filled with fun and growth and discovery. Then the rumors began. The Air Force was closing the base, and we would all be transferred back to the States that summer, headed for different assignments, hundreds or thousands of miles apart.

As promised, Opal and I wrote occasional letters (on military salaries, long distance phone calls were out of the question) until we were sixteen. I was in boarding school when her last letter came. She'd fallen in love with an older man—nineteen—an airman first class. She'd left her family in England and returned to the States to marry him. She had just given birth to a beautiful baby girl.

I wrote back right away but didn't get an answer. Knowing how Opal found writing an awful chore, I wrote again and again. Finally my letters were returned: forwarding address unknown. How I worried about her! To be married and have a baby at sixteen! I knew her so well: I knew she'd be a wonderful mother, but I also knew she was too young to be married.

I graduated from boarding school and then college, was married, had three babies, divorced, remarried. My children grew up, went to college, and my daughter was now a mother. And so often I thought of Opal, wondering where she was, if she was all right, if she was happy. I'd talk about our blissful years together, and my family knew all about my best friend.

One sweaty hot August day in 1991 the telephone rang. "Is this Louise?"

"Yes."

"Is this Louise Ladd?"

"Yes."

"Is this Louise Ladd from Japan?"

"Who are you?" I roared.

"This is Opal."

I screamed. I was outside on the porch and the entire town must have heard me. Dancing around and jumping up and down, I shouted out my joy.

Thirty-four years after we said good-bye, she had found me. Sorting through piles of stuff after a recent move, she had opened an ancient box marked "papers." My letter from 1959 was in it. Immediately she called everyone named Ladd who lived anywhere near my old address in Maryland; then, refusing to give up, she called my boarding school. After much begging and pleading (she swears she was literally down on her knees), the alumnae office finally gave her my phone number.

That Christmas, Opal and her second husband drove from Omaha, Nebraska, to spend a few days with us in Connecticut. She looked exactly the same. She sounded exactly the same. She radiated the same warmth and love I'd always known. She'd missed me as much as I'd missed her. She'd been through difficult times, but as always, had managed to find the good in life. Twenty-four-karat gold does not tarnish.

And now we are together again: best friends, forever.

Louise Ladd

The Giving Trees

For it is in giving that we receive.

Saint Francis of Assisi

I was a single parent of four small children, working at a minimum-wage job. Money was always tight, but we had a roof over our heads, food on the table, clothes on our backs and, if not a lot, always enough. My kids told me that in those days they didn't know we were poor. They just thought Mom was cheap. I've always been glad about that.

It was Christmas time, and although there wasn't money for a lot of gifts, we planned to celebrate with church and family, parties and friends, drives downtown to see the Christmas lights, special dinners, and by decorating our home.

But the big excitement for the kids was the fun of Christmas shopping at the mall. They talked and planned for weeks ahead of time, asking each other and their grandparents what they wanted for Christmas. I dreaded it. I had saved $120 for presents to be shared by all five of us.

The big day arrived and we started out early. I gave each of the four kids a twenty dollar bill and reminded them to look for gifts about four dollars each. Then everyone scattered. We had two hours to shop; then we would meet back at the "Santa's workshop" display.

Back in the car driving home, everyone was in high Christmas spirits, laughing and teasing each other with hints and clues about what they had bought. My younger daughter, Ginger, who was about eight years old, was unusually quiet. I noted she had only one small, flat bag with her after her shopping spree. I could see enough through the plastic bag to tell that she had bought candy bars—fifty-cent candy bars! I was so angry. *What did you do with that twenty dollar bill I gave you?* I wanted to yell at her, but I didn't say anything until we got home. I called her into my bedroom and closed the door, ready to be angry again when I asked her what she had done with the money. This is what she told me:

"I was looking around, thinking of what to buy, and I stopped to read the little cards on one of the Salvation Army's 'Giving Trees.' One of the cards was for a little girl, four years old, and all she wanted for Christmas was a doll with clothes and a hairbrush. So I took the card off the tree and bought the doll and the hairbrush for her and took it to the Salvation Army booth.

"I only had enough money left to buy candy bars for us," Ginger continued. "But we have so much and she doesn't have anything."

I never felt so rich as I did that day.

Kathleen Dixon

An Elf's Tale

It was six o'clock at the mall, and I was as exhausted as an elf on Christmas Eve. In fact, I *was* an elf and it *was* Christmas Eve. That December of my sixteenth year, 1995, I'd been working two jobs to help my parents with my school tuition and to make a little extra holiday money. My second job was as an elf for Santa to help with kids' photos. Between my two jobs, I'd worked twelve hours straight the day before; on Christmas Eve, things were so busy at Santaland that I hadn't even had a coffee break all day. But this was it—only minutes more, and I'd have survived!

I looked over at Shelly, our manager, and she gave me an encouraging smile. She was the reason I'd made it through. She'd been thrown in as manager halfway through the season, and she'd made all the difference in the world. My job had changed from stress-filled to challenging. Instead of yelling at her workers to keep us in line, she encouraged us and stood behind us. She made us pull together as a team. Especially when things were their craziest, she always had a smile and an encouraging word. Under her leadership, we'd achieved the highest number of mall photo sales in California.

I knew it was a difficult holiday season for her—she'd recently suffered a miscarriage. I hoped she knew how great she was and what a difference she'd made to all her workers, and to all the little children who'd come to have their pictures taken.

Our booth was open until seven; at six things started to slow down and I finally took a break. Although I didn't have much money, I really wanted to buy a little gift for Shelly so that she'd know we appreciated her. I got to a store that sold soap and lotion just as they put the grate down. "Sorry, we're closed!" barked the clerk, who looked as tired as I was and didn't sound sorry at all.

I looked around and, to my dismay, found that all the stores had closed. I'd been so tired I hadn't noticed.

I was really bummed. I had been working all day and had missed buying her a present by one minute.

On my way back to the Santa booth, I saw that Nordstrom was still open. Fearful that they, too, would close at any moment, I hurried inside and followed the signs toward the Gift Gallery. As I rushed through the store, I began to feel very conspicuous. It seemed the other shoppers were all very well-dressed and wealthy—and here I was a broke teenager in an elf costume. *How could I even think I'd find something in such a posh store for under fifteen dollars?*

I self-consciously jingled my way into the Gift Gallery. A woman sales associate, who also looked as if she'd just stepped off a fashion runway, came over and asked if she could help me. As she did, everyone in the department turned and stared.

As quietly as possible, I said, "No, that's okay. Just help somebody else."

She looked right at me and smiled. "No," she said. "I want to help *you.*"

I told the woman who I was buying for and why, then

I sheepishly admitted I only had fifteen dollars to spend. She looked as pleased and thoughtful as if I'd just asked to spend $1500. By now, the department had emptied, but she carefully went around, selecting a few things that would make a nice basket. The total came to $14.09.

The store was closing; as she rang up the purchase, the lights were turned off.

I was thinking that if I could take them home and wrap them, I could make them really pretty but I didn't have time.

As if reading my mind, the saleslady asked, "Do you need this wrapped?"

"Yes," I said.

By now the store was closed. Over the intercom, a voice asked if there were still customers in the store. I knew this woman was probably as eager to get home on Christmas Eve as everybody else, and here she was stuck waiting on some kid with a measly purchase.

But she was gone in the back room a long time. When she returned, she brought out the most beautiful basket I'd ever seen. It was all wrapped up in silver and gold, and looked as if I'd spent fifty dollars on it—at least. I couldn't believe it. I was so happy!

When I thanked her, she said, "You elves are out in the mall spreading joy to so many people, I just wanted to bring a little joy to you."

"Merry Christmas, Shelly," I said back at the booth. My manager gasped when she saw the present; she was so touched and happy that she started crying. I hoped it gave a happy start to her Christmas.

All through the holidays I couldn't stop thinking about the kindness and effort of the saleswoman, and how much joy she had brought to me, and in turn to my manager. I thought the least I could do was to write a letter to the store and let them know about it. About a week later, I got a reply from the store, thanking me for writing.

I thought that was the end of it, until mid-January.

That's when I got a call from Stephanie, the sales associate. She wanted to take me to lunch. Me, a fifteen-dollar, sixteen-year-old customer.

When we met, Stephanie gave me a hug, and a present, and told me this story.

She had walked into a recent employee meeting to find herself on the list of nominees to be named the Nordstrom All-Star. She was confused but excited, as she had never before been nominated. At the point in the meeting when the winner was announced, they called Stephanie—she'd won! When she went up front to accept the award, her manager read my letter out loud. Everyone gave her a huge round of applause.

Winning meant that her picture was put up in the store lobby, she got new business cards with Nordstrom All-Star written on them, a 14-karat gold pin, a 100-dollar award, and was invited to represent her department at the regional meeting.

At the regional meeting, they read my letter and everyone gave Stephanie a standing ovation. "This is what we want all of our employees to be like!" said the manager who read the letter. She got to meet three of the Nordstrom brothers, who were each very complimentary.

I was already a little overwhelmed when Stephanie took my hand. "But that's not the best part, Tyree," she said. "The day of that first store meeting, I took a list of the nominees, and put your letter behind it, with the 100-dollar bill behind that. I took it home and gave it to my father. He read everything and looked at me and said, "When do you find out who won?"

"I said, 'I won, Dad.'

"He looked me right in the eye and said, 'Stephanie, I'm really proud of you.'"

Quietly, she said, "My dad has never said he was proud of me."

I think I'll remember that moment all my life. That was when I realized what a powerful gift appreciation can be. Shelly's appreciation of her workers had set into motion a chain of events—Stephanie's beautiful basket, my letter, Nordstrom's award—that had changed at least three lives.

Though I'd heard it all my life, it was the Christmas when I was an elf—and a broke teenager—that I truly came to understand that the littlest things can make the biggest difference.

Tyree Dillingham

The Beloved

Where love is, there is God also.

Leo Tolstoy

I was called to the delivery room one night to assist with a term infant because of a small amount of meconium that was present. Meconium is the substance within the bowels of the infant before delivery, and it can sometimes signal distress or abnormality in the infant. It generally requires a pediatrician or other qualified individual to be in attendance. However, most of the time these babies are born without complication and are healthy and normal.

In the delivery room, both mother and father were anxious yet happy as they anticipated the birth of their first baby. The pregnancy had been uneventful. But when the baby was born, it was immediately apparent that there was a significant problem. The baby was anencephalic. This means that there is essentially no upper brain, and the dome of the calvarium, or skull, is also absent. These babies generally don't survive the immediate newborn period, and often they have other significant abnormalities.

The obstetrician immediately handed the baby to me.

Even the father, beside himself in anticipation and excitement, could see that the baby was not normal. The mother had not been sedated and, of course, wanted to see her baby right away. The baby did not cry significantly, but it was not in any serious respiratory distress. It did maintain a deep bluish color, indicating the possibility of severe heart disease, which is common in these infants.

The almost instantaneous emotional sweep that takes place under these circumstances is impossible to describe. One moment everyone is joyous and laughing, joking and high with the expectation of a beautiful baby being born and all the possibilities that life holds. Then, in an instant, emotions sink to the abysmal depth of total disbelief, anger and despair.

I put my arm around the father as we wheeled the baby over to the mother's side. I held her hand and explained the diagnosis. No one could listen carefully at that point. I wrapped the baby up and asked the father to carry the infant to the nursery. I told the mother that we needed to do some initial evaluations, but that we would be back to talk to her soon.

As we walked to the nursery, I asked the father, "What were you going to name the baby?"

He did not respond but asked me, "Will the baby live?"

I answered, "I need to evaluate him more closely." I thought about the vigorous interventions attempted to keep these babies alive for weeks or months or even years, knowing that what we *could* do was, perhaps, not even morally correct.

In the nursery, the baby began to breathe rapidly. The evaluation of the heart revealed a significant heart lesion. The chest X ray and ultrasound revealed cardiac defects that could not be successfully repaired. The baby had other problems as well, including abnormalities of the kidneys, leaving him without normal renal function.

By this time, the nurses had wheeled the mother into the room where I was examining the baby. After listening to my technical explanations about the multiple problems this baby had, she simply looked up at me and said, "His name is John. It means *the beloved one.*" Then she asked me if they could hold their child.

We went into a private room where the mother could be comfortable in a recliner and the father could sit close, and where they could both hold John and talk to him. I started to leave but they asked me to stay.

The mother prayed for the baby aloud, then sang songs and lullabies to her son. She told him all about herself and her husband, their hopes and dreams. Over and over again she told him how much they loved him.

I sat spellbound as feelings of despair and hopelessness changed to ones of intense love and caring. One of the most horrific experiences of life had been cast upon this couple, an experience that usually—and understandably—results in anger, hostility and self-pity, as hopes and dreams of watching your child grow up are shattered. But somehow within that terrible disappointment, this couple understood that what was most important was for them to give this baby a lifetime of love in the very short time they had with him. As they talked, sang, introduced themselves, and held him tight, they did not see the physical features that often have been described as grotesque. Instead, they saw and felt the soul of one small being who had only a few short hours to live. And, indeed, John died a few minutes later.

That young couple taught me that the value of a life is not dependent upon length of time on this earth, but rather on the amount of love given and shared during the time, that we have. They had given all their love to their son. He had truly been their beloved.

James C. Brown, M.D.

Ben and Virginia

In 1904, a railroad camp of civil engineers was set up near Knoxville, Tennessee. The L & N campsite had tents for the men, a warm campfire, a good cook and the most modern surveying equipment available. In fact, working as a young civil engineer for the railroad at the turn of the century presented only one real drawback: a severe shortage of eligible young women.

Benjamin Murrell was one such engineer. A tall, reticent man with a quiet sense of humor and a great sensitivity for people, Ben enjoyed the nomadic railroad life. His mother had died when he was only thirteen, and this early loss caused him to become a loner.

Like all the other men, Ben sometimes longed for the companionship of a young woman, but he kept his thoughts between himself and God. On one particularly memorable spring day, a marvelous piece of information was passed around the camp: The boss's sister-in-law was coming to visit! The men knew only three things about her: She was nineteen years old, she was single and she was pretty. By mid-afternoon the men could talk of little else. Her parents were sending her to escape the yellow fever that was invading the Deep South and she'd be there in only three days. Someone found a tintype of her, and the photograph was passed around with great seriousness and grunts of approval.

Ben watched the preoccupation of his friends with a smirk. He teased them for their silliness over a girl they'd never even met. "Just look at her, Ben. Take one look and then tell us you're not interested," one of the men retorted. But Ben only shook his head and walked away chuckling.

The next two days found it difficult for the men of the L & N engineering camp to concentrate. The train would be there early Saturday morning and they discussed their plan in great detail. Freshly bathed, twenty heads of hair carefully greased and slicked back, they would all be there to meet that train and give the young woman a railroad welcome she wouldn't soon forget. She'd scan the crowd, choose the most handsome of the lot and have an instant beau. Let the best man win, they decided. And each was determined to be that man.

On Friday evening, as the other men tried to shake the wrinkles out of their Sunday best and draw a bath, Ben sat down on a log next to the campfire. Something glinted orange in the firelight. Idly, he reached down and picked it up. His friends had been so busy and full of themselves, they'd left the girl's picture lying on the ground.

The men were too preoccupied to see Ben's face as he beheld the picture of Virginia Grace for the first time. They didn't notice the way he cradled the photograph in his big hands like a lost treasure, or that he gazed at it for a long, long time. They missed the expression on his face as he looked first at the features of the delicate beauty, then at the camp full of men he suddenly perceived to be his rivals. And they didn't see Ben go into his tent, pick up a backpack and leave camp as the sun glowed red and sank beyond a distant mountain.

Early the next morning, the men of the L & N railroad camp gathered at the train station. Virginia's family, who had come to pick her up, rolled their eyes and tried unsuccessfully not to laugh. Faces were raw from unaccustomed shaves, and the combination of men's cheap colognes was almost noxious. Several of the men had even stopped to pick bouquets of wildflowers along the way.

At long last the whistle was heard and the eagerly awaited train pulled into the station. When the petite, vivacious little darling of the L & N camp stepped onto the platform, a collective sigh escaped her would-be suitors. She was even prettier than the tintype depicted. Then every man's heart sank in collective despair. For there, holding her arm in a proprietary manner and grinning from ear to ear, was Benjamin Murrell. And from the way she tilted her little head to smile up into his face, they knew their efforts were in vain.

"How," his friends demanded of Ben later, "did you do that?"

"Well," he said, "I knew I didn't have a chance with all you scoundrels around. I'd have to get to her first if I wanted her attention, so I walked down to the previous station and met the train. I introduced myself as a member of the welcoming committee from her new home."

"But the nearest station is seventeen miles away!" someone blurted incredulously. "You walked seventeen miles to meet her train? That would take all night!"

"That it did," he affirmed.

Benjamin Murrell courted Virginia Grace, and in due time they married. They raised five children and buried one, a twelve-year-old son. I don't think they tried to build the eternal romance that some women's magazines claim is so important. Nor did they have a standing Friday night date. In fact, Ben was so far out in the sticks while working on one engineering job that one of their children was a full month old before he saw his new daughter. Ben didn't take Virginia to expensive restaurants, and the most romantic gift he ever brought her was an occasional jar of olives. If Virginia ever bought a fetching nightgown and chased him around the icebox, that secret remains buried with her to this day.

What I do know is that they worked on their relationship by being faithful to one another, treating each other with consideration and respect, having a sense of humor, bringing up their children in the knowledge and love of the Lord, and loving one another through some very difficult circumstances.

I am one of Benjamin and Virginia's great-grandchildren. He died when I was a baby, unfortunately, so I have no memory of him. NaNa (Virginia) died when I was twelve and she was eighty-five. When I knew her she was a shriveled old woman who needed assistance to get around with a walker and whose back was hunched over from osteoporosis. Her aching joints were swollen with arthritis and her eyesight was hindered by the onset of glaucoma. At times, though, those clouded eyes would sparkle and dance with the vivaciousness of the girl my great-grandfather knew. They danced especially when she told her favorite story. It was the story of how she was so pretty that once, on the basis of a tintype, an entire camp turned out to meet the train and vie for her attention. It was the story of how one man walked seventeen miles, all night long, for a chance to meet the woman of his dreams and claim her for his wife.

Gwyn Williams

Don't Hope, Friend . . . Decide!

While waiting to pick up a friend at the airport in Portland, Oregon, I had one of those life-changing experiences that you hear other people talk about—the kind that sneaks up on you unexpectedly. This one occurred a mere two feet away from me.

Straining to locate my friend among the passengers deplaning through the jetway, I noticed a man coming toward me carrying two light bags. He stopped right next to me to greet his family.

First he motioned to his youngest son (maybe six years old) as he laid down his bags. They gave each other a long, loving hug. As they separated enough to look in each other's face, I heard the father say, "It's so good to see you, son. I missed you so much!" His son smiled somewhat shyly, averted his eyes, and replied softly, "Me, too, Dad!"

Then the man stood up, gazed in the eyes of his oldest son (maybe nine or ten) and while cupping his son's face in his hands said, "You're already quite the young man. I love you very much, Zach!" They too hugged a most loving, tender hug.

While this was happening, a baby girl (perhaps one or

one-and-a-half) was squirming excitedly in her mother's arms, never once taking her little eyes off the wonderful sight of her returning father. The man said, "Hi, baby girl!" as he gently took the child from her mother. He quickly kissed her face all over and then held her close to his chest while rocking her from side to side. The little girl instantly relaxed and simply laid her head on his shoulder, motionless in pure contentment.

After several moments, he handed his daughter to his oldest son and declared, "I've saved the best for last!" and proceeded to give his wife the longest, most passionate kiss I ever remember seeing. He gazed into her eyes for several seconds and then silently mouthed, "I love you so much!"

They stared into each other's eyes, beaming big smiles at one another, while holding both hands. For an instant they reminded me of newlyweds, but I knew by the age of their kids that they couldn't possibly be. I puzzled about it for a moment, then realized how totally engrossed I was in the wonderful display of unconditional love not more than an arm's length away from me. I suddenly felt uncomfortable, as if I were invading something sacred, but was amazed to hear my own voice nervously ask, "Wow! How long have you two been married?"

"Been together fourteen years total, married twelve of those," he replied, without breaking his gaze from his lovely wife's face.

"Well then, how long have you been away?" I asked.

The man finally turned and looked at me, still beaming his joyous smile. "Two whole days!"

Two days? I was stunned. By the intensity of the greeting, I had assumed he'd been gone for at least several weeks— if not months. I know my expression betrayed me, I said almost offhandedly, hoping to end my intrusion with some semblance of grace (and to get back to searching for my friend), "I hope my marriage is still that passionate after twelve years!"

The man suddenly stopped smiling. He looked me straight in the eye, and with a forcefulness that burned right into my soul, he told me something that left me a different person. He told me, "Don't hope, friend . . . decide."

Then he flashed me his wonderful smile again, shook my hand and said, "God bless!" With that, he and his family turned and strode away together.

I was still watching that exceptional man and his special family walk just out of sight when my friend came up to me and asked, "What'cha looking at?" Without hesitating, and with a curious sense of certainty, I replied, "My future!"

Michael Hargrove

Love That Lasts

To get to a woman's heart, a man must first use his own.

Mike Dobbertin, age thirteen

I have a friend who is falling in love. She honestly claims that the sky is bluer; she's noticed the delicate fragrance of the lilacs beside her garage, though she previously walked past them without stopping; and Mozart moves her to tears. In short, life has never been so exciting.

"I'm young again!" she shouts exuberantly. I have to admit, the guy must be better than Weight Watchers. She has lost fifteen pounds and looks like a cover girl. She's taken a new interest in the shape of her thighs.

As my friend raves on about her new love, I've taken a good look at my old one. My hubby, Scott, hasn't yet had his mid-life crisis, but he's entitled to one. His hairline is receding. He's gained fifteen pounds. Once a marathon runner, all muscles and sinew, he now only runs down hospital halls. His body shows the signs of long work hours and too many candy bars. Yet, he can still give me a certain look across a restaurant table, and I want to ask for the check immediately and head for home.

My natural glow has dimmed a bit after twenty-five years. I can look pretty good when I have to, but I don't think twice about hanging around the house in my baggy sweat pants, old softball jersey and my husband's gray wool socks.

My friend asked me, "What will make this love last?" I told her the truth: "I don't know." Then she asked, "Why does *your* love last?" I told her I'd think about it.

I've run through all the obvious reasons: commitment, shared interests, unselfishness, physical attraction, the ability to communicate. Yet, there's more.

We still have fun. Spontaneous good times. Yesterday, after slipping the rubber band off the rolled-up newspaper, he flipped it playfully at me: this led to all-out war. Last Saturday, while at the grocery store, we split the list and then raced each other to see who could gather the required items and make it to the check-out stand first. We've made an art form out of our prepared gourmet dinners. Even washing dishes together can be a blast. We enjoy simply being together.

And there are surprises: surprises in daily living. One time I came home from work to find a note on the front door. This note led me to another note, then to another, until—many notes later—I was directed to the walk-in closet. I opened the door to find Scott holding a "pot of gold" (my cooking kettle) and the "treasure" of a gift package. He had been jumping back in the closet for an hour, every time he heard footsteps on the stairs. Ever since then, I often leave him notes on the mirror or slip little presents under his pillow.

There is understanding. I understand why he must play basketball with the guys regularly. And he understands why, about once a year, I must get away from the house, the phone, the kids—and even him—to meet my sisters somewhere for a few days of nonstop talking and laughing.

There is a lot of sharing. Not only do we share the bills, the household worries, the parental burdens and the cooking, we also share ideas. Scott came home from a medical convention last month and presented me with a copy of a thick historical novel. Then he touched my heart by telling me he had read the book on the plane. This confession comes from a man who loves science fiction and Tom Clancy thrillers. He read it because he wanted to be able to share ideas about the book after I'd read it.

There is comfort. It's the comfort in knowing that I can tell the waitress waiting for our dessert order, "Just bring me a fork. I'll have a bit of his." I know that one bit is allowed. If Scott really wants every single bit of his dessert to himself, I know he will say, "Sorry, order your own!" And if he's not up to sharing, I'm not offended.

There is blessed forgiveness. When I'm too loud and crazy at parties and have embarrassed us both by not knowing when to shut up, Scott forgives me. He knows I can't resist a good one-liner. I forgave him when he came home and confessed he'd lost some of our investment savings in the stock market. I gave him a hug and bravely said, "It's okay. It's only money."

There is "synergism." That is, we can produce something that is greater than the two of us. (Take, for instance, our kids.) When we put our heads together to identify a problem and all the possible solutions, sometimes we're absolutely, as a team, nothing short of brilliant.

There is sensitivity. I know not to jump all over him for being late when he comes home from the hospital with a certain look in his eyes; I can see that it's been a tough day. Last week, he walked through the door with that look. After he'd spent some time with the kids and had eaten his warmed-up dinner, I asked, "What happened?" He told me about a sixty-year-old woman who had a stroke.

He'd worked with her for hours, but she was still in a coma. When he'd returned to her hospital room to check on her, he had been moved to tears by the sight of the woman's husband standing beside her bed, stroking her hand. Scott wept again as he told me he didn't think the woman would survive. And how was he going to tell this husband of forty years that his wife would probably never recover?

I shed a few tears myself. Because of the medical crisis. Because there are still people who have been married for forty years. Because my husband is still moved and concerned, even after twenty-five years of hospital rooms and dying patients.

There is faith. We both know that God loves us; and that, though life is difficult, He will strengthen and help us. Last week, Scott was on call and already overloaded by the necessary extra hours he spent at the hospital. On Tuesday night, a good friend from church came over and tearfully confessed her fears that her husband, who has cancer, is losing his courageous battle. We did our best to comfort and advise her.

On Wednesday, I went to lunch with a friend who is struggling to reshape her life after her husband left her. Together, we talked, laughed, got angry and figured out the blessings she could still count. On Thursday, a neighbor called who needed to talk about the frightening effects of Alzheimer's disease, because it was changing her father-in-law's personality.

On Friday, my dearest childhood friend called long-distance to break the sad news that her father had died. After a minute, I hung up the phone and thought, "This is too much pain and heartache for one week." After saying a prayer, I descended the stairs to run some necessary errands. Through my tears, I noticed the boisterous orange blossoms of the gladiolus outside my window, I heard the delighted laughter of my son and his friend as they created Lego spaceships in our basement.

After backing my van out of my driveway, I caught sight of three brilliantly colored hot air balloons floating in the distant turquoise sky. Moments later, I looked left just in time to see a wedding party emerge from a neighbor's house. The bride, dressed in satin and lace, tossed her bouquet to her cheering friends.

That night, as I told my husband about these events, we acknowledged the cycles of life and the joys that counter the sorrows. We also recognized the satisfaction we felt when we assisted people with the weight of their burdens. It was enough to keep us going.

Finally, there is knowing. I know Scott will throw his laundry just shy of the hamper every night; he'll be perennially late to most appointments; he'll leave the newspaper scattered across the floor three out of five times; and he'll eat the last chocolate in the box. He knows I sleep with a pillow over my head; I'll lock us out of the house or the car on a regular basis; I'll have a pre-trip fit before we leave on vacation; and I will also eat the last chocolate in the box.

I guess our love lasts because it's comfortable. No, the sky is not bluer—it's just a familiar hue. We're not noticing many new things about life nor each other, but we like what we've noticed and benefit from relearning. Music is still meaningful because we know the harmonies. We don't feel particularly young. We've experienced too much that's contributed to growth and wisdom, taken its toll on our bodies, and created our mixed bag of treasured memories.

I hope we've got what it takes to make our love last. As a naive bride, I had Scott's wedding band engraved with this Robert Browning line: "Grow old along with me!" We're following those instructions.

Annette Paxman Bowen
Submitted by Sandra Dow Mapula

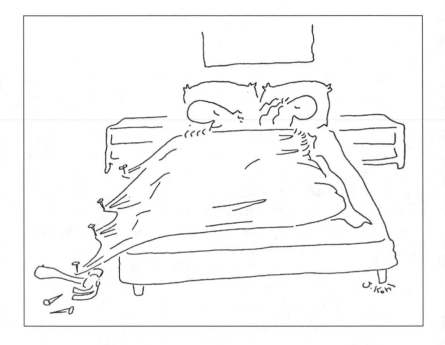

Reprinted by permission of Joe Kohl.

The Beauty of Love

Grow old along with me!
The best is yet to be,
the last of life for which the first was made.

Robert Browning

The question is asked, "Is there anything more beautiful in life than a boy and a girl clasping clean hands and pure hearts in the path of marriage? Can there be anything more beautiful than young love?"

And the answer is given. "Yes, there is a more beautiful thing. It is the spectacle of an old man and an old woman finishing their journey together on that path. Their hands are gnarled, but still clasped; their faces are seamed, but still radiant; their hearts are physically bowed and tired, but still strong with love and devotion for one another. Yes, there is a more beautiful thing than young love. Old love."

Anonymous

The Decade Diary: A Love Story

November 1918

Dearest,

Thanks be to God! The war's at end!
I'm now on bended knee.
Not just for prayer—I'll soon be home!
Will you still marry me?

We've known each other all our lives.
When did our love begin?
You were my Princess Elsa then;
And I, your Lohengrin.

Remember what you promised me
When we were just thirteen?
But that was ten long years ago . . .
Will you still be my queen?

November 1928

Dearest,

As I was rummaging among
The keepsakes in our chest,
I found the yellowed poem above
And thought how I've been blessed.
For when you answered it with "Yes!"
We hardly could delay.
And before the month was even out,
We wed—on Thanksgiving Day.

So now, ten years have passed; it seems
To me like yesterday.
You still have all the beauty any
Flower could display.

November 1938

Dearest,

Has it been ten more years, my love?
And nothing still has changed?
Save one important thing that came
From love we have exchanged.

For what we thought we'd never have . . .
The gift of progeny . . .
My love, I thank you for the son
That you have given me.

November 1948

Dearest,

How ineffectual I feel
When trying to express
How much your love has meant to me . . .
Your kiss and your caress.

You give so freely of yourself
To me and to our son . . .
There is no way I can repay
The things that you have done.

November 1958

Dearest,

Another decade now has passed.
Can it be forty years
That we have shared this life that's seen
Such happiness and tears?

You've stood beside me through it all
(Sometimes behind—and shoved).
What e'er success has come my way
I owe to you, Beloved.

November 1968

Dearest,

We almost made it, didn't we?
This would have been the Golden . . .
Oh, how I miss you every day.
Our lives so interwoven!
Though you are gone and I am here,
It pleases me to write you,
And to just pretend that once again,
Our love and vows continue.

"Till Death Do Us Part"— this I reject.
For even that can't sever
The love we had . . . the love we have!
Oh, Dearest, it's forever!

November 1978

Dear Reader,

Above you've read the poetry
My father wrote my mother.
I found them after Daddy's death,
First one place, then another.

The bulk were found in Mama's chest,
A ribbon held them tightly;
The last was found beneath her urn,
With tear stains, oh so slightly.

Their wedding anniversary
Was celebrated yearly
Thanksgiving day, no matter if
The date was late or early.

He always said it was the day
Most fitting and most proper
To celebrate the thanks they gave
For having one another.

And now, Dear Reader, I have shared
My daddy's little lines,
The intimate love story of
A tie that truly binds.

Henry Matthew Ward

Could You Have Loved as Much?

Love, true love, is that which can give the most without asking or demanding anything in return.

Mazie Hammond

The story begins early in 1950 in the Taylors' small apartment in Waltham, Massachusetts. Edith Taylor was sure that she was "the luckiest woman on the block." She and Karl had been married twenty-three years, and her heart still skipped a beat when he walked into the room. As for Karl, he gave every appearance of a man in love with his wife. If his job as a government warehouse worker took him out of town, he would write Edith each night and send small gifts from every place he visited.

In February 1950, Karl was sent to Okinawa for a few months to work in a new government warehouse. It was a long time to be away, and so far. This time no little gifts came. Edith understood. He was saving his money for the house they had long dreamed of owning someday.

The lonesome months dragged on. Each time Edith expected Karl home, he'd write that he must stay "another

three weeks." "Another month." "Just two months longer."
He'd been gone a year now, and his letters were coming
less and less often. No gifts she understood. But a few pen-
nies for a postage stamp?

Then, after weeks of silence, came a letter:

> *Dear Edith,*
>
> *I wish there were a kinder way to tell you that we are
> no longer married . . .*

Edith walked to the sofa and sat down. He had written
to Mexico for a mail-order divorce. He had married Aiko,
a Japanese maid-of-all-work assigned to his quarters. She
was nineteen. Edith was forty-eight.

Now, if I were making up this story, the rejected wife
would fight that quick paper-divorce. She would hate her
husband and the woman. She would want vengeance for
her own shattered life. But I am describing here simply
what did happen. Edith Taylor did not hate Karl. Perhaps
she had loved him so long that she was unable to stop.

She could picture the situation. A lonely man. Constant
closeness. But even so, Karl had not done the easy,
shameful thing. He had chosen divorce, rather than taking advantage of a young servant girl. The only thing
Edith could not believe was that he had stopped loving
her. Someday, somehow, Karl would come home.

Edith now built her life around this thought. She wrote
Karl, asking him to keep her in touch with his life. In time he
wrote that he and Aiko were expecting a baby. Maria was
born in 1951; then, in 1953, Helen. Edith sent gifts to the little
girls. She still wrote to Karl and he wrote back: Helen had a
tooth, Aiko's English was improving, Karl had lost weight.

And then the terrible letter. Karl was dying of lung cancer. His last letters were filled with fear. Not for himself,

but for Aiko and his two little girls. He had been saving to send them to school in America, but his hospital bills were taking everything. What would become of them?

Then Edith knew that her last gift to Karl could be peace of mind. She wrote that, if Aiko was willing, she would take Maria and Helen and bring them up in Waltham. For many months after Karl's death, Aiko would not let the children go. They were all she had ever known. Yet what could she offer them except a life of poverty, servitude and despair? In November 1956, she sent them to her "Dear Aunt Edith."

Edith had known it would be hard at fifty-four to be mother to a three-year-old and a five-year-old. She hadn't realized that, in the time since Karl's death, they would forget the little English they knew. But Maria and Helen learned fast. The fear left their eyes; their faces grew plump. And Edith, for the first time in six years, was hurrying home from work. Even getting meals was fun again!

Sadder were the times when letters came from Aiko. "Aunt. Tell me now what to do. If Maria or Helen cry or not." In the broken English, Edith read the loneliness, and she knew what loneliness was. She knew that she must bring the girls' mother here too.

She had made the decision, but Aiko was still a Japanese citizen, and the immigration quota had a waiting list many years long. It was then that Edith Taylor wrote me, asking if I could help. I described the situation in my newspaper column. Others did more. Petitions were started, and, in August 1957, Aiko Taylor was permitted to enter the country.

As the plane came in at New York's international airport, Edith had a moment of fear. What if she should hate this woman who had taken Karl away from her? The last person off the plane was a girl so thin and small that Edith thought at first it was a child. She stood there clutching the railing, and Edith knew that, if she had been afraid, Aiko was near panic.

She called Aiko's name, and the girl rushed down the steps and into Edith's arms. As they held each other, Edith had an extraordinary thought. "I prayed for Karl to come back. Now he has—in his two little daughters and in this gentle girl he loved. Help me, God, to love her, too."

Bob Considine

A Gift-Wrapped Memory

Three things in human life are important: The first is to be kind. The second is to be kind. And the third is to be kind.

Henry James

Every holiday season since I was a teenager Dad asked, "Do you remember *that* Christmas Eve? Remember those two little children who asked us for carfare?"

Yes, I remembered. Even if my father had not reminded me of that strange event every season for more than thirty-five years, I would have remembered.

It was 1935, a typical Christmas Eve in St. Louis, Missouri. Streetcars clang-clanged their warnings. Shoppers rushed in and out of stores for last-minute gifts. Even then, mothers forgot a few ingredients absolutely necessary to complete the family Christmas dinner. Mother had sent Dad and me on such a mission.

Our frosty breaths made a parallel trail behind us as we hurried from the car to her favorite grocery store on Delmar Avenue. Mother liked Moll's because its shelves were stocked with exotic condiments and fancy foods.

Up and down the aisles we hurried, selecting anise and cardamom for Christmas breakfast bread, double whipping cream and jumbo pecans for pumpkin pies, and day-old bread for a fat gobbler's stuffing. We checked the last item off Mother's list and paid the cashier.

Once again we braced our backs for the frigid cold. As we stepped out of the store, a small voice asked, "Please, would you give us a dime for carfare so we can go home?"

Taken aback, Dad stopped. Our eyes met those of a little girl around nine years old. She was holding the gloveless hand of her six-year-old brother.

"Where do you live?" Dad asked.

"On Easton Avenue" was the reply.

We were amazed. Here it was night—Christmas Eve night—and these two children were more than three miles from home.

"What are you doing so far from home?" Dad asked her.

"We had only enough money to ride the streetcar here," she said. "We came to ask for money to buy food for Christmas. But no one gave us any and we are afraid to walk home." Then she told us that their father was blind, their mother was sick, and there were five other children at home.

My dad was a strong-willed urban businessman. But his heart was soft and warm, just like the little girl's brown eyes. "Well, the first thing I think we should do is shop for groceries," he announced, taking her hand. Her brother promptly reached for mine.

Once again we hurried up and down Moll's aisles. This time Dad selected two plump chickens, potatoes, carrots, milk, bread, oranges, apples, bananas, candy and nuts. When we left the store, we had two huge sacks of groceries to carry to the car and two small trusting children in tow.

They gave us directions to Easton Avenue. "Home" was upstairs in a large, old brick building. The first floor housed commercial establishments, while rental units were on the second. A bare light bulb on a long cord hung from the ceiling at the landing, swaying slightly as we climbed the long flight of worn wooden steps to their apartment.

The little girl and her brother burst through the door announcing the arrival of two sacks of groceries. The family was just as she had described: The father was blind and the mother was ill in bed. Five other children, most of them with colds, were on the floor.

Dad introduced himself. First on one foot and then the other, concerned that he would embarrass the father, he continued, "Uh ... er ... Merry Christmas." He set the groceries on a table.

The father said, "Thank you. My name is Earl Withers."

"Withers?" Dad turned sharply. "You wouldn't know Hal Withers, would you?"

"Sure do. He's my uncle."

Both Dad and I were stunned. My aunt was married to Hal Withers. Although we were not blood relatives, we felt related to Uncle Hal. How could the sad plight of this family be? Why were they in such need when they had so many relatives living in the same city? A strange coincidence, indeed.

Or was it?

Through the years the incident haunted us. Each succeeding year seemed to reveal a different answer to the question, "What was the meaning of that Christmas Eve?"

At first, the phrase repeatedly quoted by elderly aunts, "God works in strange and mysterious ways," surfaced. Perhaps Dad acted out the Good Samaritan role. That was it! God had a job for us to do and fortunately we did it.

Another year passed. It was not a satisfactory answer. What was? If I am my brother's keeper, am I also my wife's sister's husband's brother's blind son's keeper? That was it! This tied the incident into a neat package.

Yet it didn't. The years rolled by, and each year Dad and I would again toss the question around. Then Dad, who was born in the Christmas season of 1881, died in the Christmas season of 1972. Every December since, though, I still hear him ask me, "Do you remember *that* Christmas Eve?"

Yes, Dad. I remember. And I believe I finally have the answer. We were the ones blessed when two children innocently gave a middle-aged father and his teenaged daughter the true meaning of Christmas: It *is* more blessed to give than to receive.

This gift-wrapped memory became the most beautiful Christmas I ever celebrated. I think it was your best one, too, Dad.

Dorothy DuNard

A Tribute to Gramps

The following letter about our grandfather, Harold Poster, was written by our mother, Patricia Levin. Our grandfather attended Harvard University. For his fiftieth reunion book, a form letter was sent out asking what official titles, achievements, awards, etcetera people had received and what they had accomplished since leaving Harvard. Our mother was very upset about the way the letter was written, as it implied that unless you had achieved some higher goal, you were a failure.

As my mother's letter will attest, our grandfather was a wonderful man, whose goal was to keep his family happy. He succeeded 110 percent! Our grandpa passed away eight years ago, and not one day goes by that our hearts don't ache from missing him so much.

Dear Class Secretary of 1934,

I am answering this questionnaire on behalf of my father. My father suffered a stroke about four months ago. Although he understands mostly everything, he is not able to write or speak clearly.

You ask on your questionnaire for a list of offices

*held, honors and awards received, and I am at a loss to
think of any official titles my father has held. However,
this is not to say that he has led an uneventful or
uncharitable life. If awards were to be given for
"Wonderful Father," "Exceptional Grandfather" and
"Devoted Friend," then surely he would have won them
all. Never in my memory has there not been time for my
father to be with his children, never a problem too large
that Grandpa couldn't solve it. And when his friends
tell me what a fine person he is, what a devoted friend,
what an understanding man, I want to tell them, "I
know, I know, he's my father; I've always known this."
So, although these honors were not gained by a higher
education or written on diplomas or awards, they are
nonetheless meaningful. They were acquired by living
every day to its fullest and bringing happiness to his
children, grandchildren and friends.*

*So, under the titles of honors on your questionnaire,
the best honor of all, I suppose, is mine. I am honored
to say Harold Poster is my father.*

Sincerely,
Patricia Levin

The response to our mother's letter followed a few days
later:

Dear Mrs. Levin:

*As Secretary of the Class and Editor of the Fiftieth
Report, I have the task of reviewing all of the questionnaire returns before they proceed to the printer. I say
"task" but generally speaking, it usually is a pleasure.
Of all those reviewed, I couldn't help but write you
about the one I considered the most warm and satisfy-
ing contribution for our fiftieth Report. I can tell you*

without reservation that it served to describe a person who has achieved honor and success in his life far exceeding the vast majority who have listed paragraph after paragraph of alleged honors and successes (financial, to be sure!).

My only regret is that I did not know your father in college and in the intervening years. Now I know what a truly fine man he is and a lucky person to have produced his replica in you. I do hope he is well on the road to recovery.

Many thanks for your wonderful reply!

Sincerely,
John M. Lockwood, Secretary
Class of 1934

Dana O'Connor and Melissa Levin

The Canarsie Rose

In 1931 I was eleven. Grandma was ninety-three. It was during the Great Depression, and she lived with us in a cold water tenement, five floors up. She was bent, wrinkled, and had only one tooth left in her mouth. But, boy, she had a thousand years of magic stored in her head. And to a kid like me, she knew everything. She had all kinds of powders and colored liquids in her room, and when she mixed them up and we slugged them down, no one ever got sick.

She refused to learn English. When I asked her why, she'd shrug and say in Yiddish, "English won't help when the Cossacks come. They'll still break our heads."

"But, Grandma, this is America, we don't have Cossacks here."

She'd stare at me for a second and then mumble, "Cossacks are everywhere!"

"You know," Mom said one day, "Grandma was once very famous."

"What for, Ma?"

"She grew a rose and it was beautiful. It was six inches wide and white like the cream from the top of the milk. It was so famous that two men from the Czar even came to look. They gave her a paper and it was such an honor that the Rabbi himself read it to us from the *shul*."

"Was it like a medal, Ma?"

"Yeah, some medal. A week later the Cossacks came riding through the *shtetl* breaking our heads and tearing the rose to pieces. Right after that we were all on a boat sailing for America."

The story of the rose bugged me, and I begged Pop to find her another. Where we lived a blade of grass was considered a plant. A rose bush? Unheard of. Leave it to Pop; a week later he lugged a pot up five flights and handed Grandma a tiny new rose bush.

She immediately sifted the soil in her hands and nodded her head in pleasure. After gently placing it on the fire escape, she kissed Pop on both cheeks and cried.

That summer I could see why the Czar sent his men to give her a prize. She fed and rubbed her rosebush with different concoctions. Even the thorns became her friends. The bush grew sturdy and when a bud finally appeared, she nurtured it like another child. At night she would sit near the fire escape and speak tenderly to it in Slavish, Polish, Romansch, and a few more languages that I didn't understand.

In the beginning of July six souls crouched on the fire escape, dizzy with excitement, watching as the huge bud unfolded its creamy white petals. She had grown a perfect white rose.

Not long after that Pop gave us some good news. The bunch of us, me, my two sisters, Grandma and Mom and Pop were moving to Brooklyn. To a section called Canarsie out in the boondocks. Around us were miles of farmland stretching into the distance.

We were homesteading in a part of Brooklyn that was like the plains of Iowa and Kansas. Flat rolling land, green with eggplant, zucchini and tomatoes growing every-where. Grandma took one look and started to cry. Ninety-three and she had finally discovered America.

The house came with a back yard, and Pop started a vegetable garden. Mom planted hollyhocks and some other stuff, but the centerpiece was the rose bushes, Grandma's private preserve. That summer she planted six in different colors: reds, pinks, peach, and her creamy white that was going to look like the top of the milk. They bloomed and were gorgeous. But still, Grandma wasn't satisfied.

"I need a horse," she said. "Not just a horse, a special horse."

"For what, Grandma?"

"With the right horse I can use the manure for the rose. Maybe this time the Cossacks won't come."

"Isn't all horse manure the same, Grandma?"

"What are you, *meshugas*? There are hundreds of quali-ties and I need the best!"

So Mom and I were always on the lookout for the right kind of horse manure. We carried a shovel and filled bag after bag. They all failed Grandma's acid test. Like a fine wine sniffer she would pulverize the manure in her hand, take a whiff, and proclaim our fertilizer no good. Poor Grandma, she was looking for the perfect bouquet.

And then one day we had a big surprise; new neighbors moved in next door. They arrived with a big horse and wagon that said "Borden's Milk" on the side. Grandma and Mom were at Bill and Grace Hart's door the minute the furniture was inside. They carried a big welcome basket filled with Jewish goodies: hamantaschen, strudel, even the ruggelach that I was counting on eating that night. The Harts were Irish, and their brogue was as foreign to Grandma as the man in the moon. The gesture, thought, brought tears to the old milkman's eyes. His horse Buck and the Borden's wagon were still at the curb, and when Grandma looked him over, she swooned!

"You see that horse," she said. "He has a golden *tuchas*. When he *kvetches*, diamonds will come out!"

"How do you know, Grandma?"

"How do I *know*, boychick? With a horse like that, the Czar gave me a medal."

Bill was a kindred spirit in his love for flowers and never failed to leave a bag of fertilizer at our front door with two quarts of milk. By now they were old pals with a friendship based on shrugs, grimaces and red and blue liquids that they both shared. With the mixture of Grandma's voodoo and Bill's manure they were developing gargantuan flowers and rose buds as big as a fist.

Just when he was needed most, Buck developed a severe case of constipation. No more diamonds were tumbling out. It was a crisis, and in a few days the Borden Milk company sent a replacement, a horse called Nick. I thought Nick was great, but Grandma pined away for Buck. More bad news. Bill told us Buck had three days to get well or he'd be turned into dog food.

"Murderers! Murderers!" Grandma screamed. She was positive the Cossacks were out to get her new rose.

"Not this time, boychick!"

The next day Bill took Grandma and me to the Borden stable and we got ready for the cure. A gallon of prunes, plums and other stuff from her arsenal of medications produced nothing but a little wind. This was much more than Grandma expected. We slept that night in the barn with Buck and toward dawn we watched as the old magician started her mysterious incantations. Bill was hypnotized. She was calling for the same spirits that his sainted mother invoked when he was a boy. He crossed himself a couple of times, and we watched as Grandma whipped out a Star of David and swung it in front of Buck three times. Nothing, not even a little gas. But she was biding her time.

When the sun rose in the east, she made her big move. "Boychick," she shouted, "what we need is a tub full of *Shmetina*. You understand? *Shmetina!*"

"What do you need sour cream for, Grandma?"

"Don't ask, just get it!"

So Bill and Pop got a ton of sour cream and ladled it into Buck's trough. Not just plain sour cream, but stuff that she fortified with a royal blue broth. That horse Buck lapped up the sour cream like an old *Galitziana* (member of a neighboring Jewish tribe), licking his chops. Suddenly there was an explosion that almost blew off the rafters and caused the other horses to stampede out of Borden's front gate. Fertilizer came pouring out of Buck like a burst dam. Fertilizer so rich in enzymes and proteins that it revolutionized Canarsie farms forever. A teaspoon of Buck's manure now accomplished what fifty pounds did before. Grandma and her blue sour cream had produced a new strain that created monsters in the garden. Cantaloupes as big as basketballs, dahlias as big as your head, and roses . . . oh boy, what roses!

The Canarsie Chamber of Commerce and Brooklyn Botanical Gardens awarded Grandma and Bill their highest honor for the creamy white rose. This new strain was even given a Latin name: "Buckitus Shemtinitus."

When she accepted her medal, Grandma leaned over and whispered in my ear, "Boychick, get ready! Tonight the Cossacks will come for this rose."

Mike Lipstock

2

ON PARENTS AND PARENTING

Children are a poor man's riches.

English Proverb

The Pitcher

My father was always "permanent pitcher" in our backyard baseball games when I was growing up.

He got this special honor in part because no one else could pitch well enough to get the ball over home plate. If we had any hope of moving a game along at a fair pace, we needed him to do the pitching.

But he also pitched because, with one wooden leg courtesy of Adolf Hitler, he didn't do too well in the field. Running after a fly ball that got hit into the cornfield out back just wasn't his strong suit.

And so he stood under the hot sun throwing endless numbers of pitches to my sister, brother and me, while we took our turns at bat and in the field.

I never questioned the rightness of it.

"Fathers pitch," was a fact of life I'd internalized without giving it any real thought. When I'd play ball in other children's backyards, it always seemed odd to me that their fathers played the outfield and ran the bases. It was somehow childish, the way fathers were sprinting around out there.

Fathers pitched.

He ran our games with the authority of a Yankees team

manager. He was boss of the field, and there were requirements if we wanted to play. We had to chatter in the outfield. I must have said, "Nobatternobatternobatternobatter," 5,000 times growing up.

We had to stand properly, too, both in the field and at bat. And we always had to try to outrun the ball, no matter how futile it might seem. This was baseball, by God, and there was only one way to play it. The way the Yankees played it.

Going up to bat against my father was not exactly like playing T-ball. None of this self-esteem stuff for him, trying to make kids feel good about hitting a ball that's standing still.

It was perfectly fine with him if he struck me out, and he did it all the time. He never felt sorry about it at all.

"Do you want to play ball, or don't you?" he'd ask, if I began whining about his fast pitches.

I wanted to. And when I'd finally connect with one of his pitches—oh, man—I knew I deserved the hit. I could tell by the feel of it. And I'd be grinning all the way down the first-base line.

Then I'd turn around to look at my father standing on the pitcher's mound. I'd watch as he took off his glove and tucked it under his arm. And then he'd clap for me.

To my ears, it sounded like a standing ovation at Yankee stadium.

Years later, my boy was to learn those same rules about baseball from my father.

"Grandfathers pitch," was his understanding. By then, though, his grandfather was pitching from a wheelchair. By some medical fluke, my father had lost his other leg sometime between my childhood and my son's.

But nothing else had changed. My boy was required to chatter from the outfield. He had to stand properly at bat and in the field. He had to try outrunning the ball, no matter how futile it might have seemed.

And when he whined that the ball was coming at him too fast—my father could still get steam behind it, even sitting in a wheelchair—he got the ultimatum: "Do you want to play ball or don't you?"

He did.

My boy was nine years old the spring before his grandfather died. They played a lot of ball that season, and there was the usual litany of complaints about my father pitching too hard.

"Just keep your eye on the ball!" my father would holler at him.

Finally, at one at-bat, he did.

He swung the bat around and connected with the ball dead center. Then the ball headed back out where it'd come from, straight down the middle. Straight and hard at my father.

He reached for it, but it got past him. And in the process, his wheelchair tilted backward. In ever such slow motion, we watched him and his chair topple until he came down on his back with a thud.

My boy stood stock still halfway to first.

"You don't ever stop running!" my father roared at him from the ground. "That ball's still in play! You run!"

And when my boy stood safe at first base, he turned to look at my father lying on his back on the pitcher's mound. He saw him take off his glove and tuck it under his arm.

And then he heard his grandfather clap for him.

Beth Mullally

THE FAMILY CIRCUS®　By Bil Keane

10-29
©1996 Bil Keane, Inc.
Dist. by Cowles Synd., Inc.

"I'm a real superhero. I'm Daddy."

Hall of Fame Dad

To Wendy MacBlain, the second-floor exhibit area at the National Baseball Hall of Fame and Museum in Cooperstown, New York, felt cavernous without its displays. They had been placed in temporary storage so that a new humidification system could be installed. On that winter morning early in 1994, MacBlain moved around the empty room, cleaning up the litter that had slipped underneath and between the display cases. As she neared the spot where the World War II display had been, she noticed a small black-and-white photograph lying face up on the floor.

Picking up the picture she headed downstairs. "I found this," she said, handing the snapshot to Ted Spencer, curator of the museum. "Maybe it fell out of one of the exhibits."

Spencer glanced at the photo. He knew immediately that the man was not one of the 216 baseball giants immortalized at the Hall of Fame—including players such as Ty Cobb, Babe Ruth, Lou Gehrig and Ted Williams. Who was he?

Intrigued, Spencer studied the photograph more closely. The smiling stocky man wore a bulky baseball uniform of the 1940s and his bat over his right shoulder, obscuring the team name on his shirt. On his left sleeve, however, Spencer could see a small dinosaur—the logo, he guessed of an industrial league team sponsored by the Sinclair Refining Company.

"This isn't from any of the exhibits," Spencer said slowly. So how did it end up in the Hall of Fame? Turning the picture over, he found no name, but a short message written by the man's son. The signature looked like "Pete."

The curator was fascinated by the small mystery. To him, the unidentified man became a symbol of many American fathers who play baseball with their kids. He sent a copy of the photo and its message to a friend, writer Steve Wulf, at *Sports Illustrated*. And in early April 1994, a few weeks after the picture was discovered, an article about the mysterious ballplayer appeared.

Some 150 miles from Cooperstown, in the village of Wellsville, New York, Neal Simon read the article. A reporter for the *Wellsville Daily Reporter*, Simon knew the town had once been the location of a Sinclair refinery. He looked carefully at the copy of the photograph. The rolling foothills in the background resembled those surrounding the valley community.

Hoping to unravel the mystery, Simon began showing the picture to longtime residents. For five days he drew a blank. Sinclair had sponsored teams all over the country. One resident said, "You'll never find this guy."

Finally, just as he was about to give up, Simon struck gold. "That's Joe O'Donnell," said an older man who saw the picture. "His son Pat runs the Blarney Stone Tavern in Andover."

Pat? Simon wondered. On the office copier a colleague enlarged the "Pete" signature reproduced in *Sports Illustrated.* The name was Pat!

He called Pat O'Donnell in neighboring Andover and told him who he was. "I'm trying to identify a photo," the reporter said. "I think it may be your father."

"Does he have a bat over his right shoulder?" O'Donnell asked.

"Yes, he does."

"Yeah, that's my dad."

Simon could tell O'Donnell was fighting back tears. "This is quite a thing you've done," he said gently. "Why the Hall of Fame?"

"Well," O'Donnell answered, "you'd have to know my dad to understand that."

And in a halting voice he began at the beginning.

> *"Let's see whatcha got!" Joe O'Donnell called out to his son, pounding his big fist in the pocket of his old black fielder's glove. Nine-year-old Pat went into a windup, drew back his left arm and sent the ball sailing—over his father's head.*
>
> *Sighing, Joe stood up and trotted after the ball. He was tired after a long day working at the nearby Sinclair refinery. But it was the spring of 1957, and the baseball season was approaching.*
>
> *Tossing the ball back to his son, Joe dropped into his catcher's crouch again. This time Pat threw dead center into his father's glove, amazing them both. Joe wondered how his southpaw son could throw so wildly one moment and so on target the next.*
>
> *As the ball sailed back and forth between them, Pat felt a singular closeness with the man on the other end of the throw. The two were in rhythm, synchronized in movement and thought. His father's total focus made Pat feel proud and important.*
>
> *The two had been playing catch almost since Pat had learned to walk: The family photo album held a picture*

of Pat, age two, with a baseball glove on his hand. Now, nearly ten, he'd soon be moving up to Little League. And thanks to his dad and other volunteers, he'd be playing in a brand new ballpark.

Like his son, Joe O'Donnell had fallen in love with baseball at an early age. A heavy hitter on his high school team in Genesee, Pennsylvania, he joined the town team after graduating. "Joe, you ought to think about trying out for a pro team," manager Harry Hurd had told him one day. "You're good enough."

Joe smiled. By then he was married to his high school sweetheart, Mary Charlantiny, and was thankful to have steady work in the Pennsylvania oil and gas fields. Turning pro was a dream he simply buried deep inside.

In 1941 Joe went to work for a Sinclair refinery in Wellsville. He won a spot on the refinery team, playing right field and catcher. Then World War II broke out, and Joe joined the U.S. Army Air Forces. When he returned from the Pacific, he went back to Sinclair. But his baseball-playing days were over.

"I hardly ever get a hit," Pat complained. In his first year of Little League, the youngest member of the team, he was discouraged.

"Nobody's going to give you a hit," Joe told him one day. "You've got to want a hit and then you have to go out and get it. It's jut like anything else in life."

Several evenings later, Pat stood at the plate, burning with anger and shame. Jim Euken, one of the team's best hitters, had just been deliberately walked so Pat would come to bat. The game was in the last inning, with Pat's team down a run and men on first and second—one more out and it would be over. Now came eager shouts from the opposing team: "Easy out! Easy out!"

The pitcher went into his windup and threw.

"Strike one!" the umpire yelled. ". . . Strike two!"

"Time!" Pat called, and the umpire held up his hand. Pat stepped out of the batter's box and glanced at his father on the sidelines. Joe had a broad smile, and he was nodding. If you want a hit, he seemed to be saying, go out and get it!

Then, stepping back to the plate, the boy took a determined stance. I'm going to blast the next pitch a mile, he thought.

Pat swung hard at the pitch. He felt a solid crack as the bat met the ball. But it wasn't until he reached second base that it all sank in: The game was over—and he'd driven in the winning run.

Pat's teammates steamed out of the dugout. Off to the side, Jim Euken's dad slapped Joe on the back. Pat's father had a grin as big as Yankee Stadium.

It was Pat's final year of Little League. Playing center field one day, the twelve-year-old was running toward the fence chasing a long fly ball. Time and again, Joe had said, "Always keep your eye on the ball." Pat did just that as it sailed out of the field—and he slammed into the fence. Fortunately he only had the wind knocked out of him.

After the game, as Pat and Joe walked toward Joe's pickup truck, another father caught up with them. "If you keep Pat alive," the father told Joe, winking, "maybe he'll make it into the Baseball Hall of Fame."

On the drive home Pat turned to his father. "Dad, how do people get into the Hall of Fame?" he asked.

"You get there by being the best of the best," Joe said. "You have to be very special."

Pat thought of Lou Gehrig, who'd played in over 2,000 games without missing a day. Joe DiMaggio, who'd gotten a hit in 56 straight games. Ty Cobb, whose lifetime batting average was .367. They were special.

The boy looked over at his father. He wished he could

have seen him play baseball. Even if Joe O'Donnell hadn't averaged .367, he was special, too.

Four years later, Pat found himself in a pickup game on the very diamond where his father had played with the Sinclair team many years before. Suddenly he noticed his father watching from the far sidelines and walked over to him.

One of the other boys yelled, "Hey, Mr. O'Donnell, wanna play?" Joe smiled and shook his head. "No, baseball's for you young guys."

Pat noticed a faraway look in his father's eyes as Joe watched the action on the field—a look he'd never seen before. "Y'know," his father said softly, "I just might've had a chance out there. But things just sorta slid away from me."

Pat knew people had once suggested that Joe try out for a pro team. He might have gone far, he thought. But standing there, he knew nothing he could say would comfort his father about the past, with all its mistakes and regrets. At that moment, staring into his father's eyes, Pat hoped he would always remember that rule.

On the evening of March 29, 1966, at the age of fifty, Joe suffered a massive heart attack and died. Hundreds of people stopped by the funeral home in Wellsville to pay their respects. Some had known him as a ballplayer, some as a coworker. All knew him as a friend.

Joe O'Donnell's sudden death devastated his eighteen-year-old son. By then Pat was married to his high school sweetheart and was soon to be a father. His difficulty adjusting to his new responsibilities was compounded by his deep grief. After Pat's son was born, his marriage fell apart.

Before long, the tensions in Pat's personal life affected his work, and he lost his job at the steam-turbine plant in Wellsville. With the loss of father, wife *and job, Pat felt adrift. Over the next few years he worked on and off, traveling from town to town.*

By the spring of 1970, Pat had reached his lowest point. Seeking relief, he visited the one place he'd been avoiding: his father's grave. As twilight edged toward the darkness, he sat and leaned back against the cool tombstone and tried to think through his troubles.

After his marriage had failed, his former wife and their son, Rick, had moved over seventy miles away. I'm not there for my son the way my dad was there for me, *Pat realized. He still hadn't found a steady job. As he looked down at his father's grave, the truth hit him like one of Joe's hardest fastballs.* If you want something, *he could hear his father say,* you just have to go out and get it!

Shortly after that, Pat landed a draftsman's job, and before long he was moving up in the company. But he'd always wanted to go into business for himself. In 1980 he took the plunge and bought a tavern. After renovating the existing structure, he added one final touch. He had an eight-by-ten enlargement of a small snapshot of his dad hung behind the bar. The photo showed Joe O'Donnell in his Sinclair uniform with a big smile on his face.

Then, in 1987, Pat was married a second time—to Ann Barnes, a vivacious woman who brought new energy and enthusiasm to his life. Pat felt there was only one last loose thread in his life: his relationship with his son.

In the spring of 1988, Rick, now in his early twenties, came to Andover for a visit. Talking with his son, Pat found himself struggling with his emotions.

"Rick, I'm sorry," he suddenly blurted. "I'm sorry I didn't get to watch you grow up. I wasn't there to teach you how to swing a bat or to play catch with you like your Grandpa Joe did with me."

"That was then and this is now," the young man said. "And right now, Dad, we're together—that's what counts."

"I love you," Pat said quietly. As the two hugged, Pat felt the distance and guilt start to melt away.

Several weeks later Rick came by for Pat's birthday. Getting out of the car, he tossed something to his father. "Here, catch," he called. It was a new baseball glove. Rick carried another in his hand.

Together, father and son went to the parking lot behind the Blarney Stone. As the ball sailed back and forth between them, Pat once again felt the old rhythm—the closeness, the unity—of father and son.

On a warm, quiet night in August 1989, Pat sat in a hotel room in Cooperstown, looking at a small photograph of his father. Turning the picture over, Pat wrote:

"You were never too busy or tired to play catch. On your days off you helped build the Little League field. You always came to watch me play. You were a Hall of Fame Dad. I wish I could share this moment with you. Your son, Pat."

The next day, Pat O'Donnell toured the Baseball Hall of Fame and Museum. On the second floor he found pictures of players in bulky uniforms like the one Joe O'Donnell had worn. At the World War II exhibit, Pat noticed a small opening between the bottom of the display case and the floor. He looked around. There were no other people nearby. Kneeling down, he slid the photo beneath the case. "Now you're in the Hall of Fame, Dad," Pat said. "This is where the best of the best get to go. And you're the best of the best."

In the fall of 1994, Hall of Fame curator Ted Spencer put Joe O'Donnell's photo in an envelope, along with the article from *Sports Illustrated* and Neal Simon's stories for the

Wellsville Daily Reporter. He also enclosed a letter of his own, addressed to any future curator who might come across the envelope and wonder. Spencer then put the package back near where Pat had originally hidden the photograph.

This gave Joe O'Donnell a permanent place in the National Baseball Hall of Fame and Museum.

Ben Fanton
Submitted by Nancy Mitchell

The Puzzle

I grew up on a farm in Iowa, the youngest of four boys. My dad had made it through the eighth grade and then started working. My mom was the valedictorian of her small high school class, but started working on the family farm rather than going to college. Even though neither had gone to college, education was very important in our house. My parents said that they didn't care if we read comic books, so long as we were reading. I later realized that they were two of the more intelligent people I would ever meet, but when I was in high school, I thought they were incredibly dumb. I am not sure if my brothers felt the same, but I could not wait to get away from home and go to college.

I first saw the Rockwell picture during the Christmas season of my sophomore year at college. It hit me with a lot of emotions I didn't know I had inside me. I was walking with my girlfriend (who eventually became my wife) down an aisle of jigsaw puzzles, utterly bored. Puzzles had never been part of my family, but they were very popular in hers. The picture caught my eye because it had been made into a puzzle. I took one look at it and went to pieces.

The son could have been me: anxious to go to school, looking beyond the father, not considering what he might be thinking. I was the son who went to college and never wrote home. The father represented what I thought of my father: a hard-working farmer wondering about his son, but not able to express his thoughts or his feelings. The final straw was the collie. When I was growing up, we had a beautiful collie named Lassie.

I immediately started crying and bolted from the store. My girlfriend finally found me, standing outside with tears running down my cheeks. I took her back inside and showed her the puzzle and started crying again. She gave me the strangest look. Emotional outbursts were not something Iowa farm boys did.

I bought the puzzle and wrapped it up for Christmas for Dad. I added a note: "Dad, I got this present, not because it was a jigsaw puzzle, but because of the picture on it. Somehow, it really struck home when I saw it." I had some concern about giving it because it was an emotional gift. Emotions were not something easily shared among the males in our house.

Christmas morning came, and I kept a close eye on Dad when he picked up my gift to open. I really did not know what to expect—whether to be excited or embarrassed. Dad took off the paper and looked at the box, his expression never changing. It was clear to me that he did not think much of the present. Just as well—we never did puzzles in our house. He put the box down and without a word left the room. After about a minute, Mom noticed he was gone. She went out to the kitchen and found Dad crying. She could not understand what had happened.

When Mom brought Dad back into the family room and I saw Dad crying, I started crying and laughing at the same time. I had never seen my dad cry before. Dad showed Mom the picture. He explained that when he saw that the father had a tobacco bag just like the one he used to roll cigarettes, the emotions became too much. Like any good farmer, he did not think it was right to cry in front of his family, so he had left the room. My older brother somehow missed the magic of the moment and looked at us both as if we were losing it.

I have often wondered how Norman Rockwell drew a picture with details that fit our family so perfectly: the eager son, the weathered father, the collie and the tobacco bag. If we had paid him to paint a picture summarizing the first eighteen years of my life, he could not have done better. We put the puzzle together and Mom glued it to a board so they could hang it in their bedroom.

Dad is now eighty-four and slowed by Parkinson's disease. I live in Minneapolis and visit him several times a year. A few years ago, Dad decided to give us a hug when we were leaving. He said he did not want to die without hugging his boys. It has taken years to get used to a hug from him.

Every time I drive back to Iowa to see my parents, I think of the picture hanging in their bedroom. It still reflects what I think of my dad. How he worked so hard to get us through college, something he really did not understand but knew was important. How he never really told us how much he thought of us. And I am still ashamed by how it embodies me at that time. How I went to college never thinking how my parents might feel about me, just ready to get away. I still get tears in my eyes when I think of that picture.

Several years ago, I decided I would talk about this picture when the time came for my father's funeral, and how this picture was able to say things to my dad on that special Christmas that I was not able to say myself. But then I thought, "Why am I going to wait? Let me write it down now so Dad can read about it while he is still alive." So I have. Only one more thing to say: "I love you, Dad."

Jerry Gale

My Dad's Hands

Bedtime came, we were settling down,
I was holding one of my lads.
As I grasped him so tight, I saw a strange sight:
My hands . . . they looked like my dad's!

I remember them well, those old gnarled hooks,
there was always a cracked nail or two.
And thanks to a hammer that strayed from its mark,
his thumb was a beautiful blue!

They were rough, I remember, incredibly tough,
as strong as a carpenter's vice.
But holding a scared little boy at night,
they seemed to me awfully nice!

The sight of those hands—how impressive it was
in the eyes of his little boy.
Other dads' hands were cleaner, it seemed
(the effects of their office employ).

I gave little thought in my formative years
of the reason for Dad's raspy mitts:
The love in the toil, the dirt and the oil,
rusty plumbing that gave those hands fits!

Thinking back, misty-eyed, and thinking ahead,
when one day my time is done.
The torch of love in my own wrinkled hands
will pass on to the hands of my son.

I don't mind the bruises, the scars here and there
or the hammer that just seemed to slip.
I want most of all when my son takes my hand,
to feel that love lies in the grip.

David Kettler

One Small Stone, Unforgotten

To some people, a cemetery can be a frightening, sad place, full of unfinished business and painful memories. But, not to me. When I was a young child growing up in rural Indiana, cemeteries were my playgrounds. My father was the groundskeeper for several state-run and private cemeteries in the county.

He had come to America from Russia after the war as a young man and met my mother, also a recent immigrant, through mutual friends. Somehow they ended up in a small town in Indiana where my father found work as a landscape gardener. He worked hard all his life and his little business grew. He tended all the cemeteries in the county as well as all the lawns of the private homes in the area. Often, he would take me with him to work.

My father chose his profession partly because his English remained poor all his life and landscaping was something he could do well without extensive communication skills. That and the fact that he loved to make beautiful spaces, spaces that would cause one to pause and appreciate the serene loveliness in Nature.

When I was very little, I loved to go to the cemeteries

with him. To me, the cemeteries were quiet, calm places full of life stories—millions of them which I conjured in my own imagination. Just the name and dates of a person's life were enough for me. I would imagine whole scenarios about how that person lived and what kind of family he had had. I would infuse the dead of rural Indiana with all manner of mystery. Some of the graves belonged to long-lost royalty or heroes who had perished saving others. And, sometimes, I imagined that a grave bore a lover who, having met an untimely demise, would finally be forever united with the loved one in a better place. (I really believe that adults read obituaries each day in the newspaper for pretty much the same reason—to catch a glimpse of another's life encapsulated, with all the details left to the imagination.)

All of my childish imaginings were given vent in the cemeteries because my own life was painfully devoid of any drama or excitement. By the time I reached my teens, I had grown so bored with my sheltered, quiet life in rural Indiana that my invented scenarios were my only means of escape.

My parents, I was sure, could not possibly have been able to understand my growing frustration. I considered them just ignorant immigrants who lived and worked where they did because that was all they could do. It never occurred to me to wonder about their lives before they arrived in America. To me, my parents were simple, uncomplicated people. They had settled in a place where settling was what life was about. They had no dreams, no desires to be anything other than exactly what they were.

But, I wanted more, much more.

Throughout my college years—tumultuous years of experimentation and rebellion—I searched for a way to leave my own personal mark on the world. I wanted to be defined, to feel myself important, significant. My parents had only been ordinary but, I, with all the fervor of my young heart, longed to really experience life.

While I was away at university, my parents grew quietly older. One winter vacation, I went home for a visit.

The years had taken their toll on my father and he could not work as he once could. He missed the feel of dirt in his hands and he said, he missed something else, too. While I had spent my time lost in my fantasies in the cemeteries, my father had done his work—mowing and edging and planting—making the cemeteries lovely. And just before we left each time, my father would take a handful of small pebbles from the back of his pick-up truck. These he would lay carefully on the headstones of some of the graves. It had never occurred to me to ask why he did this. I had just accepted that this was part of his work. But, I knew this act was as important to him as bringing beauty to these resting places.

On this particular visit home, my father asked a favor of me. He wanted me to take his truck out to one of the cemeteries and lay some of the stones on several of the markers. For some reason, this was very important to him and it had to be done that day.

I was beginning to outgrow some of my teenage rebelliousness so I agreed to do this for him. And, in fact, I wanted to revisit the scene of some of my happy childhood moments.

When I reached the cemetery, I parked on the hill overlooking the group of graves that my father had directed me to. Immediately, I could see that I was not alone. A woman, bareheaded against the cold November wind, had come to visit one of the graves I was to leave a stone on. As I bent to leave it, I heard her whisper softly, "Thank you."

It was then that I noticed that the date of death on the grave was that same November day. The grave was that of a child, only five years old when he died some fifteen years before. I looked at the woman. She appeared to be around fifty, her face lined appropriately. I expected to see sadness in her bearing; instead I saw quiet dignity and calm acceptance.

"He was my son," she said. "But, where is your father? He was always the one to leave the stone."

I was so surprised that it took me a minute to find my voice. Then I told her that my father was not well but that he had asked me to come and leave the stones. It had been very important to him, I said. She nodded in a way that implied she knew my father and appreciated just how important this small act was to him. And so I asked her to explain. "I don't know your father well. But, I knew his nature anyway. His kindness has meant more to me than anything else in my life. You see, when my child died, I came often to the grave to visit him. It is our custom to leave a stone on the marker. It lets everyone know that the one who is buried her is not forgotten but is thought of and missed. But, then we moved away from here . . . so many painful memories . . . all of us moved . . . family . . . friends. There was no one left to visit the grave and I was so afraid that he would be all alone. But your father marked the grave every time he came. Each time I have returned here, I have seen that stone and it has always comforted me. Your father is the kind of man who would ease the suffering of a mother's heart even though we are strangers."

The wind whipped my hair into my face and for a moment I could not move. But the woman reached out and touched my arm. "Just tell him you saw me today, won't you?" she said. Then she turned and was gone.

As I sat in the old pick-up truck, waiting for it to warm up, I understood. Leaving the stones may have been something my father learned in his youth in Russia or maybe he just saw people like this woman do it here in

Indiana. In any case, it was a gesture that touched and comforted the survivors. That small stone had marked the grave of a child and the heart of his mother.

The heater in the old truck must have worked because I was suddenly comfortably warm. But it was a warmth that penetrated all of me. I put the truck in gear and went home.

Marsha Arons

Sending Kids Off to School

The mother's heart is the child's schoolroom.

Henry Ward Beecher

I could see how the scene was going to play itself out as clearly as if it had been written in a movie script.

"Five more minutes, honey, then we have to leave," I called to my five-year-old daughter, who had been frolicking in the Pacific Ocean for the past hour. It was a partial truth. Although I did have a million things to do that day, I decided to collect my child when I saw that she had found some older kids to frolic with. They were bigger and stronger, and the waves didn't knock them down as easily as they did my daughter. With exuberant five-year-old confidence, she kept following them out farther and farther toward the breaking waves. She was a proficient pool swimmer, but the deep blue sea was a different matter.

Maybe she didn't hear me calling her name above the roar of the ocean; maybe she did hear and was just ignoring me—it was impossible to tell. It had been an impromptu trip to the beach, so I wasn't wearing my swimsuit. Reluctantly, I hiked up my shorts and plunged into the ocean. Even in August I drew in a sharp breath as the water came in contact with my thighs.

"Hey, time's up, we have to go now." She turned, gave me a "see ya, Mom" look and headed farther into the surf. I splashed out and grabbed her arm. My shorts were soaked. I wondered if anyone was watching our little drama unfold.

"No!" she screamed, "I don't want to leave!" (Why is it that kids never want to get out of the water?) She jerked her arm away from me and pushed her defiant little body closer to Tokyo. I could see the headline now: "Child drowns while pursued by irate mother."

Now she was in over her head. Overcome with fear and rage I grabbed her, firmly this time, and began to drag her out. She did not come willingly. She screamed more intensely with every breath. It didn't stop when we got on shore. She wriggled and kicked, struggling violently in the sand to rid herself of me and charge back into the water. Now people were staring. I didn't care. I had to get her far enough away so that she couldn't plunge back into the powerful waves. She screamed and thrashed about like a wild animal caught in a trap, growling and scratching. The gritty sand clung to our wet skin.

By now I was shaking. I could hardly believe what happened next. A firm believer in nonviolent discipline—until now, that is—I smacked her on the bottom, hard. It stunned her enough to make her freeze and stop her hysterical ravings. She stood there almost completely covered in sand and with her mouth wide open, unable to take a breath.

"Come on!" I said through clenched teeth as I pulled her along toward the path that would lead us away from the beach. She hopped alongside of me, seething and jibbering. I realized she was trying to tell me something. Her unintelligible words alternated with jagged sobs as she shifted her weight from one foot to another. Her feet! Now that we were out of the surf, the sand was scalding hot. I had been clutching her thongs all along. "I'm so sorry, sweetie. Put these on." I slipped her thongs on her trembling feet, then we climbed the path toward the car and headed home.

That was weeks ago. Now it was September, and I was back on the beach, alone. This time the sand was cool. It yielded softly beneath my feet as I walked along the edge of the receding water line. The morning sun had not been up long enough to work its magic. As I walked the beach, tears welled up in my eyes. I could see the image of my daughter earlier that morning, heading into her freshly painted kindergarten classroom for her first day of school. Her new day pack was slung proudly over her shoulder. The design of yellow and purple puppies and kittens verified her tender years.

I'd driven straight to the beach after dropping her off. There was something so reassuring in the never-ending cresting and breaking of the waves. I hoped the pounding surf would soothe my anxious thoughts.

"I love you, Mommy!" she had called out cheerfully from the window as I walked back to my car.

"I'll pick you up after school," I called back. I turned to blow her a kiss, but she had already turned from the window.

I had dreamed of this day for years—five to be exact. I dreamed of this day soon after I brought her home from the hospital. I tried holding her, rocking her, and singing to her. When all that failed, I would give her a bottle, her "binky," her bear . . . anything.

I dreamed of this day when she was only a year old and she spent her days lurching through the house unsteadily, learning to walk. I was so concerned that she might maim herself, I followed her around, hovering with arms outstretched like a giant bear. There was the time she ran smack into the corner of a door at full toddler speed. The blood gushed like a fountain from above her eye, but she was much more calm and brave about having it stitched than I was.

When she was two, I needed a break from full-time mommyhood badly. I had never been away from her for even one night. But there I was, halfway around the world in Austria. I had left her with my parents and had finally taken my break. But when I heard her tiny little voice over the long-distance phone lines, my voice cracked so badly that I could hardly answer her back.

And this past summer, our days on end of being constantly together caused her to demand my unfailing attention. As the summer's heat grew more oppressive, I got listless but she became more spirited. She wanted more of everything—more pool time, more ice cream, more Popsicles, more playtime, more of me. Every day I heard, "Mom, let's go to the park, let's go to the beach, let's go to the Wild Animal Park, let's go, let's go, let's go!"

Why the tears then? I stopped walking and sat on a rough outcropping of rocks, on a lovely beach on a glorious day feeling miserable. I watched the seagulls wheel and dive, their constant motion distracting the thoughts running through my mind.

I should be happy, I thought. No more incessant chatter bombarding me twelve hours a day. Now I could think free, uncluttered thoughts in a stream of connected ideas. I would be free to go back to school or start the business I'd been thinking about. I could have lunch with friends at restaurants that didn't hand out crayons and coloring menus as you were seated. I could go shopping by myself without having my daughter stand in the middle of the clothing carousels spinning the rack, perilously close to tipping it over while the sales clerk glared with disapproval. I could roll up the windows in my car, pick a CD that wasn't Raffi or Barney and sing at the top of my lungs without hearing her say, "Don't sing, Mommy! Don't sing!" I could even go to the grocery store without having to deal with bribery and blackmail.

The truth is, I'd miss having her by my side. I'd become used to having a constant companion for the past five years. "Don't worry, Mom, we'll still have our afternoons together," she had reassured me at the breakfast table that morning.

With that thought in mind, I collected my things off the beach and headed for my car. It was time to go pick up my baby—oh, my kindergartner—from her first day of school. I was looking forward to spending the afternoon together.

Susan Union

Let's Go Bug Hunting More Often

Kids spell love T-I-M-E.

John Crudele

One fall afternoon I rushed home from the university where I taught. I prepared a hasty dinner, threatened my nine-year-old daughter, Christi, to hurry and finish her homework "or else," and properly reprimanded Del, my husband, for leaving his dusty shoes on the good carpet. I then frantically vacuumed the entryway because a group of prestigious ladies were coming by to pick up some good used clothing for a worthwhile cause; and then later a graduate student would be at our house to work on a very important thesis—one that I was certain would make a sound contribution to research.

As I paused to catch my breath, I heard Christi talking with a friend on the telephone. Her comments went something like this: "Mom is cleaning house—some ladies we don't even know are coming by to pick up some old worn-out clothes . . . and a college student is coming out to work on a thesis . . . no, I don't know what a thesis is . . .

I just know Mom isn't doing anything important . . . and she won't go bug hunting with me."

Before Christi had hung up the phone, I had put on my jeans and old tennis shoes, persuaded Del to do likewise, pinned a note to the door telling the graduate student I'd be back soon, and set the box of used clothing on the front porch with a note on it that Del, Christi and I had gone bug hunting.

Barbara Chesser, Ph.D.

A Mother's Day Review

Ah, Mother's Day. Used to be it was a day to sit back and relax. Who could ask for more than a wake-up call of toast heaped with chunky peanut butter and dripping with jam, coffee lukewarm, half sugar, half cream? I loved being able to take it easy for at least that one holiday.

But a recent conversation with a neighbor gave me a case of the guilts. "How can you let such a great opportunity for self-improvement pass you by?" she chided. "Now's the time to examine how you're doing in your role as a mother. Think about all you've learned that you never read in books! Think about all you've learned about yourself. Think about what it means to be a real mother!"

As much as I try to avoid getting too philosophical while piecing together Mr. Potato Head or trying to pull gum out of someone's socks, I decided to give the self-evaluation stuff a try. I started with thinking about the early days.

Amazingly enough, I realized I did know something I'd never read in a book—all babies are born with an innate sense that urges them to cry and demand immediate attention if their mother should attempt any of the following: a warm meal, a long-distance phone call, a good book, a hot bath or sex. My kids are older now, and about the only changes I've noticed are that food can be good cold, magazines are quicker to read than books and cold showers diminish the desire for sex.

Then I thought of something else I learned. It's perfectly normal for kids to get sick when the doctor's office is closed. This habit used to send me into a panic, trying to determine what rare disease my child had and if I should call the doctor's service or just head straight for the hospital. I'm smarter now. My first call is to a friend who has five kids, for her opinion.

I've learned some unpublished facts about nutrition, too. I know a two-year-old can survive on yogurt, Cheerios and raisins for extended periods of time; that at first, raisins come out looking pretty much like they did going in, and that anything covered in ketchup is gourmet to kids. I also know that peanut butter, besides being almost impossible to clean off a high chair, is a great hair conditioner.

Further thought made me realize that I have learned some things about myself. I've learned that if I could find someone who would pay me a nickel for every time I thought, "My kids will never . . ." and they did, I'd be a millionaire. And even though my wonderful offspring sometimes do not react at all when I'm speaking, I do still speak English and can be heard and understood by other people in the room. In addition, I've discovered that if I don't have some time to myself, I tend to get ugly. I've learned that for me to be a good (most of the time) and sane (some of the time) mother, I need a good friend who shares the same ideas and ideals of motherhood. I've also learned that if every once in a while I think how peaceful it would be without my kids, it doesn't mean I don't love them—it simply means I need a break.

And I do know what it means to be a real mother! It means that on our very bad days, my method of survival relies on reciting, "This, too, shall pass" and that on most days, I know that *this, too, shall pass*—too quickly.

Bring on the toast!

Paula (Bachleda) Koskey

"Happy Mother's Day"

READER/CUSTOMER CARE SURVEY

If you are enjoying this book, please help us serve you better and meet your changing needs by taking a few minutes to complete this survey. Please fold it & drop it in the mail.

Name: _____

Address: _____

_____

Tel. # _____

(1) Gender: 1) ____ Female 2) ____ Male

(2) Age:
1) ____ 18-25 4) ____ 46-55
2) ____ 26-35 5) ____ 56-65
3) ____ 36-45 6) ____ 65+

(3) Marital status:

1) ____ Married 3) ____ Single 5) ____ Widowed
2) ____ Divorced 4) ____ Partner

(4) Is this book:
1) ____ Purchased for self?
2) ____ Purchased for others?
3) ____ Received as gift?

(5) How did you find out about this book?

1) ____ Catalog 2) ____ Store Display
Newspaper
3) ____ Best Seller List
4) ____ Article/Book Review
5) ____ Advertisement
Magazine
6) ____ Feature Article
7) ____ Book Review
8) ____ Advertisement
9) ____ Word of Mouth
A) ____ T.V./Talk Show (Specify) _____
B) ____ Radio/Talk Show (Specify) _____
C) ____ Professional Referral _____
D) ____ Other (Specify) _____

Which Health Communications book are you currently reading? _____

As a special **"Thank You"** we'll send you exciting news about interesting books and a valuable Gift Cerfificate.
It's Our Pleasure to Serve You!

(6) What subject areas do you enjoy reading most? (Rank in order of enjoyment)

1) ____ Women's Issues/ Relationships
2) ____ Business Self Help
3) ____ Soul/Spirituality/ Inspiration
4) ____ Recovery
5) ____ New Age/ Altern. Healing
6) ____ Aging
7) ____ Parenting
8) ____ Diet/Nutrition/ Exercise/Health

(14) What do you look for when choosing a personal growth book?
(Rank in order of importance)

1) ____ Subject
2) ____ Title
Cover Design
3) ____ Author
4) ____ Price
5) ____ In Store Location

(19) When do you buy books?
(Rank in order of importance)

1) ____ Christmas
2) ____ Valentine's Day
3) ____ Birthday
4) ____ Mother's Day
5) ____ Other (Specify _____

(23) Where do you buy your books?
(Rank in order of frequency of purchases)

1) ____ Bookstore
2) ____ Price Club
3) ____ Department Store
4) ____ Supermarket/ Drug Store
5) ____ Health Food Store
6) ____ Gift Store
7) ____ Book Club
8) ____ Mail Order
9) ____ T.V. Shopping
A) ____ Airport

Additional comments you would like to make to help us serve you better.

_____

_____

Thank You !!

FOLD HERE

BUSINESS REPLY MAIL
FIRST CLASS MAIL PERMIT NO 45 DEERFIELD BEACH, FL

POSTAGE WILL BE PAID BY ADDRESSEE

HEALTH COMMUNICATIONS
3201 SW 15TH STREET
DEERFIELD BEACH, FL 33442-9875

What I Want

I don't want a pipe and I don't want a watch.
I don't want cigars or a bottle of Scotch.
I don't want a thing your money can buy.
I don't want a shirt or a four-in-hand tie.
If you really would make this old heart of mine glad,
I just want to know you're still fond of your dad.
You women folk say, and believe it I can,
"It's so terribly hard to buy things for a man!"
And from all that I've heard I am sure it must be.
Well, I don't want you spending your money on me.
I just want to know you're still fond of your dad.
Get on with your shopping; give others the stuff!
For me just a hug and a kiss are enough!

Edgar Guest
Submitted by Floyd Burkey

My Dad

I think I was his favorite. My brothers and sister probably thought *they* were his favorite. He had the ability to
make each of us feel special, even after we'd done something wrong. He didn't understand me as a teenager but
knew enough not to try. He didn't offer advice unless I
asked him and even then it was more of a soul-searching
exercise with him. He knew I could figure things out on
my own, without him, but I continued asking for his
advice for as long as I could. My father and I shared a lot
of similarities. We loved animals, liked the same movies,
enjoyed the same adventures. We also shared the same
commitment to our families—something that I learned
from him.

My two brothers, my sister and I were raised in a very
creative environment with many opportunities. Both my
mother and my father were always there for us. They
gave us the stability and the life that is so important for
children. When I was about ten, I would try on my
mother's wedding gown and my dad would run in from
working in the yard, brush off his hands and play "The
Wedding March" on the organ for me as I walked slowly

down the stairs, believing my prince had come. We would do this over and over again until I got tired. He would never tell me he was too busy.

To see the way he treated other people and the helping hand he offered was a great gift to give a child. He forever wanted to stop and help people stranded on the highway. It was only because there were four tired kids in the car and my mother reassuring him that other people were stopping to help that my father could continue on. He also wanted to pick up hitchhikers, as he hated to see anyone needing something that he could give them. He felt is was our duty as citizens to help other people in need.

He was frugal but generous. He loved to have as many people as we could squish into our mountain cabin near Yosemite, and he was always baking. Pies were coming out of the oven as fast as anyone could eat them. He gave to many charities and sponsored children overseas. He was very proud of that and showed off the letters from those children whenever he could.

As I grew up, married and moved away from home, I realized the importance of having Dad in my life. He was still my rock—my stability, my security. The foundation that Dad provided for me had given me the opportunity to enjoy my marriage and my children. While many people cannot accept challenges or inconveniences in their lives, my dad taught me how to clear the hurdles that can cause complications in life.

And so it has happened. On the coldest day of the year in February 1996, my father passed away after battling cancer for almost a year. It's okay, though. After all, he wasn't thirty-five, forty-five or even fifty-five. He was a sixty-five-year-old man. His children were all happily married and living their own busy lives. He had eleven grandchildren and a great-grandchild on the way. Many people would say he had lived a full life. Which he had— but I still wasn't ready to let him go.

We worried about Mom going on without him. We worried that somehow our childhood chapter would close if he died. We worried that he would be in pain. He fought without complaining, and we now know he fought it for us. Battling lymphoma for ten months showed his four children the courage it takes to be a good father.

In his final days, we spent as much time with him as possible. In those few short months, I tried to pay him back for everything he had done for me in my thirty-six years. I wanted to do it all and could only do so little. Many days I just sat with him.

I believe he chose his night to die. All of us were in town. We had a big family dinner and I walked him to bed before I left that evening. I kissed him on his head and told him I would see him tomorrow. I know my brothers and sister left after me and went in to say goodnight also. They each had their moment: that last great moment. My mother had him in the end. As she walked him from the bathroom back to bed around 3:00 in the morning, he silently collapsed in her arms. She gently lowered him to the floor, put a pillow under his head and covered him with a blanket. That's how we saw him when we showed up minutes later, after my mother called us all together. My brother said that he heard it was the coldest day of the year, that day in February.

The days following his death just confirmed to me how important he was in my life and in the lives of my sister and brothers. Each of us has our special memories that are just of "me and Dad." As my life goes on he continues to help me make important decisions. Sometimes I can hear his voice. Standing in line to buy flowers for his grave one day, I could hear him so clearly saying, "Oh Brenda, don't buy those for me. Spend the money on yourself."

What's important for you to understand about me, Dad, is that in a way, I *was* spending money on myself. I've learned from you that doing things for other people is the best gift I can give to myself.

Brenda Gallardo

Father's Day

When I was five, my biological father committed suicide. It left me feeling as though I'd done something wrong; that if I had been better somehow, maybe he'd have stayed around. My mother remarried shortly thereafter, and this man was my dad until I was nineteen. I called him Dad and used his name all through school. But when he and my mother divorced, he just walked away. Once again, I wondered what was wrong with me that I couldn't keep a father.

Mother remarried again, and Bob was a wonderful, kind man. I was twenty now and no longer living at home, but I felt a great love and attachment for him. A few years later my mother was diagnosed with cancer and was not given long to live. Shortly before she died, Bob came over to my house alone one day. We talked about a lot of things, and then he told me that he wanted me to know that he'd always be there for me, even after Mother was gone. Then he asked if he could adopt me.

I could hardly believe my ears. Tears streamed down my face. He wanted me—me! This man had no obligation to me, but he was reaching out from his heart, and I accepted. During the adoption proceedings, the judge commented on all of the undesirable duties of his profession and then with a tear in his eye, thanked us for brightening his day as he pronounced us father and daughter. I was twenty-five, but I was his little girl.

Three short years later, Bob, too, was diagnosed with cancer and was gone within the year. At first I was hurt and angry at God for taking this father away too. But eventually the love and acceptance that I felt from Dad came through again, and I became, once more, grateful for the years we had.

On Father's Day I always reflect on what I've learned about fatherhood. I've learned that it is not dependent on biology or even on raising a child. Fatherhood is a matter of the heart. Bob's gift from the heart will warm my soul for eternity.

Sherry Lynn Blake Jensen Miller

A Lesson from My Son

I was one of those lucky children for whom learning came easy. So, when I became a parent, I naturally assumed that if I read to both of my children faithfully and offered them fun, educational playtimes, they would follow in my footsteps. They, too, would learn, retain materials and receive all As as I had done.

Amanda, my first child, was right on target. She learned quickly and earned good grades. However, even though I practiced the same methods with my second child, Eric, I sensed that life would be a challenge, not only for his teachers, but for Eric and myself personally.

I did my part for this sweet, loving youngster who was never a discipline problem for anyone. I made sure his homework was completed each night, kept in touch with his teachers, and enrolled him in every assistance program the school had to offer. But, no matter how hard he struggled, report cards with Cs were met with frustration and tears. I could see his discouragement and feared he would lose all interest in learning. Soon I doubted myself.

Where had I failed my son? I wondered. *Why couldn't I motivate him to help him succeed?* I felt if he didn't excel in school, he would be unable to create a life of his own or support himself—and perhaps a family someday.

Eric was a sixteen-year-old blonde when my eyes were opened. We were sitting in the living room when the phone rang; a message that my father had suffered a massive heart attack and died at age seventy-nine.

"Papa," as Eric had called him, had been such a part of my little boy's life during his first five years. Since my husband worked nights and slept days, it was Papa who took him for haircuts, ice cream and played baseball with him during those earlier times. Papa was his number-one pal.

When my father left and moved back to the town where he grew up, Eric was lost without him. But time healed those wounds. Gradually, he came to understand his grandfather's need for old friends and roots of the past. For Eric, phone calls and visits from the grandfather he loved became a way of life. And his Papa never forgot him.

When we entered the funeral parlor, I stood in the doorway and looked at my father, so still, so unlike the man I knew. My children were on either side of me, and I felt Eric take my hand as we walked up to his grandfather. We shared our moments together then took our places on the side of the room as hundreds of friends filed by. Each person shared sympathies and memories of my father's life. Others just touched my hand and walked away.

Suddenly, I realized Eric wasn't beside me. I turned to look around the room and noticed him near the entranceway helping the elderly in need of assistance with the stairs or the door. Strangers all, some with walkers, others with canes, many simply leaning on his arm as he led them to his grandfather to pay their last respects.

Later that evening the funeral director mentioned to me that one more pallbearer was needed. Eric immediately said, "Please Sir, may I help?"

The director suggested he might prefer to stay with his sister and myself. Eric shook his head. "My papa carried me when I was little," he said. "Now it's my turn to carry him." When I heard those words I started to cry. I felt as though I could never stop.

From that moment on, I knew I would never berate my son for imperfect grades. Never again would I expect him to be someone I had created in my own mind, because that individual I envisioned was nowhere near the fine person my son had become. His compassion, caring and love were the gifts God had blessed him with. No book could have taught him these things. No degree framed behind glass would ever convey to the world the qualities Eric possessed.

He is now twenty years old and continues to spread his kindness, his sense of humor and compassion for his fellow man wherever he goes. Today I ask myself, "What difference do science and math grades make? When a young man does the best he can, he deserves an "A" from the heart.

Kathleen Beaulieu

Blessed Are the Pure in Heart

Blessed are the pure in heart.
So often we are told
Of saints whose names and daily deeds
Inscribed in books of gold
Are certain to be seeing God
In well-rewarding joy—
But when I see the pure in heart
I see a little boy.

He shins up trees and barks his knees,
Has lizards in a box;
He loves to read of dinosaurs,
Collects bright-colored rocks.
His grubby hands are gentle
On the coats of dogs and birds,
And he has a quiet wisdom in naiveté of words.
I listen to his little prayers
At night with quiet joy—
And when I hear the pure in heart
I hear a little boy.

He hasn't reached the age as yet

To question and to doubt;
He gravely takes his mother's words,
And that's what life's about.
Each day is gold, a shining thing
Without a wrong alloy—
And when I hold the pure in heart
I hold a little boy.

Gwen Belson Taylor

Slender Thread

As his mother drove away, eleven-year-old Billy stood by the curb and cried. His mother was an abusive drug addict; still, she was all he had. Now he was to live with his aunt. A wave of desolation mounted in his chest.

Aunt Val had no interest in caring for him, either. Billy was left alone, living off peanut butter, stale bread and cereal. In the evenings he spent his time listening to the voices of the five children who lived next door, the laughter and shouts, and the firm voice of their mama sending them to bed.

On Sunday morning, as they packed into the car for church, Mama noticed Billy watching her kids from the shadow of his doorway. He looked like trouble: His face was defiant and his shabby clothes hung loose on his thin frame. What kind of life did this boy have? He made her uneasy; yet she saw the hurt that showed in his dark eyes.

Billy's face haunted her while she sat through the service. When they got home, he was still there. His eyes followed the children as they piled chattering from the car.

Mama's heart caught as her boy, Cecil, paused and asked, "What's your name?"

"Billy."

"How old are you?" Cecil asked.

"Eleven, almost twelve," said Billy.

"Me, too. Want to come inside? We're going out to play basketball after we change clothes."

Mama bit her lip as Billy followed Cecil inside.

The next afternoon, Billy came home with Cecil after school.

"Billy's aunt ain't never home, so I said he could come over here," Cecil said.

But Billy didn't fit in with the rhythm of their household. When the children did their homework Billy was a distraction, chattering thoughtlessly while they tried to concentrate. He used foul language and bullied the younger children. A sour feeling settled in Mama's stomach. Billy was not going to be a good influence on her kids.

The following day, Mama saw Billy hanging around the front of the apartments when she got back from her job driving the school bus. A cigarette hung in his mouth. He ducked away when he saw her, which only made her dislike him more. After basketball that evening Billy came inside with Cecil. The boys had found an expensive tennis shoe at the courts and wanted to show it to Mama.

"I'm gonna buy shoes like these some day," Billy bragged. "I'm gonna have all the money I want."

Mama shivered. She could imagine how Billy would get the money to buy what he wanted. She didn't like the man she feared he would become. Cecil was looking at Billy and the flashy shoe with envy. It made Mama angry; she didn't want Billy's kind leading her children astray.

When Billy left, she told Cecil, "I won't have you hanging out with Billy. He's not going where I want you to go."

Cecil's expression clouded. "Don't, Mama. There's something good in Billy. I know it. He needs us."

Mama shook her head. She was adamant. Her family came first, and Billy was bad news.

That night she dreamt of Billy, crying while his mother drove away. He turned to Mama but she only shook her head. In her dream an older Billy faced her, his face hardened, his eyes cold. He wore the expensive tennis shoes. He stared at her in agony with a bullet wound in his chest, then collapsed and lay still on the concrete. Light flashed and an angel stood beside her. He asked: "Did you do your best?"

Mama woke and tried to push the dream from her mind. It could not be erased. Life had failed Billy. Would she fail him, too?

It was early. Light dawned outside. Mama tried to sleep, but when she closed her eyes she saw Billy sprawled on the concrete. She got up and went into the kitchen to start some coffee. The Billy of her dream was fresh in her mind—a lost little boy trying to act tough in a frightening world. Billy's future hung by a slender thread. She could either hold it tightly or release it to the wind. She knew what she would want someone to do for her Cecil, if anything were to happen to her.

Later that morning, when Cecil came into the kitchen she said, "You were right about Billy. But there has to be some rules. You bring him home after school. I want to talk to him."

That afternoon, Mama drew Billy aside. "I think there's a lot of good in you and I want us to be friends. But there are going to be some rules. You come home with Cecil each day and do your homework without any talking. If you have any questions, you ask me. You and Cecil need to help me start supper, and you may stay and eat with us. If you work hard and stay in school, someday you'll get those shoes you want."

Billy looked into Mama's face. She met his searching eyes. Then he nodded.

Mama patted his shoulder. "It won't be easy. If you goof off, I'll send you home. But I really hope you'll choose to stay."

Right off, Billy tested Mama and got sent home. But as the weeks passed, more and more often he stayed for supper. On Sundays he often went with the family to church.

Over the years Billy changed. His hardness fell away, he trusted Mama and her firm guidance, and he came to her whenever he had problems. Mama kept in touch with Billy's teachers and followed his progress at school.

On the day of his high school graduation, Billy grinned as Mama snapped a picture. He raised the edge of the long green robe to reveal a present to himself, bought with money he'd saved from his summer job. Tears came to Mama's eyes when she saw the new tennis shoes. She could almost feel the angel's hand resting on her shoulder. Yes, she'd done her best.

Karen Cogan

Neither Have I

Nature cannot be tricked or cheated. She will give up to you the object of your struggles only after you have paid her price.

Napoleon Hill

It has been my experience that one stumbles across life's most profound lessons in the most unexpected places—places like a neighborhood Little League baseball diamond.

Our sons' first game of the season was scheduled for an evening in early May. Since this particular league included grades six through eight, our older son was a third-year veteran on the team, while his younger brother, a sixth-grader, was among the new recruits. The usual crowd of parents had gathered as I took my seat on a weather-beaten plank, third row from the top. Sandwiched between a cotton candy-faced youngster and somebody's mother, I checked the scoreboard. Fourth inning already. Because the boys had anticipated my late arrival, they instructed me to watch the first base and catcher positions. As my attention moved between them,

I glanced at the pitcher's mound. Jason Voldner?

Jason was undoubtedly the most well-liked and good-natured boy on the team, but athletically, his participation had been limited to the alternating positions of right field or bench—the latter, unfortunately, more frequently. Having spent an uncountable number of hours as a spectator (on an equally uncountable number of varying bleachers), it is my belief that every ball field has its own version of Jason Voldner.

The Jasons of the world show up at a tender young age for their first Saturday morning T-ball practice, oiled glove in hand. By the end of this long awaited "chance to play ball," the heavy-hearted Jasons return home remembering the boy who hit farther, the boy who ran faster and the boy who actually knew what he was supposed to do with the glove.

Ability is not only recognized but utilized, allowing for the exceptional players to become even more so, while the Jasons wait their turn to play the seventh inning. Right field. Their allotted playing time is not only limited, it's conditional: only if the team is already winning. If not, the Jasons have simply been waiting to go home. And yet here was Jason Voldner pitching what I would say was the game of his life.

Turning to comment to anyone willing to listen, I now realized that the "somebody's mother" sitting beside me belonged to Jason. "Such talent," I offered. "I've never seen your son pitch before." In a voice of quiet resolve she responded, "Neither have I." And then she told me this story.

Four weeks ago, she had chauffeured a car full of boys, her son included, to this same baseball diamond for their first spring practice. Just before dusk she had sat on her porch swing, dodging the sudden downpour and waiting for the next carpool mother to drop Jason off after practice. As the van pulled up, Jason emerged from behind the sliding door. "His face was a combination of dirt smudges and rain streaks and would have masked from anyone but me that he was upset," she said.

"My immediate concern was for an injury," Jason's mother continued. But there was none. Probing questions led her no closer to the elusive pain. By bedtime, she knew no more than she did back on the porch. This would change shortly.

"Sometime in the hours that followed, I was awakened by choking sobs. Jason's. At his bedside, broken words were telling his story. 'Waiting. Eighth grade. Sick of right field. Eighth grade.'" As Jason's mother calmed her son, he further explained that Matthew, a sixth-grader, was going to play second base "because his dad is coaching"; John, a sixth-grader, was assigned to shortstop "because he's Matthew's friend"; and Brian, yet another sixth-grader, was the new catcher "because his brother is on the team."

I found myself bristling here and wondered where her story was going. Brian was my younger son.

"Not fair. Not fair. Not fair." Listening to Jason, his mother's heart ached for him. There should be a word that takes empathy to another level; a word for the exclusive use of parents.

"While my son was waiting for me to agree with him," said his mother, "I was making the difficult decision not to. One has to be careful when having a direct and lasting effect on another person's negative emotions. Agreement may appear to be the most caring and loyal means of help, but in reality, it can work to the contrary as you reinforce the negative feelings.

"So first I explained to Jason that until we were ready to assist the coach with his responsibilities, we would trust his judgments.

"Secondly, I reminded him how seldom we passed the vacant lot on the corner of our block without finding the three sixth-graders in question involved in a random, unscheduled game of ball. Playing infield is not about being in the sixth grade or the eighth; it's about working hard and capability, not preferential treatment. All through your life you are going to come into contact with individuals possessing a natural talent for what they are pursuing—on the ball field, in the classroom, in the workplace. Does this mean you are unable to achieve what they have? Certainly not. You simply have to choose to work harder. Resentment, blame and excuses only poison potential."

Finally, Jason's mother tucked him back into bed. As she smoothed the covers over him, she said to her son, "You're disappointed that the coach doesn't believe in you, Jason, but before you can expect others to believe in you, you have to believe in yourself. The coach is basing his placements on the performance he has seen thus far. If you truly feel you deserve a position other than right field, then prove it." With those words she kissed him goodnight.

Jason's mother laughed softly. "We spoke more in those few minutes than we have pretty much in the weeks since. Our contact recently has been through notes that Jason leaves me on the kitchen table: 'Gone to practice. Gone to prove it.'" She paused. "And he did."

Yes, it has been my experience that one stumbles across life's most profound lessons in the most unexpected places—like the neighborhood Little League baseball diamond, while sitting on a weather-beaten plank, third row from the top.

Rochelle M. Pennington

THE FAMILY CIRCUS® By Bil Keane

"Stay!"

The Thing About Goldfish

There are many good things about having a goldfish for a pet. It teaches even a small child a little responsibility. You don't have to walk it. It won't mess up the house. It doesn't shed. And one goldfish looks pretty much like another.

This last trait is very important, I found, in light of the one bad thing about goldfish—they have a relatively short life span.

There are twelve years and two sisters between my oldest daughter, Anna, and my youngest, Elliana. But the two of them have always been close. So I wasn't surprised when it was Anna who solved the problem created by Elli's fear of the dark.

We have four bedrooms in our house. When Elli graduated to a bed at age two and a half, we moved her in with her next oldest sister, Kayla. That left the two oldest girls with their own rooms, much to their delight. But Elli was afraid of the dark and Kayla couldn't sleep with a light on. Anna knew she would have to come up with something if she wanted to keep her personal space.

The answer was a goldfish.

Anna bought Elli a bowl, a little plastic house for the fish to swim through, some colored gravel and a small light that kept the little aquarium illuminated. Elli kept the bowl on the nightstand next to her bed. That way, she had enough light to make her feel safe and a "friend" to murmur to quietly before she fell asleep. The light from the fish bowl was dim enough so that Kayla wasn't bothered. And both of them liked having a pet.

Elli fed that fish like clockwork and reminded us to clean the bowl more often than we would have liked. She was always careful about adding the anti-chlorine drops to the fresh water, lest her fish die a toxic death. And she named her fish creatively. Some days the fish would be "Jaws," other days, it would be "Swimmy." A few times, Elli decided its name was "Patsy" or "Mabel," or some other name that struck her fancy at a particular moment. The fish's gender also varied according to my daughter's whim.

But goldfish don't live very long. As a result, all of us became co-conspirators in the game of making sure that Elli always had a live goldfish in that bowl. Every night when I kissed her goodnight, I would check the fish. If I covered up my sleeping children in the middle of the night, I would check the fish. I found that Anna checked the fish, too, many times before she went to bed herself. If any of us noticed the fish looking a bit peaked around the gills, a quiet trip to the pet store was quickly scheduled. For fifty cents, we kept a little girl very happy. It was a small price to pay, to be sure, and Elli certainly never questioned her fish's longevity.

Elli turned six years old two weeks before Anna left for college. I was having a separation problem of my own sending my oldest off. But I was more worried about how Elli would react.

In fact, Elliana became quiet and spent a lot of time in her room for the first days after Anna left. But assured that she could send her sister pictures and talk to her on the phone, Elli, like the rest of us, adjusted. Still, it did feel odd to have five of us around the dinner table where there had once been six. But Anna was happy at school, and her enjoyment of her new surroundings made the transition easier for all of us.

One evening as I was putting the two little ones to bed, Elli said to me, "Mommy, when this fish dies, will Anna come home and get me a new one?"

I don't know why I was surprised. Children don't really miss much, I guess. But I smiled at her and asked her how long she had known that her goldfish kept getting replaced every time one died.

Elli just shrugged. I asked her if it bothered her that the present goldfish wasn't the same one her sister had bought for her almost four years before.

No, it didn't bother her, Elli said. It never had. It had made Anna happy to play the game that way, so she just went along with it.

And so, I understood. The little love token from one sister to another and back again was swimming happily beside my daughter's bed. The fish may not have been the original, but the message had never changed.

As I turned out the overhead light and watched the little aquarium glow softly, I thought to myself, "Now I know one more good thing about goldfish!"

Marsha Arons

3

ON TEACHING AND LEARNING

Education is not preparation for life; education is life itself.

John Dewey

The Day We Became Brothers

In the darkest hour the soul is replenished and given strength to endure.

Heart Warrior Chosa

I was ten years old when my father died. Eight months later, my mother, believing I needed more structure and male role models, enrolled me in the Milton Hershey School in Hershey, Pennsylvania.

A knot in my stomach grew tighter as our car approached the school that February day in 1964. I told myself over and over, *be brave.* Be the man you're supposed to be now that your father is dead. Actually, I had little idea how to be a man, except to act stoically. So I never uttered a word of protest, though every fiber of my body resisted the trip. What was my life going to be like? How would the other boys react to me?

When we arrived, my mother and I were given a tour of the spotless ranch-style house, which accommodated the sixteen boys in my unit, with an apartment for our houseparents. My mother remained behind while I was shown the bedroom I would share with another boy.

I returned to an empty living room. "Where's my mom?" I asked.

"Oh, she left," someone said.

Left? My legs went limp. The school's counselor, I learned later, urged my mother to slip away without saying good-bye so as to avoid a scene.

I spent the afternoon sitting in my new bedroom. When the boys returned from school at four o'clock, they came to look at me. "Boy, you're short," said one kid.

"Lee, he's not short. He's tiny."

"Let's call him 'Ant,'" Lee said.

"No, 'Bug' is better."

"I like those extra eyes he's got," said another, pointing to my glasses.

"Maybe we should call him 'Bug Eyes.'"

With that, they went about their after-school chores.

After dinner, we were allowed an hour of free time until study period. I picked up a book and started reading, but my roommate, Jim, interrupted: "There's some things you should know if you don't want to be laughed at. Somebody might ask you to go get a bucket of steam or a left-handed wrench. Your toothbrush will sometimes disappear. Oh, and you'd better keep those glasses in sight all the time."

"Thanks for the warning."

He shrugged. "You'll also probably have to fight somebody soon if you don't want to be treated like dirt."

I sat quietly for a while, absorbing what Jim had told me. Suddenly he asked, "It was your father who died, right?"

"Yes."

He looked into his book. "Nobody's going to want to hear about that."

That night I did my best not to cry. I failed.

Jim's predictions turned out to be true. I got into a fight after two boys played catch with my glasses. Angry, I rammed my head into the stomach of one and we began to slug each other.

I never mentioned my father to anyone, and no one mentioned his or her lost parents to me. The unspoken code that Hershey boys held was not just the denial of feeling, but the denial that our dead parents had existed at all.

One of the favorite games among the boys was tackle. A football was thrown into the air and whoever caught it tried to run directly through the rest without being brought down. Tackle was less of a game than an excuse to deliberately smash our bodies into each other for the main purpose, I realized later, of dissipating our frustration and anger.

Late that first spring, Mr. and Mrs. Carney became our new houseparents and loosened the reins on us. Soon, however, chores were not being done well, and some boys spoke to the Carneys rudely.

Mr. Carney's response was to hold a meeting in which the boys could air their beefs and the Carneys could express their expectations of us. To me, the Carneys were not the "enemy" but surrogate parents who genuinely cared about us. During the meeting I pointed out, "If anything, the Carneys are too nice. Some of you guys are taking advantage of that."

Cold shoulders promptly turned my way. As if to relieve me from the others, the Carneys took me that Friday evening to their weekend house, where I spent most of the time fishing.

When I returned to the unit, Jim notified me, "Everybody thinks you kissed up to the Carneys. You have a lot of guys mad at you."

Great. I had spent months trying to fit in, and in a minute I had ostracized myself. I was not surprised to find my toothbrush in the toilet the next morning.

Two months later, I overheard Lee, Bruce and Jim trying to decide how to pass a long August afternoon.

"Let's go down to the pond," Jim suggested.

"I say we go to the hideout," said Lee, referring to a mysterious place I had not yet seen.

"Why don't we just hike," Bruce offered, "and see where we wind up?"

"I'll go for that," Jim said.

"Me, too," I added.

"Who invited you, twerp?" Lee said to me.

"Don't call me that."

"Okay, Four Eyes."

Wanting to avoid another fight, I swallowed my anger.

"I'm heading that-a-way," Bruce said, motioning to the open spaces. "If anybody wants to come, fine. If not, *adios*." He started off, and Jim and Lee followed. I lingered briefly, then joined the group.

After crossing meadows dotted with wildflowers, we found a thin stream. Jumping over it, we soon came to a cornfield that stretched as far as we could see. "Let's go in," Lee said, and without hesitation we did.

We quickly became hidden, but pushed deeper into the field. The broad leaves slashed at our faces, and the ears of corn clunked us on the head. We crossed perhaps thirty rows before we halted and sat on the ground.

"Is this the hideout?" I asked.

"Hardly," Lee said, removing cigarettes from his pants.

"I don't think you should smoke in here," Jim said.

"Me neither," Bruce added.

Lee shrugged. "All right, no sweat." This surprised me, but I soon learned there was something about the cornfield that changed our usual behavior. It was a place that melted inhibitions and tough-guy exteriors. Here, hidden from the world, we found ourselves on those roads into our interiors that we traveled only in private.

Bruce was the first to talk. "My father was a salesman," he said, "and one day a truck ran a stoplight and smashed into his car. He died right there. I was in school, and they called me home. I knew something big had happened, but I never thought it was that."

"Mine died of a heart attack," Jim said. "But I hardly knew him. I was four. He was a schoolteacher."

After a pause, Lee said, "My old man was a carpenter. He made me a boxcar one summer. He took me to a couple of Yankees games, and once we went to the circus. Then he got bone cancer. He was a big man, but by the time he died, he was like a string bean." Lee's eyes had become wet. He looked away into the depths of the cornfield.

The others did, too. They were wearing expressions I had never seen before. No one spoke for a long time. All I heard was the rustling of the cornstalks and the cry of a distant crow.

Bruce broke our silence. "You didn't tell us about your father," he said to me.

I wasn't sure I wanted to. I had survived Hershey by remaining "strong," and I now felt reluctant to allow myself to weaken. But like them, I was eager to unburden myself of something I simply couldn't keep bottled up any longer.

"Mine had diabetes for a long time," I said haltingly, "but it was his kidneys that went bad, and that's what killed him. My mother was called away by the hospital one night. I was in bed when I heard the door open and her footsteps coming up the stairs. They sounded . . . sad, so I knew before she said, 'Your father passed away.'"

We didn't talk much about how we felt when our fathers died; we could tell from our faces. Instead we talked about our fathers' lives. What they were like. Who they were. If we'd had pictures, we would have shared them. But none of us had a photo, not even in our rooms, it being generally accepted that such a thing was too much of a reminder of a life more bright and normal than the one we now lived.

The talk about our fathers gave way to other, less weighty matters, and soon we were back to a lighter mood. But when we stepped out into the sunlight, we did so with a common understanding—that life handed out its losses, but we did not have to suffer them alone. For the first time, we realized that we held in common not only parental loss but also the need to release the sorrow that came with it.

As we made our way home, we stopped to drink at the stream. Jim was next to me, and I watched him remove his baseball hat, splash his face and rub his wet fingers through his hair. Then instead of putting the cap back on his own head, he reached over and placed it on mine. The others gathered around, and together we jumped over the stream. And I knew as we returned to the unit that we walked as brothers.

Albert DiBartolomeo

Drop Earrings

Blessed is the influence of one true, loving human soul on another.

George Eliot

We had come to the park that day to celebrate my thirty-fifth birthday. We were two enduring friends, mothers with three children apiece.

From a picnic table we watched as our kids laughed and leapt their way through a playground fragranced with scarlet apple trees and lavender lilacs.

It was a good day for a picnic. Dressed in shorts, denim jackets and sunglasses, we unpacked a basket bulging with bologna sandwiches, Doritos, and Oreo cookies.

We toasted friendship with clear bottles of mineral water.

It was then I noticed Laurie's new drop earrings—tiny interlocking loops of silver laced with stones of indigo blue. For the thirteen years I'd known Laurie, ever since college, she'd always loved drop earrings.

Over the years I'd seen her wear pair after dangling pair—threaded crystals cast in blue, shiny silver loops, strands of colored gemstones, sapphire hoops, beaded pearls in pastel pink, diamonds set in golden links.

"There's a reason why I like drop earrings," Laurie said. She began revealing saved images from a childhood memory that changed her forever. A tender tale of truth and its power to transform . . .

When Laurie was in the sixth grade, her desk was the last one in a row of seven near a bank of brick-framed windows. She remembered with amazing detail the way her classroom looked one spring day—the yellow May Day baskets suspended on clotheslines above her desk, the caged hamsters that rustled through shredded newspapers, the window shelves where orange marigolds curled over cut-off milk cartons, the cursive writing charts above the blackboard. That classroom felt safe to Laurie, a sharp contrast to a home riddled with dysfunction.

"Mrs. Moline made that classroom feel so safe," Laurie mused. She recalled the way her teacher looked on that long-ago morning; how her auburn hair flipped onto her shoulders like Jackie Kennedy's, how her kind, hazel-green eyes were full of light and sparkle.

But it was her teacher's drop earrings that Laurie remembered most, golden teardrop strands laced with ivory pearls. "Even from my back row seat," Laurie recalled, "I could see her earrings gleaming in the sunlight from the windows." They provided a beacon of hope in a dark, depressing life.

That year her father's alcoholism had escalated. Many late nights she had fallen asleep despite the sounds of the disabling disease: whiskey being poured into shot glasses, can openers piercing metal beer tops, ice cubes clinking in glass after glass, the loud slurred voices of her father and his friends in the kitchen, her mother's sobs, slamming doors, pictures rattling on the wall.

The previous Christmas she had saved babysitting

money to buy her dad a shoeshine kit, complete with varnished footrest, a buffer brush, and a copper can of cordovan shoe polish. She had wrapped the gift with red and green Santa Claus paper and trimmed it with a gold ribbon curled into a bow.

On Christmas Eve she had watched in stunned silence as he had thrown it across the living room, breaking it into three pieces.

Laurie took off her sunglasses and began to rub her eyes. I handed her a napkin . . . I knew the pain of that Christmas memory still lingered.

When she continued the story of that day in the classroom, Laurie said, "That spring day had been set aside for end-of-the-year conferences. Mrs. Moline stood in front of the class reminding us that both parents and students would participate in these important progress reports." On the blackboard an alphabetical schedule assigned a twenty-minute conference slot for each family.

Laurie was puzzled that Mrs. Moline had placed her name at the end of this list, even though her last name began with a B. She wasn't sure why, but it didn't matter much—her parents would not be coming. She knew this despite the three reminder letters she'd seen at home and the phone calls her teacher had made.

All day long she listened as the volunteer room mother called out her classmates' names. Laurie watched each child being escorted past her desk to a doorway five feet away, a doorway where parents greeted their sons and daughters with proud smiles and pats on the back and sometimes even hugs. The door would close.

Though she tried to distract herself with assigned projects, she couldn't help but hear the muffled voices just beyond the door as interested parents asked questions, children giggled nervously, and Mrs. Moline offered affirmations and solutions.

She imagined how it might feel to have her parents greet her at the door.

When at last everyone else's name had been called, Mrs. Moline quietly opened the door and motioned for Laurie to join her in the hallway.

In silence she slipped out without one of her classmates noticing. There were three folding chairs set up in the hallway across from a desk covered with student files and projects.

Curiously she watched as Mrs. Moline began to fold up two of the folding chairs. "These won't be necessary," she said. While Laurie sat down in the remaining chair, her teacher looked through her files and smiled.

All Laurie could do was fold her hands and look down at the linoleum floor; she was embarrassed her parents had not come.

Moving her chair next to the downcast little girl, Mrs. Moline lifted Laurie's chin so that she could make eye contact with her. "First of all," she began, "I want you to know how much I love you."

Laurie lifted her eyes. In Mrs. Moline's face, she saw things she'd rarely seen—compassion, empathy, tenderness.

"Second," she continued, "You need to know that it is not your fault that your parents are not here today."

Again Laurie looked into Mrs. Moline's face. No one had ever talked to her like this. No one had ever given her permission to see herself as anything but worthless. No one.

"Third," she went on, "you deserve a conference whether your parents are here or not—you deserve to hear how well you are doing and how wonderful I think you are."

In the following minutes, Mrs. Moline held a conference with Laurie—just Laurie. She showed her grades and Iowa test scores and academic charts that placed her in the upper national percentile. She scanned papers and projects that Laurie had completed, always praising her efforts, always affirming her strengths.

She had even saved a stack of watercolor paintings Laurie had done.

"You would be a great interior designer," she said. Laurie didn't know exactly when, but at some point in that conference she remembered hearing the voice of hope in her heart, somewhere in that inner place where truth takes hold and transformation starts.

And as tears welled up in her sixth-grade eyes, Laurie could see Mrs. Moline's face becoming misty and hazy, all except for the golden curls and ivory pearls of her drop earrings. The irritating intruders in two clams' shells had been surrounded and transformed into pearls of beauty.

It was then that Laurie realized, for the first time in her life, that she was lovable.

We sat together in the comforting silence that follows a story worth remembering. In those quiet moments, I thought of all the times Laurie had worn the drop earrings of truth for me.

I too had grown up in an alcoholic home, and for years I had buried my childhood stories. But Laurie had met me in the symbolic hallway of empathy.

There she had given me the courage to name the truths hidden within each of those carefully concealed tales: that alcoholism is never a child's fault; that self-worth is a gift from God that everyone deserves, a shimmering jewel, bestowed at birth, to be worn with pride for a lifetime; that even adulthood was not too late to don the dazzling diamonds of newfound self-esteem, to finally define myself as lovable.

Just then the kids ran to the table, dramatizing famine by flopping onto the grass and picnic benches.

For the rest of the afternoon, we found ourselves

immersed in the interruptions of parenthood. We cut bologna into small pieces, wiped up spilled milk, praised off-balance somersaults and glided down slides much too small for us.

But in the midst of it all, Laurie handed me a small box, a birthday gift wrapped in red floral paper trimmed with a gold bow.

I opened the box. Inside was a pair of drop earrings.

Nancy Sullivan Geng

A Genius for Loving

I grew up knowing I was different, and I hated it.

I was born with a cleft palate, and when I started to go to school, my classmates—who were constantly teasing—made it clear to me how I must look to others; a little girl with a misshapen lip, crooked nose, lopsided teeth, and hollow and somewhat garbled speech. I couldn't even blow up a balloon without holding my nose, and when I bent to drink from a fountain, the water spilled out of my nose.

When schoolmates asked, "What happened to your lip?" I'd tell them that I'd fallen as a baby and cut it on a piece of glass. Somehow it seemed more acceptable to have suffered an accident than to have been born different. By the age of seven, I was convinced that no one outside my own family could ever love me. Or even like me.

And then I entered second grade and Mrs. Leonard's class.

I never knew what her first name was—just Mrs. Leonard. She was round and pretty and fragrant, with chubby arms and shining brown hair and warm, dark eyes that smiled even on the rare occasions when her mouth didn't. Everyone adored her. But no one came to love her more than I did. And for a special reason.

The time came for the annual "hearing tests" given at our school. I was barely able to hear anything out of one ear, and was not about to reveal yet another problem that would single me out as different. And so I cheated.

I had learned to watch the other children and raise my hand when they did during group testing. The "whisper test," however, required a different kind of deception: Each child would go to the door of the classroom, turn sideways, close one ear with a finger, and the teacher would whisper something from her desk, which the child would repeat. Then the same thing was done for the other ear. I had discovered in kindergarten that nobody checked to see how tightly the untested ear was being covered, so I merely pretended to block mine.

As usual, I was last, but all through the testing I wondered what Mrs. Leonard might say to me. I knew from previous years that the teacher whispered things like, "The sky is blue" or "Do you have new shoes?"

My turn came. I turned my bad ear to her, plugging up the other solidly with my finger, then gently backed my finger out enough to be able to hear. I waited, and then came the words that God had surely put into her mouth, seven words that changed my life forever.

Mrs. Leonard, the pretty, fragrant teacher I adored, said softly, "I wish you were my little girl."

Mary Ann Bird
Submitted by Dorothy Sandland

Thank You for Changing My Life

I met Frankie the day I walked into his sixth-grade classroom as a fledgling student teacher full of fear and trepidation. I had just spent two years assisting at a day care center and had decided to go to teacher's college to become a kindergarten teacher. What was I doing in a sixth-grade classroom?

Frankie wasn't hard to miss. He was sitting at the back of the class, leaning back on his chair with his feet up on the desk. A miniature Fonz, Frankie's clothes were spattered with dried mud—not an easy feat in this frozen Canadian town of Winnipeg, where none of us had seen mud for months, only four feet of ice and snow. His hair hadn't seen a comb in a long time and his eyes glared, "Just try and teach me!"

The regular classroom teacher was wrapped up in trying to complete his master's thesis, so the students were given individual contracts at the beginning of each week and then sent to the library or wherever else they could keep out of trouble to do "individual research." The teacher decided to give me the one group his conscience hadn't let him contract out—the bottom math group—all boys, all restless and all as motivated to learn about math as I was to learn about hang gliding. Frankie was included. The teacher explained that Frankie's only obligation was to show up every day. If he came, he got full credit, even if he only just sat there with his feet up.

Racking my brains for a math unit that could capture the attention of these nine rowdy boys, I was inspired to base the unit on fractions and taught it using recipes. We made everything from chocolate chip cookies to my one and only loaf of home-baked bread. At first, Frankie hung out at the back of the group totally uninterested. Then I promised the boys a trip to McDonald's for lunch for anyone who completed the unit. Frankie said I couldn't do that. I said I could and would.

Each day, Frankie became more and more involved. As the second week of my adventure with these boys began, a miracle happened. Frankie showed up, all scrubbed up and in clean clothes. By the end of the third week, all nine boys—including Frankie—had completed the whole unit, and I realized I had to make good on the McDonald's promise. Those boys had worked hard! What a blow it was when I learned the school administration would not allow a student teacher to take students off school property. Frankie was right—I couldn't do it. An even greater blow came as the classroom teacher handed me the most derogatory evaluation I would receive during that whole year of classroom teaching experiences.

Depressed and defeated, I apologized profusely to the boys, thanked them for all their hard work and packed up my materials. That last afternoon in their classroom was also the Valentine's Dance for the entire sixth grade. It was a true classic in the genre—all the boys stood on one side of the gym and all the girls stood on the other. A handful of girls were dancing together at the girls' end and that was it. Another student teacher victim and I sat up on the bleachers, savoring our last look at middle school before finishing the year back at our elementary school haven.

Suddenly the ear-splitting rock-and-roll ended and a beautiful waltz filled the gym. Frankie separated himself from the wall of boys, climbed the bleachers and asked if I would dance with him. All alone in the middle of the dance floor, with every eye glued on us, Frankie and I waltzed in silence. As the last notes faded away, he stopped dancing, looked me right in the eyes and said, "Thank you for changing my life."

It was not the magic of recipes and fractions. It was not the promise of a Big Mac. The only thing I figured had wrought the miracle was that someone cared. If I had changed Frankie's life, so had he changed mine. I had learned the power of love, kindness and respect in a classroom. This kindergarten-bound student teacher switched her major to special education and spent many a rewarding year teaching in classrooms in Canada and the United States searching out every Frankie I could find. Thank *you*, Frankie, for changing *my* life!

Randy Loyd Mills

When Children Learn

When children learn that happiness is not found in what a person has but in who that person is,

When they learn that giving and forgiving are more rewarding than taking and avenging,

When they learn that suffering is not eased by self-pity, but overcome by inner resolve and spiritual strength,

When they learn that they can't control the world around them, but they are the masters of their own souls,

When they learn that relationships will prosper if they value friendship over ego, compromise over pride, and listening over advising,

When they learn not to hate a person whose difference they fear, but to fear that kind of hate,

When they learn that there is pleasure in the power of lifting others up, not in the pseudo-power of pushing them down,

When they learn that praise from others is flattering but meaningless if it is not matched by self-respect,

When they learn that the value of a life is best measured not by the years spent accumulating possessions, but by the moments spent giving of one's self—sharing wisdom, inspiring hope, wiping tears and touching hearts,

When they learn that a person's beauty is seen not with the eyes but with the heart; and that even though time and hardships may ravage one's outer shell, they can enhance one's character and perspective,

When they learn to withhold judgment of people, knowing everyone is blessed with good and bad qualities, and that the emergence of either often depends on the help given or hurt inflicted by others,

When they learn that every person has been given the gift of a unique self, and the purpose of life is to share the very best of that gift with the world,

When children learn these ideals and how to practice them in the art of good living, they will no longer be children—they will be blessings to those who know them, and worthy models for all the world.

David L. Weatherford

"I swear I didn't use a calculator."

Reprinted by permission of Oliver Gaspirtz.

Academic Excellence Begins with a '51 Studebaker

What the teacher is, is more important than what he teaches.

Karl Menninger

David Ford, my best friend in September 1956, and I were playing kick-the-can on our way to our third-grade class. It was a typical September morning in Jal, New Mexico. The smell of crude oil and dust hung heavy in the desert morning air. Until that time, I had been an A student and liked school, but this year things were different. Although we didn't do many difficult things, school was turning out to be a place I would rather not be. These long fall days were spent coloring, adding, subtracting and looking at a dead snake in a pickle jar. I was a towheaded boy with a cowlick that would not quit. My jeans were worn through at the knees before it was popular to wear them that way.

Our classroom was also known as Mrs. Writt's dungeon of torture. Mrs. Writt was a stickler for proper appearance and pointed out daily the sins of untidiness. I seemed to be her favorite target and to my chagrin, she would inevitably find dirt under my fingernails and my Keds improperly laced.

Although I didn't recognize its significance until much later, this one particular day was to be a defining time for me. This would forever be the moment at which I could look back and say, "That's when it happened."

We had all colored the same picture the day before: a curly-haired, dimple-faced girl sitting on a hobby horse. The same image was used, no doubt, for comparison purposes. Now, I never saw the purpose in coloring; it was something I had decided that girls did. David and I had discussed this at length and had decided that, indeed, boys couldn't be good at this activity. Any boy who was adept at coloring a curly-haired, dimple-faced girl most certainly wasn't capable of excelling at "boy things" like shooting rabbits or playing football.

When I took a seat, my classmates were giggling and pointing at the chalkboard. To my surprise, my rendering of color on the curly-haired girl was taped prominently on the left side of the chalkboard, and labeled with broad chalk lettering: "Terry's picture." On the right side of the board was another coloring of the same picture, labeled "Sherry's picture." Sherry's picture had been done by "perfect" Sherry Peirson. Sherry was pretty, clean and always well dressed. Her coloring was always perfect, with the correct hues and of course, *always* within the lines.

As Mrs. Writt called roll, I got a knot in the pit of my stomach and I felt my face getting hot as I slid further down into my seat. Suddenly, I felt like my feet were grotesquely oversized and I didn't know what to do with my large, dirty hands, so I put them in my pockets. I felt dizzy and my vision narrowed to where all I could see was my coloring taped to the chalkboard. There it was, the girl with curly purple hair and green lips sitting on a red hobby horse, crayon marks irregularly straying over the lines. Oh how I wished that I had done better, or had a chance to do it again. Maybe the principal would call a fire drill or even better, the school would catch fire and burn down. Maybe now the Soviets would drop the bomb on us and we could jump under our desks and watch the searing heat burn all the paper products in town. Before salvation could come in any form, Mrs. Writt called my name. "Terry, Terry Savoie, come and stand under your work. I want the class to see who is responsible for this.

"Sherry, please stand next to your work. Now class, which of these is acceptable, Terry's work or Sherry's work?"

"Sherry's, teacher."

"Class, please notice how the appearance of the person matches the appearance of the work. I want you to be like Sherry; she is a shining example of excellence. Don't do what Terry has done; Terry is an example of failure. This is what failure looks like and this is what excellence looks like. Okay, children, you may take your seats."

So this was my position, the class failure. Oddly, at the moment I sat down I felt comfortable with my new position. My parents had told me, "Do what you do well." I could most certainly do this well. I could, in fact, be the best class failure Jal Elementary ever had. It was a liberating feeling. I would have this position unchallenged and indeed be a clown, or sleep, or work feverishly at failing and forever own the official title of Class Failure. I found that I was particularly good at my new-found talent. I took pride in my position and never again had to feel that knot in my stomach for poor performance.

David, being my best friend, was impressed with my new ability and began to compete with me for my position, but he was never any real competition because he had never gotten the recognition from the authority on this subject like I had. I was the best at failure and had the credentials to prove it.

I found that there was a price to pay for my position. I had to deal with my parents' disappointment every six weeks. I spent many long hours being lectured to and also had to endure regular spankings. The most difficult price for me to pay were my mother's tears. But a man's got to do what a man's got to do. My parents continued to tell me that I wasn't stupid. In fact, they went to great lengths to encourage me and tell me I was as smart as anyone else, even smarter than most. But they were my parents and they were supposed to say that. The "professionals" knew better and had spoken.

Life turned out to be relatively easy once I had calloused myself to my parents' grief. The school moved me on with my friends and annotated on my records "chronological promotion," which meant I was old enough to move to the next grade. They did hold me back when I failed the seventh grade and again in the ninth grade. This is when my problems began to catch up with me. My friends were leaving me, even David moved up, and I was left with the younger kids. After I failed the ninth grade, Mom suggested that I get a tutor in algebra and English. It was then decided that I would spend the summer of 1964 in summer school, and that until my grades came up I would spend every summer in school.

The high school principal, Mr. K. B. Walker, called a meeting with my parents and me. He got so close to me that I could smell the oil in his red hair, and he said some very scary words to me that went something like this: "Savoie, you need to understand that I don't care how long it takes, you will stay in the ninth grade until you meet the same standards everyone else does before you move on." Then he looked at my dad and said, "Herman, you're backing me on this, aren't you?"

"Yes sir."

At this time my interests were in cars and trucks. I was

fascinated with all sorts of mechanical things. My dad had helped me buy a 1951 Studebaker and we spent many weekends together working on it. When we pulled it into the garage, it was rusty red and nothing worked, but to me its sleek rocket shape was the most exciting thing I had ever seen. We removed the hood and began our project by first removing all the dirt daubers' nests from around the carburetor. We cleaned and scraped and I worked part time at Alexander's grocery store, putting every dime I made into parts.

Eventually the car came back to life. We rebuilt the old flathead six and put in a new six-volt battery. I remember clearly the Friday evening in July waiting on the porch for my dad to get home so we could connect the battery and start the engine. Dad came straight in and we told Mom to skip supper—we had important things to do. I brushed the cables gently with a wire brush. Then I reverently tightened the seven-sixteenth-inch post clamps. Dad decided to check to see if the six volts were now coursing life through the old rocket. He pulled the headlight switch and the right headlight burned brightly. The light reflected my white T-shirt and Dad spit some Beech-Nut tobacco out the driver's side window and raised his eyebrows. He stuck his head out and said, "Son, pour about two tablespoons of gas in that carburetor and let's see if she cranks."

He pumped the accelerator pedal twice and pulled the choke half closed, turned the key on and pushed the chrome-plated start button. The starter rotated the engine once, then twice, the rotations quickened. A bright orange flame shot from the open exhaust pipe, the engine spun to life with a cloud of black smoke and then the air cleared. The engine settled to a smooth, even idle. I whooped, Dad grinned and Mom came into the garage. She put her arm around my shoulder and said, "It's running, you made it run, you're good at this, aren't you?"

I said, "Yeah, with Dad's help, I guess I am." We went on to paint the car and with the help of wet concrete mortar for rubbing compound, we got all of the tarnish off the chrome bright work. It was truly a work of art.

I tell you about the Studebaker because the work I did on this car became a recurring topic of conversation during my algebra summer school. To understand the metamorphosis that was to take place the summer of 1964, I must introduce you to Montrella Ruffner. My parents never gave up on me and they weren't afraid to try anything. Montrella was a member of our church and was also a teacher. My parents talked her into helping me. She didn't tell me anything my parents hadn't told me but since she was a teacher, she was the expert on success and failure. Montrella was a robust and enthusiastic woman. She was rather large and usually the first thing she did when I arrived for tutoring was to give me a hug. When Montrella hugged you, you didn't come unhugged for a week. We would start each session by talking about my favorite subject, my Studebaker. Montrella was as mechanically inclined as most thirty-five-year-old algebra teachers but she seemed to really enjoy hearing me talk about connecting rods, piston rings and carburetors. She sat enthralled as I spoke eloquently about firing order and ignition timing.

Then she would ask, "Is this what you really love to do? Would you like to be a mechanic when you grow up?" Well, to me, being a mechanic wasn't anything special. Most of my friends were mechanics on their own cars. I allowed, though, that it might be what I would do. After all what else could an academic failure like me do?

This robust authority on success began to paint pictures in my mind. She talked about how it was almost magical how automobiles worked and how people who could fix them were like powerful doctors. She asked me to imagine what a world without mechanics would be like. "Why, surely we would still have to hitch up a wagon and bail our drinking water out of an open well," she said authoritatively. She talked about the mechanical magicians that had fixed her car over at the Kermit Chevy House. How they wore the professional blue coveralls with their names and "Chevy Mechanic" embroidered on them.

She told me, "Son, you are going to be one of those guys, not only that, I think I see you being a Master Technician one of these days. Can you see yourself in those clothes doing that with a reputation for being the best? Why, look at Jimmy Lewallen. He is one of the smartest, most respected men in Jal." Jimmy was our small town's resident mechanic and a man of excellent reputation.

It was at this point she caught me, she gently nudged me into algebra by saying, "You're gonna be the best, aren't you?"

"Yes ma'am."

"Son, do you know there are steps you have to take to get there?"

"Yes ma'am," nodding enthusiastically.

"Son, you know what you've got to do first to be top of the line?"

"What's that, ma'am?"

"You gotta do this algebra and anyone that can do the kind of magic you do with a broken down old car can do this algebra and do it well, do you understand that son? Do you?"

"Yes, ma'am."

Then she said, "Let's tear this algebra down and breathe some life into it, okay?"

I went on that fall to get a B in algebra—the first B that I had gotten since the second grade. It turns out that I was a solid B student with occasional abilities for receiving As. I joined the Air Force in 1969. They didn't know that I had been stupid once and I didn't tell them. In basic training, I was overjoyed when I was told I had a high aptitude for mechanics and that they were going to send me to jet school at Chanute AFB I11. To me this was like getting drafted to play linebacker for the Dallas Cowboys.

The victories, though, didn't end in mechanics. I had many different and interesting jobs in my twenty-five-year career and in 1987, I was selected as the USAF First Sergeant of the Year, "Top of the Line." I earned two college degrees going to night school and now that I'm out of the Air Force, I'm a teacher of aerospace science at Central High School in San Angelo, Texas. Academic excellence sometimes begins in strange and unorthodox places. To me, academic excellence began with a 1951 Studebaker.

Terry A. Savoie

The Second Mile

Somebody made a mistake, I thought as I skimmed the Vietnam treetops in my unarmed Cessna. My radio had reported enemy troops below, but as I circled the site, scouring the elephant grass, I saw nothing.

My job as forward air controller with the U.S. Air Force in 1966 was to spot enemy targets and radio information back so headquarters could send attack aircraft. That morning my patrol had been uneventful. Then my radio crackled, "Airedale Pup, this is Airedale."

It was Captain Jim Ahmann, using our personal code words and calling from our forward operating base at Dong Tre. I was his junior officer, so naturally I was Pup. My little single-engine monoplane, carrying only smoke rockets to mark targets, was Bird Dog.

Ahmann continued: "We have a reported sighting of 200 or 300 Viet Cong in the open." They had been spotted by an Army forward observer plane.

"On my way," I answered, banking Bird Dog toward the coordinates.

However, as I reached the given location, I could find no sign of the forward observer plane. I scrutinized the area, flying low, worrying about VC ground fire and remembering some bullet holes I had earlier found in Bird Dog's thin skin. I circled again. Still nothing.

"Airedale, there's nothing here." I heard our fighters checking in on the other radio frequency. "Have the fighters hold high." I was about to call off the search. I had done my job.

"Have you?" demanded a gruff voice. I winced. Despite the passage of years, I could almost see his sharp features in the windshield before me: Father John Mulroy, one of my teachers at Archbishop Stepinac High School in White Plains, New York.

He had nailed me to the wall when I submitted my first class paper. I had confidently handed it in, thinking it was complete.

Father Mulroy did not. He gave me a C. I was shocked. He knew I wanted to go to the Air Force Academy, and I needed good grades. When I questioned the C, he fastened me with his dark, penetrating eyes. "That's what it was worth," he snapped. He then rattled off a list of information sources. "Did you check into them?"

"I didn't think it was necessary," I said weakly.

"You only did enough to get by," he said. "When Christ asks us to go the second mile, he means making that extra effort in *everything*." Father Mulroy tapped his desk. "Out in the world, that can make a difference in getting a promotion—or saving a life. Don't try to ride Easy Street and expect to wear the stars of a general."

On my next paper I dug deeper. It still wasn't good enough for Father Mulroy. "God put more into you than you think," he said. "Don't sell him short."

Try as I might, he kept sandpapering me. The more he did, the more I gritted my teeth. "I'll show him," I muttered—which was just what he wanted.

When I didn't make the starting football team as a

fullback, I switched to defense, concentrated on becoming a fierce tackler and won a starting position. This, I hoped, would help me get into the Academy.

After the Academy turned me down, I went to the University of Pennsylvania, determined to put in a strong enough showing to make the Academy the next year. I earned high scores, won a starting spot on the football team, pored over Academy study guides, reapplied and got in.

After I graduated I volunteered for Vietnam, then as a forward air controller, one of the more hazardous flying assignments in the military. Once in Vietnam, I joined Project Delta—the elite hunter-killer teams of the Green Berets who operated behind enemy lines.

Now in Bird Dog, here was Father Mulroy again.

I radioed base. "Something's wrong," I reported. "I need some time. Give me another frequency. I've got to raise the Army forward observer."

As the new frequency came through, a swarm of Army helicopter gunships roared under me, turning in a large arc as if searching for something.

I called the Army plane on the new frequency. No response. I tried again and again to raise the mystery ship. I couldn't give up. I had to reach this guy!

Finally, a response. "This is Sundance X Ray."

"Do you have a target?" I asked.

"I've got 300 VC in the open, and I'm trying to locate our gunships."

It was obvious that Sundance was nowhere near the coordinates I had been given. But where *was* he? I had to find him. Timing was critical.

"Sundance, what do you see beneath you?" He described a meandering river, and I tried to match his description on my map. "Okay. I think I know where you are."

I shoved the throttle forward until my Cessna was making its full 115 miles per hour. Soon I spotted the observer plane high against the sky.

It was a small monoplane much like mine. "Lead me to the target," I radioed. Glancing over my shoulder, I saw the gunships following us. "Down there," he called, "along the light green field. They were heading west and disappeared in the trees."

I checked my map. We were six miles from the coordinates he had given us.

"Are you sure?" I asked, circling the location.

Then I saw them. A serpentine column moving through the elephant grass on the back of a knoll. Maybe 200 or 300 troops, all with packs. When I dipped closer, I saw they were in VC attire—a hodgepodge of dark uniforms.

As I moved to a safer altitude, I felt that familiar nudge. Something wasn't right. My mouth dry, I flew closer, expecting the zing of bullets and the whump of heavy-weapons fire. I was about to launch my smoke rockets into the column to pinpoint it for the gunships when again something stopped me. These men didn't take cover. They *had* to see me. However, we knew that VC caught in the open often behaved like friendly troops, even to the point of waving at passing aircraft.

Now the gunships, aligned for attack, began to close in. Still something stopped me from getting out of their way. In my mind's ear I heard the distant echo of Father Mulroy's voice: *Make sure, John. Make sure.*

I had to get a closer look. I cut the Cessna's power and glided toward the elephant grass close to the column, expecting a fusillade of bullets. My heart caught. They were *our* Vietnamese troops—counter-guerrilla forces who wore uniforms similar to the VC's—carrying American carbines and wearing colored scarves. *Friendlies!*

"Abort!" I shouted over the radio. But the gunships kept

coming. They couldn't hear me because they were on a different frequency.

I slammed the control stick full over, jammed the throttle forward and pulled into a gut-wrenching climb. My plane shuddered into a steep bank and stalled. I rolled out to the left, completing my climbing U-turn in front of and 500 feet below the oncoming gunships, positioning myself between them and the friendlies. They couldn't fire without hitting me.

"Sundance, get the helicopters outta here!" I shouted over the radio. "They're friendlies!"

Somehow the message got through. The choppers broke off their attack.

The Army pilot followed me back to Dong Tre. He turned out to be a lieutenant new to the country, visibly upset as he realized what had transpired. It was an honest mistake.

The Distinguished Flying Cross I was awarded for that mission meant more to me than all the other decorations I got for performance during combat.

After I returned from Vietnam, I received a note from Father Mulroy. "I had the greatest confidence in you and that God would guide and protect you," he wrote.

Today I serve on the alumni association and, like Father Mulroy, I teach school, demanding of my students in St. Francis College in Brooklyn, New York, that they go the second mile and write papers to my—and Father Mulroy's—standards. Father Mulroy died in 1994 at seventy-seven, but his message lives on. My students know they can't ride Easy Street and expect to reach the stars.

John F. Flanagan Jr.

Do You Disciple?

After teaching a lesson to my kindergarten class on Jesus and his disciples, I was feeling quite proud. It was a model lesson, an A, and included a game, a song and a story.

At the conclusion of the lesson, I opened the discussion to questions. With pride, I looked out at my students' wildly waving arms. My lesson was obviously a success. Teaching seemed so rewarding. I would now let them shower me with this new knowledge that I had so skillfully imparted to them.

I called on Brittney to respond. Since her arm was waving more frantically than the rest, surely her observation would be that much more brilliant. "Brittney, what do you have to say about Jesus and his disciples?" I asked eagerly.

"Well," she began, with true kindergarten confidence, "I just wanted you to know that I know a lot about disciples 'cause at my house we disciple everything. We have a special disciple can for plastic, a special disciple can for glass, and a special disciple can for paper. My mom says it's how we save the earth."

I paused, took a deep breath and said, "Let's get ready for lunch."

Christine Pisera Naman

DILBERT. Reprinted by permission of United Features Syndicate, Inc.

It's a House . . . It's a Cow . . . It's Ms. Burk!

When the midwife confirmed my pregnancy, I was working as a teacher's aide in a fourth-grade classroom. To avoid the inevitable barrage of questions, I tried to keep my news from the students as long as possible. But I hadn't counted on Natalye to root out the truth like a pig in search of truffles.

Natalye had recently become a big sister and considered herself the expert on pregnancy. Since her mother was no longer pregnant, Natalye figured it was someone else's turn, and no woman was above suspicion. She took a sideways glance at her slender teacher and announced, "Ms. Daily's pregnant. I can tell." Word spread rapidly, until Ms. Daily flatly denied the rumor. Next, Natalye turned her appraising eye on Mrs. Scofield, who was enthusiastically congratulated by mobs of nine-year-olds until that rumor, too, was squelched. Finally, it was my turn. I had been waiting for Natalye to turn her investigative nose my way, and I was prepared with a few creative answers because I didn't want to flat-out lie.

She approached me with her entourage of three other girls and asked me (or rather told me), "Ms. Burk, when's your baby due? 'Cause I *know* you're expecting." I responded with humor, "Oh Natalye, you always think somebody's pregnant." But she wouldn't let it go. Every morning she grinned her most appealing grin and said, "You can tell me, Ms. Burk. You fixin' to have a baby, ain't you?" I answered with a grammar lesson: "Aren't you. Not ain't you."

She persisted, improving her language so I couldn't hide behind it. I tried distracting her with "Why do you ask, am I gaining weight?" But eventually she wore me down, and I admitted that, yes, my baby was due in June. Six long months away for me. Natalye was thrilled, reigning goddess of spotting "p.g. women." Never mind that she'd been wrong at least a half-dozen times before me; she'd struck gold at last.

Morning sickness is tough on anyone, but pregnant teachers should get special martyr points for having to use the same bathroom as nine-year-old boys whose aim is far from accurate. Let it suffice to say that I tried to use the adults-only restroom in the office when I had enough advance warning.

During the ensuing school year I was asked many questions, ranging from "Does your baby like it when you eat pickles?" to "Where does a baby's fart go?" Milton was appalled that I would be happy with either a boy or a girl. "Oh, Ms. Burk, how could you want a girl? Girls are so *disgusting*. Well, except you're not so bad."

Two of the girls liked to kiss the baby good-bye every day. As a couple of the boys taunted them with, "Hope and Sheneka are in love with Ms. Burk," the girls haughtily ignored them and bent over to kiss and pat my stomach. Later at home, I'd rub a laundry stain-remover stick over my so-called waistline to remove grape-juice-kiss stains and pizza-grease fingerprints.

Kendell looked up out of his perpetual fog one day and interrupted the math lesson to blurt out, "Ms. Burk, are you pregnant?" I was amazed that this information had escaped him. At eight months, I'd been stretching the seams of my maternity blouses for weeks. My thoughts were succinctly put into words by Freddie, who hollered, "Man, where you been? She's big as a house!"

Zeke liked to tell me at every possible opportunity, "It's really gonna hurt bad, Ms. Burk. You'll probably cry." His prophecies inspired Yi-Hsuan to draw a picture of me on a bed, stick knees up in the air, and big crocodile tears streaming down my cheeks. A bubble caption over my head held one boldly printed word: OWWWCH!

On the playground during recess, Willa pointed to my stomach and asked, "Where's the baby going to come out? There, or . . ." she crooked her finger south an inch and looked at me sideways, "um, you know, down there?" Bored with my explanation about natural childbirth and cesarean sections, she was nevertheless clearly pleased to get away with saying something that bordered on dirty talk.

Jon told his P.E. class that I went into the bathroom a lot because the baby was sitting on my bladder sac.

I thought I was immune to blushing, but Moira proved me wrong when she informed the principal that after my baby was born it would milk me, "just like a cow."

Because my due date wasn't until summer, the children wanted to make presents for the baby before school was out. So one rainy day, following instructions from a magazine article, I brought in paper plates and non-toxic markers and explained that newborns love to look at pictures of faces. I asked all the students to draw pictures of themselves on the plates so I could show the baby the wonderful children I worked with. Well, the results were a far cry from the article's depiction of pug noses and toothy smiles. The "artwork" I got was more appropriate for a Stephen King dream than for a nursery crib. Purple saliva dripped from fangs, green slime oozed from nostrils. It was downright scary.

A sweet memory I have is of Crystal, a little girl who was so behind in reading that she refused to read aloud in class or even in a reading group. But she loved to come back to the classroom after lunch and read a beginning book "to the baby." She'd lean down and whisper very loudly at my stomach, "Okay, this is about a cat who can fly. You listening, baby?"

The baby who was loved so much that school year was born only five days after school let out, a full three weeks early. When fall rolled back around and classes started again, I arranged for "my kids" to have lunch in their old classroom, and I took my daughter, Kayla, in for a visit. The children gathered around her, and she stared somberly at all their faces until the class comedian began an impromptu and loud rendition of "Oh, what a beautiful baby!" The other kids started laughing, and so did Kayla. Then the questions and comments began again.

"Ms. Burk, can I feed her a pretzel?"

"Did it hurt real bad like I told you? Did you cry?"

"What's her favorite color, because I want to draw her a picture."

"She's pretty cute . . . for a girl."

Soon after the kids said good-bye and returned to their classes, their teacher told me she was expecting and had been walking down to the cafeteria every day to buy milk just as I had the year before. I asked her if the kids knew yet, and she said she wasn't planning to tell them for a few months. I couldn't stop smiling as I settled Kayla into her car seat and drove away. *Well, watch out for Natalye,* I thought.

April Burk

[EDITORS' NOTE: *All names have been changed.*]

What Color Are You?

As a second-grade teacher in an inner-city school, I am often faced with the task of answering questions that really have nothing to do with our course of study for the day—questions that you won't find on any national standardized tests. Some of these questions can be recycled into research for the class ("Mrs. Eastham, why are butterflies all different colors?" "How does the grass die in the winter and then come alive in the spring?") Others are much more ponderous and may not have an exact right or wrong answer.

Since I am not one to squelch curiosity, we often take these opportunities as they arise and have short class discussions on them. I let everyone comment on the subject and then tell them we can each make up our own minds. ("Why do we have homework *every night*?" "Are there really such things as angels?")

Our discussion on differences started innocently enough. I asked the class if they could tell me whether a very tall man was good or bad. They agreed that you couldn't tell if someone was good or bad just because they were tall. I told them that I knew someone who couldn't walk well and so she rode in a wheelchair most of the time. I asked if that person was bad or mean because she uses a wheelchair, and they all agreed that you couldn't tell. We went on for a while in this vein and came to the conclusion that being different doesn't make someone good or bad, it just makes that person different.

I decided to take the discussion to a more personal level and explore our personal differences. We talked about how we are all different from one another, how no two people are exactly alike, how even twins have different personalities or features that define them as individuals. I went on to tell them that I was different from everyone in the room because I was the tallest. I was also different because I lived in Red Oak and everyone else lived in Dallas.

Then I planned to have each of them tell the class how they were different. But before I could call on the first pupil, my quietest student raised his hand and announced, "Mrs. Eastham is different because she is a different color."

As I think back now, I realize that if this had been said in a room with fifteen other adults, this simple statement of truth would have laid out on the floor, floundering like a fish out of water, while embarrassed glances waited for someone to break the awkward silence. Not so in a classroom of fifteen second-graders. They jumped on it!

"Yeah, Mrs. Eastham is white."

"No, she's not, she's peach!"

"I think she's really just bright brown."

"She's creamy."

"She's kinda yellow."

"She's just really shiny."

Trying to hide my grin, I told the class they could have small group discussions on it while I turned the attendance report into the office. I barely made it out of the room before my smirk turned into a full belly laugh. I chuckled all the way to the office and related the story to a fellow teacher while there. I couldn't wait to get back to the room to hear them discuss this!

When I opened the door, they were already back in their seats. They had finished their discussion. (Darn, I had missed it!) I picked a spokesperson for the group, and he said that they knew what color I was but they wanted me to tell them if they were right or not. I said that since this question had only one right answer, I would tell them if they had guessed right or not. Then he told me that the class had decided that I was clear.

Clear? Somehow I was able to suppress my laughter. How did they come up with *that?* I was saved by the bell, as it was time for them to go to gym. I told them we could talk about it after gym and sent them on their way. Looking back now, I know *someone* was looking out for me.

While grading papers, I began to muse over our morning again. I was reminded of the times I had been at conferences and workshops and even dinner parties and had been asked, "How many of your students are black? How many white children are in your class? Do you teach many Hispanics?" So many times I have had to stop and try to count out the answers. "How many black students do I have? I know I have fifteen kids. Is it ten black and five Hispanic, or eleven and four?"

The person posing the question is very often amazed and perplexed that I don't know the ethnic makeup of my classroom. I guess it's because when I am teaching, I am teaching children, not colors. I began to realize that it was the same for my kids. They don't see me as black or white or Hispanic; they see me as a person, someone who cares about them, encourages them to do their best and works hard with them every day.

When my students got back to the room, they were all still abuzz about our morning discussion and begged me to tell them if they were right or wrong. I had to tell them the truth. They were exactly right. I am *clear!*

Now when I am asked that inevitable question at dinner parties or conventions or workshops—"How many black and Hispanic and white children do you have?"—I have a pat answer that works every time, with no fumbling or counting. I look the person straight in the eye and say, "None. They are all clear."

Melissa D. Strong Eastham

4

ON DEATH
AND DYING

*Oh, heart, if one should say to you that the
soul perishes like the body, answer that the
flower withers, but the seed remains.
This is the law of God.*

Kahlil Gibran

To Those I Love

When I am gone, release me, let me go
I have so many things to see and do
You mustn't tie yourself to me with tears
Be happy that we had so many years.
I gave you my love. You can only guess
How much you gave to me in happiness
I thank you for the love you have shown
But now it's time I traveled on alone.
So grieve awhile for me if grieve you must
Then let your grief be comforted by trust
It's only for a while that we must part
So bless the memories with your heart.
I won't be far away, for life goes on
So if you need me, call and I will come
Though you can't see or touch me, I'll be near
And if you listen with your heart, you'll hear
All of my love around you soft and clear.
And then, when you must come this way alone
I'll greet you with a smile, and welcome you home.

Anonymous

Tommy's Shoes

I had in my mind to give those shoes to Cameron and Christy if I could just remember where I'd put them. Already having looked everywhere obvious that an old pair of track shoes were likely to be, I was straining for new possibilities. Even though I'd kept them for the better part of twenty-five years, they seemed a pretty lame remembrance to give to the thirteen-year-old twins whose father had just died at the age of forty.

I'd met Cameron and Christy probably on half a dozen occasions when they were little, but I'm sure they were too young then to recognize me now. Oh, Great Gift Bearer of Worn-out Shoes. How could I explain it to them? Their father meant so many firsts in my life. Some of which I can say and others I never will.

The first time I seriously considered running away, I called Tommy. He and his brother and two sisters were all adopted. I thought it was just amazing that people would adopt four kids and actually have a functional family. I still do. I figured he might have some perspective to offer me that I hadn't imagined, and of course he did. Tommy was never short on perspective, and at times his view of

the world confused me, but that night I appreciated it
because I didn't run away.

Tommy was part magician. If he went out and caught a
twelve-inch catfish, it'd be eighteen inches by the time it
flopped into the pan, and two feet long when the butter
sizzled in the skillet to fry it up. I don't think I did right by
Tommy in this regard when we were teenagers.
Sometimes I defended him and other times I doubted. But
to Tommy, it appeared to make little difference. He was
not afraid of things like ridicule that kept many of us that
age in a wasteland, too nearsighted to catch even a
glimpse of his vision.

Tommy loved challenges. "Yeah, right, Tommy. You can
get me a summer job." The next Saturday I was in the
fields picking watermelons. And when the land was
picked clean he got me my second job, as a painter's
helper. The summer after that I was a landscaper, thanks
to Tommy.

To say that we were best friends wouldn't be exactly
accurate, but to say we had a whole boat load of best
times together wouldn't be a lie. I guess Tommy always
made me feel like his best friend when we were together.
I'm sure I wasn't the only one.

He used to wear these blue running shoes made out of
some kind of parachute canvas when he'd do the mile and
the half-mile in high school. He wasn't the greatest long-
distance runner in the state, but for a boy with a bad heart,
he placed respectably in quite a few meets. I'd holler at
him from inside the track all the way around, telling him
where his closest competitor was. "Dig in, Tommy! Stretch
it out! You're the man!" And when it was my turn to run
my quarter of the mile relay, there was no one in the stadium shouting louder or harder for me than him.

When I had my first near-death experience, he was
there. We were on our way home from the beach. I was

driving, my girlfriend's head resting on my lap. Tommy had pulled the back cushions out of his red Barracuda convertible so he could get to the trunk from the inside, where he was sleeping. Everyone in dreamland with me cruising along at about eighty-five miles an hour in a drizzly rain. When I hit that curve, I could feel the air swirling around me thick and fast, lifting the car completely off the surface of the pavement, as if a huge window had been cracked open and then slammed shut in almost the same instant. The four tires grabbed the asphalt road again. But I know we'd have all been dead if God had wanted it so.

It was three days later before Tommy ever acknowledged the event. He came up to me in the locker room, popped me with a towel and said, "You nearly lost it on the beach road Saturday, didn't ya?"

"I thought you were asleep," I said. He laughed at me, and I punched him in the arm as many times as I could before he got even.

Punching was a big thing for us. I remember Tommy nearly broke his hand punching out a stop sign, he was so upset over a fight he'd had with his girlfriend. He married Melanie a short while after that. She was a country girl who matched his spirit fine. Sweet and pretty, but not inclined to take any sass from the likes of Tommy. He cried so much saying his wedding vows I didn't think he was going to make it, he was so happy to get her.

The twins were born and as the seasons passed, we seemed to drift in and out of each other's lives with less frequency. The last times that represented any consistency for us were during the University of Florida Gators' home football games. Tommy was in charge of the crew that supplied hot dogs for the entire stadium, and I was his lieutenant. Part of that responsibility meant meeting at the field by 4:00 A.M. to prepare for the assembly of ten thousand hot dogs. Let me tell you, when you get up in the middle of a weekend night to work your buns off alongside a guy passing you weenies all day just for the sheer pleasure of punching him in the arm every once in a while—well, you love him.

I think why I did so much is because when I was with him, we shared things. Partly because we were pretty close to the same size, and maybe too because sometimes it wasn't easy to feel like we fit anywhere.

I guess that's why passing back the shoes feels important. He gave me many things, including these running shoes, and I'm frustrated from looking and not finding. Rummaging through the final box in the back corner of the barn, I see a shoe toe that I recognize instantly. I pull it out like a prize from a cereal box and brush away the cockroach that has taken up residence inside. But there's only one shoe. The left mate is missing. How can I give the offspring of my old friend one beat-up, worn-out shoe that belonged to their father a quarter of a century ago? Feeling deflated, I close my eyes and ask Tommy what he thinks I should do. His response, as usual, is quick and decisive. "Give the kids the dang shoe and move on."

Tommy never did steer me in the wrong direction.

Samuel P. Clark

Broken Days

When the phone rang that day, it was a particularly hectic time in our lives. Our daughter was two, and our three-month-old son had colic. We had just come through a month of Christmas, colds and flu. My husband and I were exhausted. He was, in fact, taking an unprecedented afternoon off from work so he could sleep.

It was our friends, Otis and George, on the phone. They had just driven our mutual friend Dan to a hospital. The admitting doctor had told them, "I don't need an HIV test to tell you what you already know. Your friend is dying of AIDS. He's further along than any person I've ever examined for the first time. He could die this weekend."

We were stunned. Dan was our great friend. He was witty, bitingly sarcastic about pomposity, and tender and gentle with animals and children. His lively blue eyes sparkled when he laughed at himself or at us. We loved him.

Welcome to the grown-up world of people dying, I told myself. My father had died when I was a teenager, and my grandparents had all died in the ensuing five years, so I thought I understood pain and loss. What I didn't know—and was about to learn—was that losing those we love is not only painful, but also extremely inconvenient.

Dan rallied, and a week later he was discharged from the hospital. I joined with a close group of friends to help take care of him. Our friend Linda faithfully visited him every day, whether he was in the hospital or at home. George and Otis dealt with insurance, public aid, drawing up a will and funeral arrangements. They also notified Dan's mother and helped her around the city when she visited. I stayed in touch with Dan by phone, went to see him, and sometimes ferried him to chemotherapy sessions. During this period, I decided to hire a baby-sitter so I could keep up with my writing. But the first time she came, I used the allotted hours to cook a promised ham dinner for Dan and drive it to him through the rush-hour traffic.

Other people's crises can bring about great disruption in our lives. To varying degrees, we do what we know how to do. We send cards and casseroles. We talk on the phone. We sit with our loved ones and remember old jokes and happy occasions. In the closet of our minds, we crave for things to return to normal so we can cease all this effort, so we can find time to catch our breath and absorb the impact of the crisis, so we can be done with the guilt we feel for not doing more, so we can mourn the loss of a friend's life instead of the disorder of our own.

Most of us have an idea of how we think our days should go. We want nights of undisturbed sleep, regular meals and calm homes with a certain amount of order. We want family evenings filled with activities of our own choosing.

What we hate are broken days, interrupted schedules, unpredictable disorder and phone calls when we are asleep. If we are watching our favorite TV show, please don't let the neighbor's teenager pound on our door after being kicked out of the house. If we are trying to change jobs, don't let Mother need weekly rides to the doctor. If we are using all our resources to manage a busy life and colicky baby, please, God, don't let our friend collapse with AIDS.

I did a lot of thinking about stress during those months. I thought about the much-publicized checklist of stresses occurring in one's life in a given year, and I realized that even before Dan became ill, we were pushing our limits. It seemed overwhelming that on top of everything else, we would have to deal with this.

I will always remember one morning near the end of Dan's life. It was another hectic Saturday. I nursed the baby, and leaving him with my husband, took our daughter Lilly with me to a meeting. After it was over, I drove to Dan's place and hauled my damp, sleepy toddler out of the car and up the two flights of stairs to Dan's apartment.

He was gaunt and weak. He gave me a hug and collapsed back into the nest of pillows on his bed. I set Lilly at his dining table with water paints and paper. We silently watched her, both of us smiling as she unconsciously stuck her tongue out of the corner of her mouth, intently painting suns and flowers. The kitchen window framed her, its light illuminating her fair hair and soft neck.

I can still see Dan reclining on the bed. Sometimes his eyes were quietly shut; sometimes they were open with an unfamiliar, watery, pain-filled gaze. But when he watched Lilly, the pain seemed to leave for a moment. I could see him savoring the sweet, vibrant sight of my child.

I knew this would be one of our last hours together. But I was also anxious. The baby would need to nurse soon, Lilly needed her lunch and a nap, and my husband needed the car. How could one moment be crowded with so much love, poignancy . . . and worry?

If growing up is the process of creating ideas and dreams about what life should be, then maturity is letting go again. Dan died a few weeks later. My friend and mentor, Nancy, died the following year. My sister lost her life after two hard years of fighting cancer.

Over and over again, I find I am not capable or nurturing or insightful enough. I do not solace or comfort the way I imagined I would. At the same time, our home life is ragged at the edges. We give up some of our routines and pleasures so that we can find time and energy to make a water painting for Dan, to write an early-morning letter to Nancy, to bake Mom's special coffeecake for my sister. We are not triumphant at anything. We go along.

As the ill and dying give up their lives, we give up our claim to quiet nights and neat days. Maybe it is those who die who finally teach us that through the cracks in our days often come life and love, and moments of connection.

Mary Beth Danielson

Every Loss Is a Mini-Death

"I don't want to die, but unless there is a miracle I guess it will be soon," said my close friend. She was fifty-two years old and had been healthy until four months before.

The day she said this was the day I was leaving for a weekend family reunion at a cross-country ski resort. Our family had made plans months before for the only weekend we could all get together for our favorite sport. Normally, I would be anticipating the weekend with great joy. But today my heart was breaking. I said good-bye to my friend, wondering if I would ever see her again.

Although my friend's death could be weeks away, it could also happen at any moment. With a close friendship that spanned twenty-five years and my background as a hospice social worker, I knew my friend wanted me to be there at the time of her death to provide emotional support for her and her family. How could I possibly enjoy myself skiing when I truly wanted to be with her at this crucial time? Torn between my friend and my family, I felt an irrational anger toward the person who had organized this trip. I drove the four hours to the resort in northern New England in tears. The peaceful, cozy ambiance of the old inn made me feel like an impostor for being there.

The next day as we began skiing, I could think of nothing but my deep sadness for my friend and her family. For hours we skied ever deeper into the dark woods, hiking steep grades, gliding down long, curving slopes, climbing still higher on the mountain. Suddenly the woods ended, and we were treated to a breathtaking view that commanded us to stop and absorb the majesty of nature. At just that moment the sun emerged from behind the clouds, turning the snow into a shimmering carpet of diamonds. Rolling hills sloped down to a forest of trees next to the dollhouse-sized inn. Below that was a lake ringed by mountains. We were enveloped in total stillness, broken only by a hawk soaring overhead.

Suddenly my eyes filled with tears, as I felt blessed with a deep sense of peace and certainty that this was where I was meant to be at that moment. I had a startling revelation that my ambivalent feelings about leaving my friend for the weekend were the same dynamics of going on the journey into death we will all travel—the not wanting to go, the tears and sadness at leaving, every bit of energy fighting the change and regretting what was being left behind. Yet finding a sense of peace and beauty, joy and love, and a deep sense of well-being when we arrived. It caused me to remember the words I'd heard at a spiritual retreat: "Every loss is a mini-death. Throughout life we experience many mini-deaths—all preparing us for the final one." I knew then that even if my friend died while I was away, it was as it was meant to be.

When I returned home, I shared with my friend what I had learned from that day on the mountain. It was a sharing that confirmed what we both believed about the afterlife. A few days later I was privileged to spend the last day of my friend's life on earth with her and with her family.

Carol O'Connor

The Funeral

I don't think of all the misery, but of all the beauty that still remains.

Anne Frank

The dirt was wet because it had been raining the morning of the funeral. The mourners wore boots and picked their way carefully from their cars across the carpet that was laid out alongside the newly-dug grave. It wasn't a sad funeral. Isaac Ross was very old, in his nineties certainly. And he had been in excellent health until the morning of his death. His children, grandchildren and great-grandchildren would have wonderful memories of a vibrant, kind, loving man who enjoyed his life, his friends, family and work. No one could ask more of life than that. No, it wasn't a sad funeral.

I was there because Isaac Ross was the candy man. He was the man who sat in the front row at synagogue and dispensed pieces of candy to children who approached him during appropriate times in the service. The whole congregation knew him. For many parents who had to entice their youngsters to sit still during davening, or praying, Isaac Ross provided a valuable service. He was fond of telling parents that children should be rewarded with sweets for attention to Torah. He said that the words would therefore always be associated with sweetness and so be attractive to the young.

I looked around at the sea of faces who had come to say good-bye to the candy man. The family was very large and covered all ages. Mr. Ross had had many children, and each of them had had many children. All of them had come to say good-bye. One man, seated in the first row closest to the coffin, looked to be in his mid-sixties. His hair was completely white, but his face was marvelously unlined. He stepped forward to speak, first looking up at the gray sky. I thought he was deciding how long he had before the deluge began.

Instead of the typical eulogy, he told us this story.

"If Isaac Ross had been only a loving husband to my mother and a kind-hearted father to me, it would have been more than we could have asked for. But he was more, much more. He was our savior.

"In 1944, in Auschwitz, a young Polish Jew, Esther Lewandowski, was brutally raped by a Nazi officer. She was thirteen years old. What was unusual about this act was that the officer allowed her to live. Indeed, he forced her to come to him several times during the time he was stationed at the camp. When he left suddenly after a few months, he had no idea that the young Jewess whose life he neglected to take would have a reminder of his cold-hearted use of her other than painful memories. The reminder was an infant son.

"Esther's childish figure and the starvation rations in the camp enabled her to hide her pregnancy. Indeed, it was common for women to stop menstruating in those conditions, so it was possible that Esther did not even know for sure she was pregnant. Of course, if it had become known, she would have been put to death immediately.

"That was in January of 1945. Sometime in March, as the Germans became more and more aware that they were losing the war, Esther was part of a unit of women who were taken to work in a factory near Parsnitz. The truck in which they were riding stopped suddenly when the air raid siren sounded. All the guards ran off and the women escaped. They hid in the countryside on an abandoned farm until they were liberated by the Russians in May. The older women helped Esther through her pregnancy, and they all were sent to a refugee camp together. There Esther's baby was born in September. Esther Lewandowski was fourteen years old.

"Isaac Ross had also survived the war, after spending time in a camp. At the time of the liberation, he was twenty-five. He had lost a wife and a daughter as well as his parents and two brothers. After the liberation, Isaac arrived in the same refugee camp as Esther. They fell in love and Isaac became a husband and father once more. What the Nazis had taken from him, he now reclaimed for his own—a family.

"I am Esther's son by the Nazi officer. But Isaac Ross was my father in every sense that matters. He loved me, nurtured me, and gave me an identity I could cherish. More important, he loved my mother with all his heart.

"Esther never had any other children. Perhaps to Isaac, she was only a child herself. She died in his arms when I was twelve. My father and I leaned on each other in our grief. I knew that my father's heart was too big not to find others to love, so when he met Anna four years later, I was glad to see him fulfilled and happy. And at seventeen, I became big brother to the beginning of Isaac's third family.

"Today, as I stand before you all, our numbers have grown. Isaac had eight children. His grandchildren number thirty. And it remains to be seen how many great-grandchildren will come from Isaac Ross's line.

"But one thing I do know: I am living proof of one man's triumph over the most heinous evil that ever walked the earth.

"Good-bye, Isaac, my father. We will be your legacy."

The rain began falling just as Isaac's son finished speaking. It fell softly at first. The mourners filed by after the coffin was lowered into the grave. They each dropped fistfuls of dirt on the coffin.

One little girl, about five, was among the last of the family to approach the grave. She approached Isaac's son, took his hand and said, "Help me, Grandpa." She picked up a fistful of dirt and turned toward the open grave. I noticed how the brightness of her yellow curls contrasted sharply with the olive green of her coat and hat. She was really quite beautiful and in another setting, I probably would have smiled at her. She stopped at the side of the grave and looked up at the gray sky, as her grandfather— Isaac's son—had done. For just a moment, the raindrops mixed with the teardrops on her face, and I suppose on mine too, as I watched, transfixed. This beautiful little blond-haired, blue-eyed, Aryan-looking child appeared for all the world like a sunflower upturned to catch the rain.

And then it struck me: From one seed of evil, a family— beautiful, loving, thriving and Jewish—was growing. This little girl and the rest of Isaac Ross's family represented the ultimate vindication—the promise for the future.

No, it wasn't a sad funeral at all.

Marsha Arons

Karen, Do You Know Him?

Miracles do not happen in contradiction with nature, but in contradiction with what we know about nature.

Saint Augustine

I was an intern in pediatrics, fresh out of medical school. A lot of facts and figures were crammed into my brain, but my clinical experience was somewhat limited. But that's what it means to be an intern.

One of my most memorable first patients was a young lady named Karen. She had been referred to our city hospital from a small community in North Carolina because of symptoms of weakness and anemia. I knew when I first met Karen that I was dealing with someone out of the ordinary. She was not the least intimidated by the title "Doctor" or the white coat, and she always spoke what was on her mind. During our first interview, Karen wanted to know my credentials down to a tee, and wanted me to know that she knew that I was, indeed, "just" an intern. She was fourteen years old and full of life.

Unfortunately, our evaluations revealed that she had a

type of leukemia that was somewhat unusual, and not as responsive to different treatment modalities as were other types of leukemia. In fact, the prognosis for her surviving even one year was unlikely.

Chemotherapy was initiated, and Karen was never shy in telling us how sick we were making her with the medicine. She never spoke in a mean way, but simply in a way that always made her feelings known. If we had difficulty with an IV, she would readily point out our incompetence. However, she would just as readily forgive us and compliment us when an IV was maintained in her fragile veins on the first try.

Remarkably, within three months Karen went into remission, becoming free of her disease. She continued to come in for routine chemotherapy. During those short visits, Karen and I became friends. It was almost uncanny how, during random rotations, I would turn up as her physician. Always when she would see me coming, she'd gasp, "Oh no, do I *have* to have Dr. Brown?" Sometimes she was kidding, sometimes she wasn't, but she always wanted me to hear her.

About a year after her original diagnosis, her disease returned. When this type of leukemia returns, it is almost impossible to regain remission because all of the therapeutic modalities have already been spent. However, once again—remarkably if not miraculously—Karen went into remission. I was now a second-year resident, a little more competent and quite a bit more attached to this family. I continued to see Karen and her family over the next year and a half. She proceeded in her high school career and remained an outspoken, fun-loving teenager.

I was now in my chief residency year, spending my last month on the inpatient ward prior to completing my training. Karen came in once again with an exacerbation of her disease; she was extremely ill. There was involvement of every organ of her body, including her brain, and literally no other chemical agent to be tried. There was nothing we could do. Karen was made comfortable, given IV fluids and medication for pain. After long discussions, Karen's doctors and family decided that the goal would be to keep her comfortable and pain-free. No unnecessary heroic measures would be performed to prolong the inevitable. In fact, there were no heroic measures left.

Karen soon slipped into a coma. After viewing the CT scan and seeing the diffuse brain involvement, it was easy to see why. We expected each day to be her last. Her eyes were fixed and nonresponsive, her breathing shallow. Her heart was still strong, as we knew it would be. However, the disease was ravaging her blood system and brain, and there was evidence of opportunistic pneumonia involving both lungs. We knew that she would soon die.

I began to have a tremendous dread of Karen dying while I was on call. I did not want to pronounce her dead. It came to the point where I hoped that her death would come on nights that I was away from the hospital because I feared that I would not be any emotional support for the family, or that I would even be able to perform my duties as a physician. This family had come to mean so much to me.

It was a Wednesday night, and Karen had been in a coma for four days. I was the chief resident on call for the wards. I spoke with the family and peeked in on Karen. I noticed her breathing was very shallow and her temperature quite low. Death could be imminent. I selfishly hoped to myself that maybe she'd wait until tomorrow to die. I went about my chores until about 3:00 A.M., when I finally tried to get some sleep. At 4:00 A.M. I received a STAT page to Karen's room. This puzzled me somewhat because we were not going to make any heroic interventions. Nevertheless, I ran to her room.

The nurse greeted me outside the room and grabbed my arm. "Karen wants to talk to you." I literally thought this nurse was crazy. I couldn't imagine what she was talking about—Karen was in a coma. At this point in my life, my scientific, Newtonian way of thinking ruled my thoughts, primarily because this is the approach we are trained in day in and day out in medical school. I had neglected other, more important spiritual aspects of my being, ignoring the instinct that knows what reason cannot know.

I went into the room, and to my amazement, Karen was sitting up in bed. Her mother was on the left side of the bed, her father on the right. I stood next to the father, not saying anything, not knowing what to say. Karen's eyes, which had been glazed over for four days, were now clear and sharp. She simply stated, "God has come for me. It is time for me to go." She then went around to each of us at the bedside and hugged us tightly, one at a time. These were strong hugs, hugs that I kept thinking were impossible. I could only visualize her CT scan and the severe degree of brain damage. How could this be?

Then Karen lay down. But she popped back up immediately, as if she had forgotten something. She went around the bed to each of us again, with her penetrating eyes fixing our stares. No hugs this time. But her hands were strong and steady, squeezing our shoulders as she spoke. "God is here," she said. "Do you see him? Do you know him?" I was scared. Nothing in my experience could explain what was happening here. There was nothing else to say, so I mumbled, "Yes. Good-bye. Thank you." I didn't know what to say. The entire time, I kept visualizing that CT scan. Then Karen lay back down and died—or I should say, she quit breathing and her heart stopped. Her powerful spirit went on living.

It was years before I could tell that story, even to my wife. I still cannot tell it without feeling overwhelming emotions. I know now that this experience is not something to be understood through the limited viewpoint of the scientific realm. We are, in essence, spiritual beings in a spiritual universe, not primarily governed by Newton's laws, but by the laws of God.

James C. Brown, M.D.

The Horizon

Life is eternal, and love is immortal,
and death is only a horizon;
and a horizon is nothing save the limit of our sight.

Rossiter Worthington Raymond

I am standing upon the seashore.
A ship at my side spreads her white sails to the morning
breeze and starts for the blue ocean.
She is an object of beauty and strength.
I stand and watch her until at length she hangs like a
speck of white cloud on the horizon,
just where the sea and the sky come to mingle with one
another.
Then someone at my side says: "There, she is gone."
"Gone where?"
Gone from my sight. That is all.
She is just as large in mast and hull and spar as she was
when she left my side,
and she is just as able to bear her load of living freight to
her destined port.
Her diminished size is in me, not in her.

And just at the moment when someone at my side says,
"There, she is gone," there are other eyes watching her
  coming,
and other voices ready to take up the glad shout:
"Here she comes!"
And that is dying.

Anonymous

Keeping the Connection

As a mother grieving the loss of a child, the road ahead stretches long and difficult. Not having had the opportunity to complete your child's life to adulthood breaks a mother's heart over and over again. You wonder every day what he is doing. Is he okay? You pray that he is happy.

My first Christmas without my son, Justin, was a painful struggle. I just couldn't find the strength to decorate a tree with all the beautiful ornaments Justin and my daughter, Stephanie, had made over the years. Instead, I decorated my elderly mother's tree and my family shared Christmas with her. It helped us survive the first year.

The next year, I summoned the courage to put up the Christmas tree with lights, but once again Justin and Stephanie's precious ornaments remained packed away. That's as far as I got, but it was a major step.

Justin had loved Christmas, and for the sixteen years of his life he had always helped put up the tree. In fact, since Stephanie had been away at college, he'd taken charge of the decorating. He always assembled the nativity scene under the Christmas tree, a job he especially enjoyed. My father had made the manger out of barnboards from my grandfather's barn, and I had painted the figures in a ceramics class, so it had a very special meaning to our family.

By our third Christmas I felt stronger. I needed a connection to the Christmas times past when Justin had been alive. This time I put up the tree and lovingly decorated it with the children's ornaments. Then I went to get the box containing the nativity manger and ceramic figures, which had not been touched for three years.

As I looked inside the barnboard manger, I discovered a tiny little Christmas card. The front of the card showed a picture of a little boy carrying lots of Christmas cards to be delivered. I opened the card and read the inside verse:

> *If I could just pick up and leave*
> *I'd start this minute, I believe*
> *To be with you on Christmas Eve.*

At that moment, I knew I'd make it—not only through the holidays, but also through the long journey ahead of me without Justin. I never found out how the card got into the manger, but I viewed its presence there as a gift from my son. In my heart, I knew the tiny card with its message of wanting to be together for Christmas Eve was my much-needed connection to Justin. It would see me through that third Christmas, and ever after.

Patricia Chasse

Love Letters

When eight-year-old Andy Bremner needed hospital care to treat his cancer, get-well greetings poured in from school chums, cousins and neighbors. He Scotch-taped them on his walls and pasted them in scrapbooks. He read them over and over again. But when Andy left the Chicago hospital, the mail stopped.

Day after day his mother, Linda, watched her little boy search the mailbox for mail he could open, even fliers addressed to "occupant." It broke her heart.

Suddenly she realized there were many things in Andy's life she couldn't control—radiation treatments, chemotherapy, his getting better. But there was one thing she could control: the mail. From that moment on she started writing to him, carefully signing the letters, "Your secret pal."

Andy was thrilled to get these mysterious letters of support. One afternoon as he sat at the dining-room table where he loved to draw pictures for his mom, he noticed her watching him and waiting. "No, Mom," he said softly. "This is different. This one isn't for you." He rolled the paper into a scroll and laid it on the table top. "It's for my secret pal."

That night after she had tucked him in bed, Linda unrolled her little boy's picture. In a corner, Andy had left a message: "P.S.: Mom. I love you."

The correspondence between Andy and his secret pal continued until he passed away (in 1984). Andy and his mom never spoke about their game.

While sorting through her son's closet after his death, Linda Bremner found an address book with the names of friends Andy had met at a summer camp for kids with cancer. That's when the idea hit her. She sent a note to each child, and it wasn't long before she began receiving responses. "Thank you," wrote one youngster. "I didn't know anyone knew I was still alive."

Over the next ten years Linda continued writing to kids with cancer and other illnesses. At the same time she established a volunteer organization called *Love Letters, Inc.* based in Lombard, Illinois. On a modest budget dependent on donations, the group mails over 7,000 cards and packages to children every month, as well as 1,100 Christmas toys and goodies. Numbers increase each year.

"We must keep mailing," Linda urges. "These children need to know they are not forgotten, and we must send them all the love and encouragement we can." Then, with eyes misting, she adds, "I'll never leave one standing at the mailbox."

Kevin Lumsdon

Crying's Okay

We want people to feel with us more than to act for us.

George Eliot

My parents made me go to school that day even though I felt as if I couldn't stand to be around anyone. Where can you get away from people in a schoolhouse?

Finally I wandered into the room where I have English because no one was there except Mrs. Markle, and she was busy grading papers. I sat down across the desk from her. She just looked up at me and smiled as if there was nothing strange about a kid coming to the English room when he didn't have to.

"He's dead," I said in a strangled voice.

"John?"

I nodded. "He was my best friend."

"Yes, I know, *Kirk*." She walked over and closed the door, then came back to her desk.

"I miss him," I said.

"I know," she said again, "and that hurts. When something really hurts, it's all right to cry." She put a box of tissue in front of me and went on grading papers while I broke down and bawled. I was relieved that she didn't look at me.

"Nothing like this ever happened to me before," I said. "I don't know how to handle it."

"You don't have much choice," she told me. "John is gone and he won't be back."

"But what do I do?"

"Just keep on hurting until you begin to heal a little."

"I don't think I'll ever get over his death."

"You will someday, even though right now you can't believe you ever will."

"I guess."

"That's because we know with our minds," Mrs. Markle said, "but we believe with our feelings."

I sat and thought about that for a while.

"You might make things easier for John's family by visiting them," Mrs. Markle gently suggested.

I hadn't thought about John's family until now. If this was rough on me, what must it be for them?

"John's parents don't like me," I explained. "They think I was bad news for John."

"And probably your folks weren't wild about your running around with John."

"That's right." I was surprised at how much Mrs. Markle seemed to know. Just a plain old English teacher.

"That's how it is with parents," she said. "Young people together do things they wouldn't have the nerve to do by themselves. So parents get the idea that their sons and daughters are being led astray by their friends."

"Hey, that's about it."

"Go see John's family, Kirk. They'll change their minds about you now. You'll see. And if they don't, you will have at least given it a try."

"I feel guilty about some of the things John and I did," I

said. "Maybe God makes us feel guilty to punish us."

Mrs. Markle shook her head. "I don't think God plans for us to carry big loads of guilt along through life. He does give us a conscience, though, so we can ask forgiveness, and so we can profit from our mistakes. That's how we grow into better human beings."

That seemed to make good sense, but I didn't know how to quit feeling guilty. Mrs. Markle seemed to know what I was thinking. She said, "Guilt can be a crutch, you know."

"A crutch?"

"Yes, indeed. Guilt is a sort of self-punishment. If you feel guilty enough, you don't have to do something about yourself."

"'Something about yourself'?"

"Like improving your behavior, for instance."

The first bell rang. I stood up to go.

"By the way," Mrs. Markle said, "I'm glad you weren't with John in that car when it crashed."

"That's something else I feel guilty about," I admitted. "About John getting killed and not me."

Mrs. Markle said, "That's one thing you should not feel guilty about—being alive when someone else dies."

"Oh," I said. "Well, thanks for helping me. My folks didn't understand how I felt."

"How do you know?"

"They made me come to school."

"Perhaps that's because they did understand. They probably figured you'd be better off at school with classmates to share your grief."

"Oh. I didn't think about that. I wonder . . ."

The thought of going to see John's family was the hardest thing I can remember having to do. I wanted to talk to my parents about it, but I was afraid they wouldn't understand. Still, Mrs. Markle had said they might be more understanding than I realized.

At dinnertime Mom said, "We know you feel bad about John. Is there anything you'd like to talk about?"

That gave me the opening I needed. "I ought to go see John's family, but they probably don't want to see me."

"Why not?" Dad asked.

"On account of how John and I got into trouble sometimes."

"Sorrow sometimes brings people closer together," my mother said. "If I were John's parent, I'm sure I'd appreciate your coming."

So I forced my legs to take me to John's house. A lady I didn't know opened the door and took me to the living room. John's mother, father and sister sat there like broken dolls, staring into space. I didn't know what to do, but I tried to imagine they were my parents instead of John's. Then it seemed natural to go over and put my arm across Mrs. Roper's shoulder. When I did that, she began to cry. She put her arm around my waist and her head against my shoulder. "Forgive me for breaking down," she said. "I thought I was all cried out."

"It's all right to cry," I told her. And all of a sudden I was crying, too. John's sister, Adele, was only eleven, but she came over then and put her arms around her mother and me. I began to feel sorry for John's dad, sitting there all by himself. After a little while I went over to him and put my hand on his arm.

"I'm glad to hear you say it's all right to cry," he told me. "I keep wanting to do that."

Some other people came into the room about that time, so I said I guessed I'd better go.

Mrs. Roper walked to the door with me. "Kirk, it was so comforting to see you."

"I was afraid you didn't like me too much," I said.

"We love you because John loved you. And Kirk, don't fret about the past. You and John weren't perfect; you were just acting like teenage boys, that's all. It's no one's fault John is dead."

"I'll come again," I promised.

"Oh, Kirk, will you? It would mean so much to us."

I walked home feeling better than I had since that end-of-the-world minute when I heard that my best friend was dead. Tomorrow I would tell Mrs. Markle about the visit to John's family.

Kirk Hill

A Blanket for a Friend

When Meghan died in a car crash at the age of sixteen, Colleen Keefe wrote the following remembrance, which she and Shauna Dickey dedicated to their friend:

Shauna and I had a chance to say our good-bye to you last week. But the reality is, we still have a long way to go together. Standing before you and being able to speak to you and about you in front of all of your family and friends helped me to cope, though only momentarily, with the sudden loss of you as our friend.

When I heard the news of you leaving us so soon, all I could do was hug my blanket to me and close my eyes, hoping that when I opened them, the nightmare would be gone. But it is still here in front of me, engulfing me in a black cloud. On my way down to comfort your mom and dad, I realized I needed to give you a part of me that symbolized our friendship in such a way that when you were walking around the clouds above, everyone would ask what it meant. I could not cut out my heart, even though it is broken at this time. So I give to you, my friend, a piece of my blanket in the shape of a heart. Attached to it is a picture of the three of us—you, me and Shauna. She is having a problem accepting the how and why of this tragedy, as are so many others.

Now, I have to explain that this blanket was given to me by my grandfather, who is in heaven with you. He will recognize the blanket. He might not recognize my picture, as he has been gone for over fourteen years. You see, we share the same birthday, and he gave this to me to keep me warm. So I give this to you to keep you warm. And when my Papa Joe stops you and he bellows in that big deep voice of his, don't be afraid—he's really a teddy bear. Give him a big hug and a kiss for me, and tell him I said to take care of you. He will anyway. He's just like my dad.

Now that we know you are being taken care of, we can move on with our lives. Your memory is secure in our thoughts, and as Shauna and I realize you are looking down on us, we are sure we will cause you a lot of laughs in our usual goofy, klutzy way. So keep smiling, for this is how we remember you.

We found out that one of the recipients of your organ donation is doing well. Even in your death you have helped others. We will be seeing your family soon, and staying in touch with everyone.

Good-bye, my friend, we miss you already. You will never be far from our thoughts. Give us a nudge when we are heading in the wrong direction and, of course, keep "dancing." Shauna wants you to say hi to Elvis for her. He's probably in the food court.

Every time I wrap my blanket around me I will feel your presence. Stay warm.

Colleen Keefe and Shauna Dickey
Submitted by Brian Keefe

When No Words Seem Appropriate

Perhaps they are not the stars, but rather open-ings in Heaven where the love of our lost ones pours through and shines down upon us to let us know they are happy.

Inspired by an Eskimo Legend

I won't say, "I know how you feel"—because I don't. I've lost parents, grandparents, aunts, uncles and friends, but I've never lost a child. So how can I say I know how you feel?

I won't say, "You'll get over it"—because you won't. Life will have to go on. The washing, cooking, cleaning, the common routine. These chores will take your mind off your loved one, but the hurt will still be there.

I won't say, "Your other children will be a comfort to you"—because they may not be. Many mothers I've talked to say that after they have lost a child, they easily lose their temper with their remaining children. Some even feel resentful that they're alive and healthy when the other child is not.

I won't say, "Never mind, you're young enough to have

another baby"—because that won't help. A new baby cannot replace the one that you've lost. A new baby will fill your hours, keep you busy, give you sleepless nights. But it will not replace the one you've lost.

You may hear all these platitudes from your friends and relatives. They think they are helping. They don't know what else to say. You will find out who your true friends are at this time. Many will avoid you because they can't face you. Others will talk about the weather, the holidays and the school concert but never about how you're coping.

So what will I say?

I will say, "I'm here. I care. Anytime. Anywhere." I will talk about your loved one. We'll laugh about the good memories. I won't mind how long you grieve. I won't tell you to pull yourself together.

No, I don't know how you feel—but with sharing, perhaps I will learn a little of what you are going through. And perhaps you'll feel comfortable with me and find your burden has eased. Try me.

Written by a pediatric nurse
Submitted to Ann Landers

The Rose with No Thorns

*Kindness is a language the dumb can speak
and the deaf can hear and understand.*

Christian Nestell Bovee

A young man carrying a guitar case boarded the afternoon school bus at Maple Street. Obviously ill at ease, he
found a seat, placed the guitar on end beside him in the
aisle, and held it upright with his arm. He looked around
anxiously, then hung his head and began shuffling his
feet back and forth on the floor of the bus.

Melanie watched him. She didn't know who he was,
but from his looks she decided he must be a real loser.

Melanie's friend Kathy looked up from her book.
"Wouldn't you know it? Crazy Carl again."

"Who's Crazy Carl?" Melanie asked, tossing her sunny
hair.

"Don't you know your next-door neighbor?"

"Next-door neighbor? The Bells moved into that house.
We met them the day we left on spring vacation."

"Well, that's his name, Carl Bell."

The bus rolled on under the big trees along Elm Street.

Kathy and Melanie stared at the newcomer and his big guitar case.

When the driver called out "Sycamore," the new boy awkwardly picked up his case and got off. It was Melanie's stop, too, but she didn't budge. When the bus started again, she rang for the next corner. "See you, Kathy."

Melanie ran home, up the steps and through the front door. She called out, "Mom, does that weirdo live next door?"

Her mother came into the hall from the kitchen. "Melanie, you must not refer to anyone as a weirdo. Yes, the Bells have a handicapped son. This morning I called Mrs. Bell, and she told me about Carl. He has never been able to speak. He has a congenital heart defect and a nervous disorder. They have found a private tutor for him, and he is taking guitar lessons to help improve his coordination."

"Just the pits! Right next door!" Melanie exclaimed.

"He's a shy boy. You must be neighborly. Just say hello when you see him."

"But he rides the school bus, and the kids laugh at him."

"See that you don't," her mother advised.

It was a week before Carl boarded the bus again. Melanie thought he recognized her. Grudgingly, she said hello. Some of the other kids started whispering and making jokes. Pretty soon spit wads were flying. "Settle down!" the driver yelled. Carl shuffled his feet. Each time a spit wad hit him he twitched. When his guitar clattered to the floor, the driver again admonished them to settle down—this time with a warning tone in his voice. The bus grew quiet but the fun didn't stop. The boys seated behind Carl started blowing on the back of his head, making his hair stand up. They thought is was funny.

When Sycamore Street came into view Carl jumped up, rang the bell, put the guitar strap over his shoulder and headed for the door. The guitar case swung wide, hitting Chuck Wilson on the neck. Carl rushed toward the door with his case still crosswise in the aisle. When Chuck caught up and took a swing at him, the shoulder strap tore loose and the case slid down the steps into the gutter. Carl stumbled off the bus and ran down the street, leaving his guitar behind.

Melanie sat glued to her seat. "I'm never getting off there again," she said to Kathy. Once again she waited until the next corner before getting off, then retraced the block back to Sycamore. The open case still lay in the gutter. She walked past it and headed toward home. *What a character!* she thought. *What did I ever do to deserve him for a neighbor?*

But by the time Melanie had gone half a block, her conscience bothered her for leaving Carl's guitar where anyone could pick it up. She turned back to get it. Both the handle and the strap on the case were broken, so she had to carry it in her arms with her books. *Why am I doing this?* she wondered. Then she remembered how terrible it had been when everybody laughed at him.

Mrs. Bell opened the door before Melanie could knock. "Melanie, I am so glad to see you! What happened? Carl was so upset he went straight to his room," she said, laying the case on a chair.

"It was just a little accident." Melanie didn't want to alarm her with the whole story. "Carl left his guitar. I thought I should bring it."

Carl didn't ride the bus after that. His parents drove him to and from guitar lessons. Melanie saw him only when he worked in his rose garden.

Life should have gone more smoothly, but kids still pestered him. They hung around his yard, threw acorns at him and chanted, "Crazy Carl, the banjo king, takes music lessons and can't play a thing."

One hot day as Carl relaxed on the grass with a soft drink, the kids came and started their chant. Melanie glanced out her window just in time to see the soda bottle shatter on the sidewalk at their feet.

The next day at school Kathy said, "Did you hear about Crazy Carl cutting those kids with a broken bottle?"

"No wonder," Melanie said, "the way they keep after him."

"Whose side are you on?" Kathy fired back.

"I'm not choosing sides, but I heard them bugging him."

"Bet you two hold hands over the fence," Kathy said sarcastically.

At noon in the cafeteria line a classmate teased Melanie, "If you're asking Crazy Carl to go with you to the banquet, I'll be glad to take Jim off your hands."

Before the day was over, somebody wrote on the blackboard, "Melanie loves Crazy Carl."

Melanie managed to keep her poise just long enough to get home. She ran in the door and burst into tears. "Mom, I told you it was the pits having a weirdo next door. I hate him." She told her mother what happened at school.

"It hurts when your friends turn on you," Melanie said, "and for nothing!" Then she thought of something she hadn't considered before. "Carl must have cried lots of times."

"I'm sure," her mother agreed.

Why do I feel so mean about Carl? she wondered. *Or maybe I don't. Maybe I just think I'm supposed to because everybody else does.*

"Sometimes, Mom, I don't bother to do my own thinking." Melanie wiped her eyes. "Jim's coming over. I have to wash my hair." She ran upstairs.

On the last day of school, Melanie came home early. Carl was in his rose garden. When he saw her, he clipped a rose and went to the gate to wait. Melanie greeted him with her usual hello. He held out the rose. As she reached for it, he put up his other hand to delay her, and started breaking off the thorns. He pricked his finger, frowned a moment, wiped the blood on his shirt sleeve, and continued breaking off the thorns.

Tonight was the banquet, and Melanie wanted to get home and be sure her clothes were ready. But she stood and waited.

Carl handed her the rose with no thorns. "Thank you, Carl. Now I won't stick my fingers," she said, in an effort to interpret his thoughts. Touched by his childlike grin, she patted his cheek, thanked him again and walked on home. At the door she looked back. Carl was still standing there, holding his hand against the cheek she had touched.

One week later Carl died of congestive heart failure. After the funeral, the Bells went away for a while.

One day a letter came from Mrs. Bell. There was a special note for Melanie.

Dear Melanie,

I think Carl would have liked you to have this last page from his diary. We encouraged him to write at least one sentence a day. Most days there was little good to write.

Mr. Bell and I want to thank you for being his friend—the only youthful friend he ever had.

Our love,
Carla Bell

Carl's last words: Mlanee is rose wit no torns.

Eva Harding

The Butterfly Gift

My four-year-old daughter Adina got up early one Sunday morning. We sat on the kitchen floor making figures out of plasticine—a man, a horse, a dog and a chicken. I went to my den after breakfast to do some reading. Adina followed and said, "Daddy, let's make something." I said, "Okay, honey. You tell me what you want to make and we'll make it."

She returned after much thought and said, "Daddy, let's make a butterfly." We used a 3" x 5" card and I showed her how to make the shape of the wings. She colored for the longest time and then we made a base so the butterfly could stand up by itself. She was very proud of that little butterfly, and when she showed me her finished work of art, I said, "But, Adina, the butterfly doesn't have a mouth!"

She worked a little longer and made a mouth with a tongue hanging out of the corner. We laughed as we set the butterfly on my desk and went outside to enjoy a beautiful autumn day.

Late that night, Adina woke and called out, "Daddy, I gots a headache. I don't feel so good." She was running a fever. The next day her mommy took her to the doctor, then we all went to the hospital where it was diagnosed that Adina had spinal meningitis.

It hit her hard. Five doctors worked all night to save her life, but by six o'clock Tuesday morning, Adina was gone. Life was over.

The next morning, I went to my den to start making some funeral arrangements for my little girl. I was tired, angry, frustrated and defeated. I was totally lost. All my efforts in life seemed so futile and the balance of life so fragile. How could this possibly happen?

Then I saw it. On my desk was that incredibly beautiful butterfly. The multicolored wings, the big round eyes, a tongue sticking out at the world, and, behind it all, blue skies. A symbol of love, beauty, and a positive outlook on life. It was an unbelievable life-altering gift from Adina to me.

Adina left so many things behind. She left marks on the windows where she gave me "window kisses" every day when I left for work. She left paths of finger marks in her new sandbox I had just built for her. She left her new swing blowing in the breeze. But the most significant gift Adina left for me was her butterfly.

I wear a butterfly ring on my finger as a constant reminder of the importance of the relationships with the people we love. Life is for living, caring, hoping and shar-ing with the people we love. Sometimes those lives are very short. Let butterflies always remind you of the importance of the relationships with those you love.

Wayne Cotton

5

A MATTER OF PERSPECTIVE

There is nothing either good or bad, but thinking makes it so.

William Shakespeare

Action Hero

A few years ago, I stopped at a neighborhood market for some late-night ice cream. As I got out of my car, a young man hailed me from across the street. He was college-aged and dressed to the nines: expensive pullover, dress shirt and slacks so sharply creased they could have cut frozen fish. I thought he wanted directions; he had that urgent late-for-a-party look. When he reached me, he pulled up his sweater and smoothly drew a pistol from inside his waistband. "Get in the car," he ordered.

My brain went into hyperspeed. I remembered watching a personal-security expert on a talk show advise victims not to stare at an assailant's face. His reasoning was that if a robber thinks you cannot identify him, he's less likely to kill you. No one asked how much less likely. Given its importance to my future, I focused instead on his weapon—a .38 Smith & Wesson revolver, blued steel, short barrel. I'd fired others like it at pistol ranges. This was no mouse gun. Nervously, I directed my gaze lower. His shoes were highly polished. Strange as it sounds, I admired his sense of style.

The click of the revolver's hammer being cocked

snapped my head up eye to eye with his. So much for not looking at his face. Contrary to the belief that when death appears imminent a person's entire life passes before him, I was completely focused on the moment. Instinct told me that a car trip with this guy would turn out to be a one-way journey for me. I held out my keys. "Take my car," I said in a tone I prayed would inspire calmness and reason. "I'm not getting in."

He hesitated, then ignoring my proffered keys, thrust out a hand and yanked off my shoulder bag. In it were my wallet and a couple of rented videos. He took a step back, his gun still aimed at me. Neither of us spoke.

Laughter broke the silence, making us both turn. Several couples were leaving a Chinese restaurant on the opposite corner. The gunman gave them a fast scan, then lowered his revolver. Holding it against his thigh to conceal it, he began to stride quickly across the almost traffic-less street, my bag clutched under his arm.

Incredibly, I took off after him. "Hey," I shouted to the people in front of the restaurant. "This guy just robbed me." I was halfway across the street when I realized my would-be posse was not mounting up. The gunman, now aware of my proximity, pivoted in my direction. As I watched him raise his gun, everything went into slow motion. A tongue of flame flashed from the snub-nosed barrel, followed by a loud crack.

I lost my balance. I felt no pain, but when I looked down, I saw my left leg flopped out sideways at my shin. A half-dollar-size spot of blood stained my jeans. When I looked up, my assailant was sprinting down a dark side street.

Later that night at a nearby hospital, I was told that the bullet had fractured my tibia and fibula, the two bones connecting the knee and ankle. Doctors inserted a steel rod secured by four screws into my leg. They also gave me a "prosthesis alert" card to show security personnel if the rod set off a metal detector.

Almost immediately a remarkable thing began to happen—my popularity soared. When friends introduced me as "the guy who got shot," women who a moment before had no interest in me came after me like groupies. Men wanted to buy me drinks. They considered me "brave" for running after the gunman. I'm reminded of war movies in which the green infantrymen behave reverentially around the grizzled vets who have "seen action."

I found it difficult to forgive myself for what I considered an act of colossal folly. Sometimes I thought I had chased the kid out of anger at being victimized; other times I attributed my actions to an adrenaline rush that needed a physical outlet. Whatever the reason, I knew it had nothing to do with bravery.

Clearly, I was being given credit for something I didn't deserve, yet I was reluctant to give up my newly acquired status. After all, it wasn't as if I were taking an active part in any deception; I was merely allowing people to come to whatever conclusions they wished. I finally rationalized my decision to maintain the status quo: I considered any misperception to be my compensation for having gone through a horrible situation.

Things went well until the day I was approached by a panhandler. On a whim, I told him I had no money because I'd been unable to work since being shot in a robbery. His eyes grew large, and it was obvious that the information impressed him. "That's heavy," he said, then leaned closer, conspiratorially. "Did you get caught?"

Rulon Openshaw

Who Was That Masked Man?

Hurricane Bertha left me in a bad mood. I had managed to maintain my sour disposition for several days in spite of the attempts of almost everybody to cheer me up. I had leaks in my ceiling at the gallery, the floors were flooded, the showcases dirty, there was no air conditioning or electricity, and I had over one hundred artists calling me to see if their work had been damaged. On top of all that, I had to drive over to Jacksonville in the pouring rain and choking heat, and the air conditioner in my truck had quit working.

I was not happy.

As I motored along North Carolina's Highway 24 to Jacksonville, my faithful truck was trying to tell me something . . . something important like . . . YOU FORGOT TO BUY GAS! For the first time in my life I had run out of gas. I'd always smirked at the friends and family who'd done this, as if to say, "How could you be so stupid? There's a gauge on the dashboard to tell you that your tank is empty, and all you have to do is read it."

I was right: There *was* a gauge, and it said EMPTY.

I was not happy.

I coasted to the side of the road, saying several things about my own mental abilities . . . several things about Hurricane Bertha . . . and vowing to sit there until the darn truck rotted and fell apart.

As I contemplated the possibility of getting a job with the French Foreign Legion, I heard a motorcycle pull up beside me: a big, throaty, rumbling, growling Harley-Davidson. I opened my door and was face to face with a throwback to the 1960s. Snakes were painted all over his face shield and helmet and tattooed all over his body. He wore the traditional Harley-Davidson garb: denim jacket, jeans and biker boots. Chains hung from every available hook or loop. His hair was so long that he had it doubled up and tied to keep it out of his wheels. The Harley was straight out of *Easy Rider*—extended front fork; suicide rack on the back; black, purple and green paint job, and the gas tank painted to look like a skull with glowing green eyes.

"S'wrong?" he said. His shield and helmet completely masked his face

"I'm out of gas," I whispered.

"B'right back." And he rode off. About fifteen minutes later he returned with a can of gas.

When I offered to pay him he said, "Wait till ya get to the station."

I started my truck and drove the two or three miles to the station as he followed along (in the pouring rain). Again I offered to pay him. He said, "Pay the guy inside. Everything okay now?" I said yes. He said, "See ya!" And off he rode down Highway 24 toward Jacksonville, hair undone and flying in the wind, Harley roaring and throwing up spray from the pavement.

After pumping twenty-four dollars worth of gas, I went into the station and gave the attendant thirty dollars. He said, "It's only four dollars. The other guy paid twenty and said to tell you to 'pass it on, Brother.'"

I will always remember the kindness of the snakes-and-chains stranger on the Harley with the glowing green eyes, and I will never again judge anyone by their looks (a promise I had often made to myself). And I will always wonder, "Who was that masked man?"

As for the twenty dollars . . . I passed it on.

Robert R. Thomas

In a Cathedral of Fence Posts and Harleys

I have had only two rules to guide which weddings I will do and which I will turn down: I need to be able to meet with the bride and groom first, and I don't do weddings in unusual places (like parachuting or underwater).

But I broke both rules once, and it was the most meaningful wedding I have ever celebrated.

I'd agreed to do this wedding on two days' notice, as the minister who was to officiate was called away on a family emergency. I had the location (well out of town, on a farm); I knew the names of the bride and groom; and I knew that they'd completed pre-marital sessions with the other minister.

I also knew something about their wedding guests and the particular setting they'd chosen for the celebration of their union. One hundred and forty bikers had come up to spend the weekend. The wedding was to be an added bonus—a surprise to all but a handful of the guests.

I confess to considerable misgivings as I turned off the highway onto the property and caught my first glimpse of the venue. Dozens of motorcycles filled the parking lot.

Most were Harley-Davidsons, the choice of serious bikers. Very loud music filled the air from a refreshment area in the center field. Tents dotted the landscape. It looked like a heavy-metal Woodstock.

Mine was the only Jetta in sight. I parked it and headed up to the house.

To my relief, things seemed to be in order there. I was introduced to the bride's parents and the groom's parents while the bride was getting dressed. It didn't take long; jeans and a black T-shirt needed little more than a few flowers in the hair. The groom was introduced to me as "Bear." It wasn't hard to know where the nickname came from—Bear outweighed me at least two to one. His beard was thick and bushy, and his arms were heavily tattooed. Bear didn't say much.

We checked to see that the license was in order, and when everything was ready, I headed down to the big tent. I don't push through crowds very well, the meek and mild sort that I am, but I managed to get to the front, asked for a microphone, waited for the music to stop, introduced myself and announced that I was here for a wedding. I wasn't sure what kind of reaction I would get.

Several of the bikers immediately headed to the parking lot. The air was filled with the throb of powerful engines revving. Then, with almost military precision, the bikes streamed out of the parking lot and straight toward the center field, heading directly toward me. A few feet away, they turned off to form a double row facing each other—an honor guard to create an aisle for the bride. With engines at full throttle, their roar echoed across the valley.

As the bride walked slowly and gracefully down this aisle, each bike she passed switched off its engine. As she passed the last pair and all the engines were stilled, you could have heard a pin drop. She walked shyly up to Bear.

His eyes were overflowing with tears. Then the birds started to sing.

All around the host couple were the congregation of their friends, members and families of the Sober Riders, each one a recovering alcoholic, each one a biker. Each one was bowed in prayer as we entered a holy moment.

The bride had given me only one instruction for the service. "Make sure you have a sermon," she said. "These people want to hear a word from God."

"These people." Her people. And for an afternoon, my people. I stood in the middle of the field, in a congregation of T-shirts, jeans and tattoos, in front of a groom and bride who knew exactly what they were doing and why, in a cathedral of fence-posts and Harleys, and together we gave thanks to God.

Reverend Neil Parker

Jackie Robinson and Me

*The opportunity to practice brotherhood pre-
sents itself every time you meet a human being.*

Jane Wyman

The news about the first black major league baseball
player wasn't the most important thing in my life that hot
afternoon in 1945. I was more concerned with filling out a
royal flush in the card game some buddies and I were playing on a Navy ship coming back to the States from Guam.

Someone hollered at the door, "Hey, Pee Wee, did you
hear? The Dodgers signed a n-----!"

I shrugged and called for another card.

Then the guy added, "And he plays shortstop!"

My head jerked up. The guy was serious.

Just my luck, I thought. *He plays my position.*

I had been playing shortstop for the Brooklyn Dodgers
since 1940 and had made the All-Star team in 1942 before
joining the Navy. Though the black player, whose name
was Jackie Robinson, would be playing for the Montreal
Royals, a top Dodgers farm team, I figured eventually we
would be on the field together.

Oh well, I thought, picking up my card. I was confident in my abilities. And if Robinson could beat me out, more power to him. I was concerned about getting home to my wife, Dorothy, and daughter, Barbara, who was only eleven days old when I had left.

Not that I had any special affection for black people. I had grown up in the small Kentucky town of Ekron, where blacks lived on one side of town and whites on the other. I'm sure most of the kids had heard that old Sunday school song: "Red and yellow, black and white, they are precious in his sight," but there wasn't any mixing, even in the marble games we played. (I got my nickname at age thirteen from the "peewee" I used as a shooter to play marbles.)

When I started playing baseball it was the same: the blacks had their leagues, we had ours. After high school, I worked in Louisville as a cable splicer for the phone company and played weekends on the New Covenant Presbyterian Church team. In 1937 we led the church league and got to go to New York to see the Giants and Yankees battle it out in the World Series. A year later I was playing shortstop for the Louisville Colonels and then went to the Dodgers under Leo Durocher. It wasn't until April 11, 1947, when Branch Rickey signed Jackie Roosevelt Robinson to a National League contract with the Dodgers, that I was directly affected.

I don't remember shaking a black man's hand before, but on that spring training day I walked over to Jack and as captain, welcomed him to the team. I knew he had something going when I saw him bat and throw.

Some of the guys weren't happy about their new teammate. Late one night while Pete Reiser and I were talking in my hotel room there was a knock on the door. I opened it to find outfielder Dixie Walker and two others. He handed me a petition stating those who had signed wouldn't play baseball with a black man. "I'm not signing it," I said. Neither would Reiser. And that was that.

I wasn't trying to think of myself as being the Great White Father. I needed the salary, and I just wanted to play the game. It didn't matter to me whether Jackie was black or green; he had a right to be there, too.

It turned out Jackie didn't play shortstop. I stayed in that slot and eventually Jackie played second base. We got to be kind of a partnership. Recently a sportswriter called us "one of the brightest double-play combinations in baseball." Well, a team's got to be strong up the middle if it's going to win pennants, and that's what we did—won pennant after pennant.

But it wasn't easy for Jackie. During that first year, after I had played cards with Jackie in the clubhouse, Dixie Walker came up to me. "How can you be playing cards with him?"

"Look, Dixie," I said, "you and Stell travel with a black woman who takes care of your kids, who cooks your food, who you trust—isn't that even more than playing cards with a black man?"

"That's different," he humphed.

"Tell me how," I said.

He couldn't come up with anything and walked away.

A lot of other team members took to Jackie, like Gil Hodges, Ralph Branca and Eddie Stanky. Jackie and I developed a kind of rapport. Once while we sat in the dugout he complained that "the pitchers are throwing at me because they're racists."

"No," I said, grinning. "They aren't throwing at you because you're black. They're throwing at you because they don't like the way you hit."

He leaned back and gave a long easy chuckle.

But Jackie did take a lot of guff on the field. There was one time when I didn't see how any human could stand what he was taking. It was on our first road trip. In

Cincinnati the heckling from the fans really became brutal. It was more than boos and jeering; the whole stadium seemed to be in a bellowing frenzy. Then somebody threw out a black cat, which scampered across the field.

I looked over at Jackie standing alone, looking so sad, so vulnerable. Something in my gut reacted. Maybe I was thinking of the hanging tree in Brandenburg, a little town near Ekron. I remembered my dad pointing to a long branch and telling me black men had been lynched from it. As a little boy it made a terrible impression on me that people would do things like that just on account of skin color. Something about the unfairness of it all, the injustice—what? I don't know. But I stepped over to the pitcher, called time out and walked over to Jackie. I said something consoling, then reached up, put my hand on his shoulder and just stood there looking at the crowd.

The jeering stopped like someone turning off a loud radio. And we began doing what we had gone there to do, play ball.

As you know, Jackie Robinson went on to greatness. He would turn the other cheek, but he also stood up for himself. He could be a tough bench jockey, and sliding into base he might plow into a guy who was in his way.

When I see the talented black players in sports today I'm grateful for having had the privilege of playing with the man who opened the door for them. But none of us were trying to put on a show. All that any of us were trying to do was best use the talent God had given us.

One of my last talks with Jackie kind of wrapped it all up. "You know, I didn't go out of my way to be nice to you," I said.

He grinned. "Pee Wee, maybe that's what I appreciated most."

Harold "Pee Wee" Reese

"It wouldn't make any difference to me if we
went to an integrated school or a segregated one,
Billy, just as long as we went together."

Department Store Angel

If the doors of perception were cleansed, every-thing would appear as it is, infinite.

William Blake

I called my eighty-nine-year-old mother early one Friday morning in October to invite her to lunch. Before accepting the invitation, she had to check her calendar to see what activities the retirement home was offering that day. She didn't like to miss anything, whether it was an exercise class, bingo game, a tea with the other residents, a birthday celebration, or any other social activity. She said yes, she would be free from 1:00 to 2:30, but she would like to be home in time to attend the style show. I told her I would pick her up at 1:00 and would have her back by 2:30.

Since my husband and I were leaving the next morning for a week of relaxation in San Diego, I needed to purchase a few last-minute items for the trip, so before picking up my mother I headed to the mall.

I was irritated with myself, knowing I was already feeling rushed and overwhelmed with all that needed to be done for the trip, and then complicating the day even more by making a lunch date with my mother. I had even taken the day off from work so that I could have more time to get ready. There was just too much to do. Maybe I shouldn't have made the lunch plans. Taking the time out for lunch would only interfere with my shopping. I was running late and now I would only have one hour to shop before picking up my mother. I knew though, that if I had not called her, I would have felt guilty about leaving for a week in California without seeing her.

As I was walking through a department store I noticed they were having a sale on the black suede, high-top Easy Spirit shoes that I had been looking at for a couple weeks. I took the first chair in a row of about eight, quickly tried them on and decided to purchase them.

"Those looked nice on you. Are they comfortable?"

I looked down the row of chairs, and in the very last one sat a lady about seventy years old. She was just sitting there, looking pretty in her pink blouse, floral skirt, pearl necklace and very sweet smile. She wasn't trying on shoes and it was obvious she was not an employee.

I answered, "Yes, and they are very comfortable."

"Do you think they would be too winter-looking for California?"

"It's funny you should say that," I replied in a surprised tone of voice, "because I'm leaving for California tomorrow morning."

"You are?" she said. "Well, I'm leaving for California on Monday morning to live in San Diego, even though I've never been to California before."

In a sad voice she proceeded to tell me that her husband passed away earlier that year. They had lived in Cincinnati and in the same house their entire married life. They had one son, and he and his family lived in San Diego. With his encouragement and help, she sold her house along with many of her furnishings, and her most

cherished possessions were being delivered to the retirement home in San Diego that her son had chosen. "Oh,
that's nice," I said. "You'll live closer to your son and you
can see more of him."

Her voice broke as she said, "But I'm afraid. I've never
lived anywhere but Cincinnati, and not only am I giving up
my home and so many of my belongings, but I'm leaving
my friends, too." As she continued her story, she rose from
her chair and moved closer to me. We sat down side by
side, and I put my shoe box and purse down on the floor.

After listening for a few moments I said, "You know, my
eighty-nine-year-old mother lives in a retirement home
and she, too, was very apprehensive about making such a
big move four years ago." I then told her that my mother
and father were married fifty-five years before he passed
away. My mother was a homemaker and mother of nine
children, so her whole life revolved around her family.
There was not much time for social activities other than
the times she volunteered to help at church functions.
Her life was her family, so when the time came for her to
make the decision to sell her home, she was afraid, too.

When she decided on a retirement home, my sisters
and I searched for the one closest to us and helped her
with the move. Of course, we were concerned whether
she would like that lifestyle. Well, she has enjoyed it from
the day she moved in! She is socializing more than she
ever has, and the home offers more activities than she can
keep up with. The nice part is that they offer so many
things, but it is ultimately her choice whether or not to
participate in the particular activity offered. I laughed as I
told the lady how my mother was involved in so much
that she had to check her calendar and squeeze me into
her busy schedule for a luncheon date.

This stranger and I talked as if we were friends who had
known each other for a long time. After a few minutes we

stood up to say good-bye. She thanked me and said she felt much better. I was hesitant to say what I said next, but since I already felt a special kinship with her and sensed a deep spirituality about this lady, I felt it was okay. I turned to her and said, "I believe that God puts certain people in our lives, even if it is for a brief encounter like this, to help us through a difficult time. I don't think this is just a coincidental meeting. I believe it's his way of saying 'It's okay, I'm with you.'

"And I believe he sent us to each other today. You see, I was feeling overwhelmed with so much to do today, and somewhat irritated that I got myself in a situation that left me with little time to myself. This sharing with you has helped me to appreciate how happy and content my mother is with her new lifestyle, and it makes me more aware of how fortunate I am to still have her with me."

"Oh," she said, "your mother is so lucky to have you for a daughter. I can see that you love her."

"Yes, and your son loves you so much that he wants you to be closer to him. I'm sure he has chosen a very nice retirement home, and being the pleasant person you are, you won't have any trouble fitting in and making new friends. Besides, San Diego is a beautiful city and you will love the weather."

We stood up and facing each other, held each other's hands. "Can I give you a hug for good luck?" I asked. She smiled and nodded. There was a special gentleness in the hug, as if we had known each other a long time. I said, "I'm definitely buying these shoes today, and every time I put them on, I will think of you and say a prayer that all is going well for you." I was at that moment touched by the beauty and warmth about her. Her face seemed to glow.

I bent down to pick up my shoe box and purse. When I stood up, she was gone. How could she disappear so quickly? I looked all around and even walked through the store, hoping to catch one more glimpse of her. But she was nowhere in sight. There are moments in life when we truly sense God's presence, and this was one of those times. I had this feeling that I had been talking with an angel.

I looked at my watch and noticed it was already time to pick up my mother. As I was driving toward my mother's home, deep in thought about this strange yet wonderful encounter, I passed a nursing home with a sign in the yard that read, "The way to feel better about yourself is to make someone else feel better."

I pulled into the guest parking spot at my mother's home, feeling suddenly relaxed. I just knew that my mother and I were going to have a most enjoyable afternoon.

Priscilla Stenger

"Hey Nurse . . . Thanks"

The supernatural is the natural not yet understood.

Elbert Hubbard

"Hey Nurse!"

It was a man's voice, loud and gruff, coming from room 254. I was taking a shortcut through the telemetry unit after another busy day in the critical care unit. These weren't my patients, so I kept going.

"Yo, blondie."

I stopped and looked around. No other nurses were in sight, so I went to the doorway of room 254 and glanced in. A large man with a big, friendly face was sitting up in bed. He spoke before I had a chance to open my mouth.

"Do you remember me? You were my nurse on the fourth floor."

"I'm sorry, sir, but I work in the critical care unit. You must have me confused with someone else."

I smiled, wished him a good afternoon, and turned to go on my way. His booming voice stopped me again.

"No, wait a minute." He started snapping his fingers.

"Your name is . . . oh, let me think . . ."

I turned around to see him looking up at the ceiling, a half smile on his face. Then he looked back at me.

"Jackie, right? You've got a long blond ponytail, don't you?"

I was dumbfounded.

"Yes," I said, peeking at my chest to make sure I'd taken off my name tag. (I had.) I reached back and touched the tightly braided bun on the back of my head. Then I studied his face, looking for something that might trigger my memory. His eyes were cool, blue and shiny. Curly salt-and-pepper hair framed his face.

"I'm sorry. I don't work on the fourth floor, and I just don't remember you."

"That's all right, Jackie. I'm just glad I got to see you again. You came into my room about three weeks ago. My heart stopped dead on me and you put those paddles on my chest. I remember you shouting out all these technical sounding words, telling everybody to clear the way. Then you took those paddles and you shocked me back to life."

Suddenly it dawned on me: I had been in his room for a code I'd forgotten about. He was a different person then—unresponsive, with dilated pupils and a red and blue face.

"Who told you I helped you that day?" I asked, my curiosity pulling me into his room.

He laughed and looked back up at the ceiling.

"Nobody told me. I was up on that ceiling there watching you. That's how I saw your long, blond ponytail. And when you turned to look at the monitor, I saw your beautiful face. I'm so glad I got to see you again."

He looked back down at me, his smile gone. I could see he was struggling with his emotions.

"I wanted to say thanks. Thanks so much . . ."

Every time I pass room 254 now, a warm feeling wells up inside me. I am grateful for the shortcut I took that day, and for the fact that I answered the call of "Hey Nurse."

Jacqueline Zabresky, R.N.

"And how do you feel about *that* perspective?"

The Little Black Box

The hardest thing a person must do is gather together the belongings of a loved one after that person's death.

For me, my dad was both Mother and Father, having lost my mom when I was only five years old. When he succumbed to liver cancer at the age of seventy-five, I was devastated. Somehow I expected that he would live forever. Now I was faced with going through his closets and bureau drawers, discarding or giving away his possessions. One never knows what can be passed on to someone needy.

When I was very young, Dad used to disappear into his room and reappear with money for me when I needed some. I never really knew where it came from and thought it strange that this room would always bear financial fruit for me. Then one day, I overheard Dad tell my older sister to go into his room and take some money out of the black box. Why had I not been allowed to see the black box or investigate its contents? Was I too young, or did my sister have special privileges I did not have?

This black box became an obsession with me. Throughout the years, it came back to haunt me. What and where was that box? What treasures were hidden there, and when would I be allowed to behold its magical contents?

The years passed, I grew up and Dad grew older. Funny how you expect your parents to stay forever young. His hair grayed, his face wrinkled and his frame bent, but the laughter remained in his eyes each time I saw him and stayed until his last breath.

While packing and sorting things in his room that day, not once did I think about that black box. With tears welling and reality for the task at hand holding them back, I had to finish this and be done with it. This was the final chapter of my dad's life, all the necessities and the memories reduced to trash bags and boxes.

With the closets finished and the bureaus empty, the room emanated loneliness. Dad was gone, his things were going, and a new era in my life was beginning. How do you go on without one that you loved so much, without that person being there when you most need him? Who will answer the phone now when I call to say, "I love you, Dad"?

One last drawer, the night stand. Such an integral part of his final days—the resting place for the telephone, his pills, the eyeglasses. I opened the drawer and my eyes beheld the little black box. Not what I expected . . . or did I know what to expect? Should it be jeweled and trimmed with satin? Knowing my dad, the box was as it should have been: a simple, leather-covered, flat metal box, edges tattered and worn, overflowing with papers.

With shaking hands I reached for it, closed the bedroom door and spilled the contents on the bed. What I found in that box brought my life back to me, every phase of it— my mother, my childhood, tragedy, happiness, love.

Inside that box were remnants of all the things my dad cherished all his life. His marriage certificate to my mom, wrinkled and crisp with age; her death certificate; a few coins that must have held some real significance for him; letters of thanks from a dear old friend, long passed away, whom my dad had helped during tough times; a favorite photo of my mom in that yellow dress my dad so loved and so often spoke about; a photo of me when I was just six years old with a child's handwritten message, "To Daddy, Love, Debbie"; and cards. Many, many cards from me to my dad—Christmas, birthday, Father's Day cards from years gone by and years just past—each with a note inscribed inside from me to him, baring my soul and letting him know how I really felt about him.

I was in that box! My mother was in that box. No money, no insurance policies, no important legal papers— just items of no consequence other than to the man for whom they meant everything. I wonder how many times he would take out this box and read and reread the items inside, smiling or crying to himself. I would guess he did that often, as the papers appeared well handled.

I had never known that I was one of the most cherished of my father's possessions. The box told me, the box showed me, and it gave me back what I had lost only a few days before—a father's spirit and undying love for his daughter.

The black box is mine now. When the time comes for my last day on this earth and my possessions are reduced to green trash bags, my children will find this box. And inside, they will find the things that I most cherished in my life. When all is said and done, my children will have the good fortune of finding themselves, along with my spirit and love, inside the little black box, and realize that the only real important thing in life is the love we have for each other.

Deborah Roberto McDonald

Dinner Out

Tragedy and comedy are but two aspects of what is real, and whether we see the tragic or the humorous is a matter of perspective.

Arnold Beisser

As my bride of many years greeted me one evening, her voice blasted through the door, "Guess what?"

I always take a deep breath on this very leading question. "What?" I asked.

"I just won a sales contest at work and the prize is dinner for two at the new fancy restaurant down by the riverfront!"

Her excitement was contagious. We knew the restaurant was posh because we could only understand parts of the menu. "See? I told you there would be a place for me to wear my new spring outfit," she coyly reminded me.

"Two can play at that game," I responded. "I will wear my gray suit, my Borsalino imported straw hat and a new silk tie. We will be dressed to the nines. This town will never be the same. Almost like our first date."

It was early spring and nearing dusk as the maitre d' escorted us to a table by a window, with a view of the river. And the table was beautifully set, with a smoke-gray tablecloth accented by bright red napkins, lemon slices in the long-stemmed water glasses, fresh flowers— the works.

We reminisced about our children and grandchildren and their impact on our lives. A delicious meal savored in such an atmosphere should be remembered a long time. As it turned out, this will probably never be forgotten.

As the shadows lengthened, the riverboats rocking in their berths, I murmured, "Why don't we sashay down the esplanade like we did in Paris a few years ago? Remember the fun we had?"

Hand in hand, we strolled by the stores. People smiled and nodded. Lots of smiling and nodding, in fact. "I never realized there were so many friendly people as we have seen this evening, dear," I observed.

"Probably your new straw hat. Or the fact that you're such a handsome devil," she countered.

We completed the walking tour past the store windows. After acknowledging many smiles, we found ourselves back at the restaurant, looking at our reflection in the window. It was then that I saw the reason for all the smiles.

Caught in the fly of my trousers and hanging down for all to see was a bright red napkin from the restaurant!

Duke Raymond

Home vs. Visitors

My grandmother was a gentle soul. She came from a time when life was simple and uncomplicated. She would shy away from anything that was new. Every Sunday morning, she would take me to church, where she felt at home with the familiar surroundings. Because her vision was poor, we always sat near the front facing a tack board that would indicate how many home parishioners and visitors had attended the Sunday service.

As I grew older, I realized how sheltered her life had been and encouraged her to try new things. One evening as I was getting ready to attend a local basketball game, I asked her to join me. To my surprise she agreed to come along. I knew she had never been to such an event before and I tried to explain the game to her. She listened intently and pretended to understand.

Actually she seemed to enjoy it, and got caught up in the excitement of all the cheering. After the game was over, we met my mother for coffee and my grandmother began telling her about the high points of the evening. Turning to my mother she said, "You should have seen all the people there. Why, there were more present than at our church service on Sunday."

"How could you tell?" Mom asked.

Innocently, my grandmother replied, "Well, there was an attendance board at the end of the gym, just like the one at church, and it said, 'Home 134 and Visitors 120.' Why, we only had 122 home members attend last Sunday, and heaven knows we've never had that many visitors!"

S. Turkaly

"There must be another way to record attendance for our services."

The Power of a Promise

Laurie, my daughter, has always had three constants in her life from birth through her life's journey: her grandfather, her mother and one of her aunts.

In May of 1993, my father was diagnosed with terminal cancer and his prognosis was six to seven months. Laurie had applied to five universities across Canada to attend law school. In June, she was accepted at the University of Alberta in Edmonton, her first choice.

She went over to talk to her grandpa, telling him how she wasn't sure if she should move to Edmonton just then or if she should postpone the move for one year since he was ill. He looked her straight in the eye, shook his head no and said, "I want you to go to university in Edmonton. This is what you've worked for all these years. It is what you've always wanted for yourself and that is what I want for you."

She made her plans to move and before she left, she went to say good-bye to him. She said, "Grandpa, I don't want you to go anywhere while I'm gone. This can't be the last time I will see you or else I can't leave." He promised her that he would not go anywhere. "I'll be right here waiting for you when you get back," he said. My father was always a man of his word.

Laurie moved to Edmonton and started law school, while the rest of the family dealt with my father's illness day by day. Dad always accepted whatever life dealt him with good cheer and optimism. He was our rock. We all depended on him so very much. Whenever we had a problem we went to Dad, and he was always there to give us encouragement and advice.

His health was failing rapidly and he prepared all of us for his ultimate death. He even made the plans for his own funeral to take the burden from us in our grief.

On November 29th, Dad asked us to take him to the hospital. He had developed a serious allergic reaction to one of the drugs he was taking, unknown to us at the time. He was very weak. A terrible rash covered his body and his skin had started to peel. The next several days, the whole family spent time at the hospital so that there would always be someone keeping him company.

He was in terrible pain, yet he kept his good spirits. I specifically remember one Thursday night. He was sitting in a recliner chair between the two hospital beds. His eyes were closed, but he was aware of everything around him. Christmas music was playing on the television's weather channel. When "Winter Wonderland" came on, he started tapping his foot to the music. Christmas was one of his favorite seasons.

I had been in constant contact with Laurie about Dad's condition. I tried not to worry her too much because I wanted her to stay focused on her studies. She was aware of this, and in one phone conversation a few weeks earlier she had told me, "Mom, I don't want you just to call me when it is time to come home for Grandpa's funeral. I want to come home before that."

On Friday morning, I mentioned this conversation to

one of my dad's doctors. He responded with, "You'd better call her today." That morning around 11:00, my dad
was put on morphine and from then on, he never spoke
again.

I tried to reach Laurie to tell her to come home as soon
as possible, but she was at school. I kept calling but I
couldn't reach her. I left messages asking her to phone me
at the hospital as soon as she returned. By this time, we
were at the hospital constantly. That evening, the night
nurse informed us that Dad was in "transition," meaning
he could pass away at any time.

I was by Dad's bedside a lot, holding his hand or rubbing his feet because this soothed him. Around 1:00 A.M.,
I noticed that his feet were cold and so were his legs, all
the way up to his knees. His hands and arms were also
cold, all the way up to his elbows. A short while later, my
sister told me that she had tried to take his pulse but there
didn't seem to be one.

Around 2:30 I got called to the phone—it was Laurie. I
apprised her of the situation and told her the end was
near. I said to her that he probably wouldn't live through
the night. She asked me to please go back to Grandpa and
tell him she would be on the first flight out in the morning, and that she would arrive in Winnipeg sometime near
10:00. She could be at the hospital between 10:30 and
11:00. I told her I didn't think I could do that because he
had suffered enough, and I didn't want to prolong his
agony, especially in his condition. She begged me. "Please,
Mom, just go back and tell him what I said."

I went to Dad's bedside, took his hand, and told him
that I'd just spoken with Laurie. I told him she was on her
way back to Winnipeg on the earliest flight and that she
would be at the hospital by 10:30, and that she wanted
him to try to wait for her. Then I said, "Dad, if it's too
painful for you to wait, it's okay. Laurie will understand."

There was no response. I wasn't sure if he was even able to hear me, but then the strangest thing happened.

I went back to his bedside and took his hand. *It was warm.* Yet from his wrist to his elbow, it was still cold! The same was true of his feet. They were warm, but his legs from his ankles to his knees were also still cold.

Laurie arrived at 10:35. I met her at the door to prepare her because she had not seen her Grandpa since she'd left in September. He had changed much in that time, especially in the past week.

She went to his side, took his hand and let him know she was there. She talked to him for about ten minutes and said her final farewell. He was actually gripping her hand as she spoke to him. Then, without letting go of her hand, he took one deep breath in and he was gone. It was 10:50 A.M.

Dad had kept his promise. He had waited for Laurie to get back before he went anywhere.

Dianne Demarcke

The Crooked Smile

As we rolled five-year-old Mary into the MRI room, I tried to imagine what she must be feeling. She had suffered a stroke that left half of her body paralyzed, had been hospitalized for treatment of a brain tumor, and had recently lost her father, her mother and her home. We all wondered how Mary would react.

She went into the MRI machine without the slightest protest, and we began the exam. At that time, each imaging sequence required the patient to remain perfectly still for about five minutes. This would have been difficult for anyone—and certainly for a five-year-old who had suffered so much. We were taking an image of her head, so any movement of her face, including talking, would result in image distortion.

About two minutes into the first sequence, we noticed on the video monitor that Mary's mouth was moving. We heard a muted voice over the intercom. We halted the exam and gently reminded Mary not to talk. She was smiling and promised not to talk.

We reset the machine and started over. Once again we saw her facial movement and heard her voice faintly.

What she was saying wasn't clear. Everyone was becoming a little impatient, with a busy schedule that had been put on hold to perform an emergency MRI on Mary.

We went back in and slid Mary out of the machine. Once again, she looked at us with her crooked smile and wasn't upset in the least. The technologist, perhaps a bit gruffly, said, "Mary, you were talking again, and that causes blurry pictures."

Mary's smile remained as she replied, "I wasn't talking. I was singing. You said no talking." We looked at each other, feeling a little silly.

"What were you singing?" someone asked.

"'Jesus Loves Me,'" came the barely perceptible reply. "I always sing 'Jesus Loves Me' when I'm happy."

Everyone in the room was speechless. *Happy*? *How could this little girl be happy*? The technologist and I had to leave the room for a moment to regain our composure as tears began to fall.

Many times since that day, when feeling stressed, unhappy or dissatisfied with some part of my life, I have thought of Mary and felt both humbled and inspired. Her example made me see that happiness is a marvelous gift—free to anyone willing to accept it.

James C. Brown, M.D.

The Most Beautiful Flower

The park bench was deserted as I sat down to read
Beneath the long, straggly branches of an old willow tree.
Disillusioned by life with good reason to frown,
For the world was intent on dragging me down.

And if that weren't enough to ruin my day,
A young boy out of breath approached me, all tired from
     play.
He stood right before me with his head tilted down
And said with great excitement, "Look what I found!"

In his hand was a flower, and what a pitiful sight,
With its petals all worn—not enough rain, or too little light.
Wanting him to take his dead flower and go off to play,
I faked a small smile and then shifted away.

But instead of retreating he sat next to my side
And placed the flower to his nose and declared with
     overacted surprise,
"It sure smells pretty and it's beautiful, too.
"That's why I picked it; here, it's for you."

The weed before me was dying or dead.
Not vibrant of colors, orange, yellow or red.
But I knew I must take it, or he might never leave.
So I reached for the flower, and replied, "Just what I need."

But instead of him placing the flower in my hand,
He held it midair without reason or plan.
It was then that I noticed for the very first time
That weed-toting boy could not see: he was blind.

I heard my voice quiver, tears shone like the sun
As I thanked him for picking the very best one.
"You're welcome," he smiled, and then ran off to play,
Unaware of the impact he'd had on my day.

I sat there and wondered how he managed to see
A self-pitying woman beneath an old willow tree.
How did he know of my self-indulged plight?
Perhaps from his heart, he'd been blessed with true sight.

Through the eyes of a blind child, at last I could see
The problem was not with the world; the problem was me.
And for all of those times I myself had been blind,
I vowed to see the beauty in life, and appreciate every
    second that's mine.

And then I held that wilted flower up to my nose
And breathed in the fragrance of a beautiful rose
And smiled as I watched that young boy, another weed in
    his hand
About to change the life of an unsuspecting old man.

Cheryl L. Costello-Forshey

6

OVERCOMING OBSTACLES

*A man of character finds a special
attractiveness in difficulty, since it is
only by coming to grips with difficulty
that he can realize his potentialities.*

Charles de Gaulle

Rodeo Joe

David was a nine-year-old who had an unusual form of cancer involving the muscle of his leg. He was diagnosed at the age of eight and underwent major surgical excision. He was now on a continual regime of chemotherapy. The surgery had left him with significant weakening of his left leg and a noticeable limp, but he was otherwise disease-free. I was told by his parents that he was still the best worker on their little North Carolina farm. David's favorite chores involved attending to his horse and best friend, Rodeo Joe. As the staff became acquainted with David and his family, we also learned all about Rodeo Joe. Joe was a twenty-five-year-old quarter horse who in his day had been a talented cow horse, and who now in his retirement had become the best friend of a nine-year-old farm boy.

At age ten, David returned to the hospital with signs and symptoms suggesting that his disease had returned. Indeed it had, with a vengeance. There was local recurrence as well as involvement of the bone marrow, bloodstream and liver. David was very, very sick. Another round of chemotherapy was initiated, with full knowledge that the odds of a good response were minimal at best.

Chemotherapy often has negative effects on the body. As these potent substances are attacking tumor cells, they can also attack healthy, normal cells that we need for survival. Chemotherapy, in fact, can in and of itself be lethal. The balance one must obtain between too much and/or too little chemotherapy is indeed a delicate art form practiced by dedicated pediatric oncologists.

David's tumor and metastasis began to respond to the medicine, but unfortunately his immune system also became significantly impaired, and he soon developed infections involving his lungs and spinal fluid. David was a bright boy. He knew he was sick and that he may be dying. The weaker he became, the more he talked about Rodeo Joe. On our medical rounds, David would tell all of us about Joe's abilities with the cattle, and about all the ribbons he had won in his younger days. He would tell us how Joe knew when the school bus was coming and would be waiting at the fence. David would often jump on for a bareback fling around the pasture before doing his chores.

Gradually David became weaker and weaker. Soon he only grasped a well-worn photo of Rodeo Joe, which he would sometimes hold up to visitors. His only articulation to us became the repeated question, "Will I see Joe again? Can I ride him just one more time . . . just one more time?" The infection was so aggressive, it was difficult to control. David soon slipped into a coma. We doctors felt certain that the disease and infection were most likely too advanced, and that he would soon die.

David's parents were like most parents, totally devoted to their son. They were not wealthy people by any means, and the demands of their small farm by which they made their living did not cease. Caring neighbors lending a helping hand were a blessing, but Mr. and Mrs. Statler still divided their time between farm chores miles away and comforting their dying son in the hospital. They took little time to eat or sleep.

Three things stand out in my mind as I recall the time of David's coma. First is the resolute strength, determination and faith of the parents and their powerful love. Mr. Statler would say to me every day, "I do believe Davey will be ridin' that ol' gelding again, I believe he will." Next, I remember the hundreds of cards and letters taped up all over his room as David was being prayed for by a number of prayer groups all over the country. Finally, I can vividly recall all the pictures of that old horse, tacked up on the headboard of that pediatric bed. We all wanted David to ride that horse one more time. We hoped that he would come out of his coma long enough to at least see him, and we devised plans to haul Joe to the hospital grounds. We also all thought this was wishful thinking, as David's condition steadily worsened.

Then truly miraculously, for reasons not well understood by this physician, David's condition improved— and improved rapidly. The infections began to clear. David's own defense cells began to come back strong. Within forty-eight hours he was awake, alert and talking to us again about Rodeo Joe. Because of the extent of his cancer, we feared that this might only be temporary, so we wanted to try to get him home for at least one last ride with Joe. However, in running tests to evaluate the extent of the cancer, there was none to be found. Not in the leg, or in the liver, or in the spinal fluid.

One week later, David went back home to the farm, back with Rodeo Joe. A couple of months went by. I decided to go see David and his family and this old horse I had heard so much about.

It was a beautiful fall day in North Carolina, the multi-colored leaves made brilliant by the bright October sun. Their little farm was just off a secondary highway and easy to find. As I turned into the drive, I saw Rodeo Joe standing under a large orange oak tree with David sitting on his back facing backward, brushing the horse's rump. David hadn't noticed me yet, and I could see he was talking to Joe. Maybe he was sharing the story about how the doctors didn't think he'd make it back to ride Joe, but how the two of them knew he would.

I sat for a few minutes trying to match this scene with the one in the hospital, trying to understand it all. I watched the cars driving by on the highway with their occupants noticing the young boy and horse under the tall oak. I had this urge to stop traffic and explain to these people that yes, this is a picturesque fall farm scene, but you are really seeing a miracle. A miracle! But I didn't; I simply sat and watched.

James C. Brown, M.D.

When Garrett Morrison, the Sunday School
class clown, got baptized.

Reprinted by permission of Jonny Hawkins.

No Excuses Good Enough

I thank God for my handicaps, for, through them, I have found myself, my work, and my God.

Helen Keller

Twenty-four years ago Jim Ritter was a typical, active high school student—into sports, involved with girls, the class clown, and always goofing off! He was captain of the high school football and wrestling teams, played baseball, and was gifted on the trampoline. He could do triple flips and one-and-a-half twists.

At age sixteen his life changed forever.

Jim was working at his father's logging business one summer in the small town of Montesano, Washington. It was on a Friday. Jim usually never went in on Fridays, but his dad woke him at 4:30 A.M. and asked if he would go in with him.

After helping his father run the loader, work the power saw and drive the logging truck, Jim crawled into the grapple that picks up the logs for an after-lunch snooze. He laid in it like a hammock, with his feet on one side and his head resting against the other.

The next thing he recalled is seeing a flash of light and feeling as though someone had hit him in the back of the head and punched him in the nose. Jim's father had started up the engines to move the grapple, not realizing that his son lay inside, asleep.

"Oh my God!" Jim's father cried out. "I broke his neck!" Immediately, Jim's dad called for help on the C.B. radio. A logging company helicopter happened to be in the area doing survey work. They heard the call for help and picked Jim up, taking him to the hospital in Olympia, sixty-five miles away. It was truly a miracle they were in the area. His father's logging business was in the middle of nowhere, and helicopters hardly ever flew around there.

Jim's third, fourth and fifth cervical vertebrae were crushed, and after surgery, the doctor told his parents he had no chance of living. They gave him three to five days at the most. All his vital signs had stopped except his heart. "He'll be on a breathing machine the rest of his life," the doctor told Jim's family. "He'll be a head with a stick in his mouth—a vegetable."

But Jim proved everyone wrong. Although he was left paralyzed from the neck down, Jim's kidneys and other vital organs began working. He was confined to a Stryker frame like a sandwich. The medical staff flipped him every two hours! After two months, Jim was very frustrated. Because of the respirator, he could say only five words at a time before being interrupted by the machine's hissing sound. He was struggling to understand why God had let this happen.

Jim was in intensive care for nine weeks, then moved to an orthopedic hospital in Seattle, where he became an inspiration to the nurses and other patients with his quick sense of humor.

One day a volunteer came by Jim's room and asked if he would like to try painting pictures.

"I can't," Jim told her. "I'm paralyzed." But she wouldn't give up. As far as she was concerned, being paralyzed was no excuse. She showed him a drawing a paralyzed girl down the hall had done by holding a pen between her teeth. Seeing the drawing convinced Jim to give it try: If a girl could do it, so could he!

Drawing with a pen between his teeth was awkward and difficult at first. Jim practiced day after day, and gradually his drawings turned from amateur scrawls into beautiful scenes. Prior to the accident, Jim had never drawn. He had never even taken an art course.

Jim's mother cared for him for the next six years, until her death of lung cancer. All the people in Montesano were very supportive—they had fund-raisers for Jim and raised $2,000 for a van. A contractor donated his time and materials to landscape and cement his backyard for a wheelchair. His friends bought him a class ring and gave him surprise parties. A retired principal (who had been a real grouch and dreaded by all the students) volunteered his time to come by the house every day to tutor Jim in math, to help him obtain his high school diploma.

In rehabilitation, Jim met Joni Eareckson, a nationally known paralyzed artist who has written a book and starred in a movie about her experience. She was an incredible inspiration to him.

Today, Jim lets nothing stand in his way. He sings in the church choir, travels and speaks at various churches, schools and nursing homes. Jim is happily married to Sandy and they are the proud parents of a four-year-old daughter, Desireé. Jim has also become a highly talented artist. He has created several hundred pen-and-ink and watercolor scenes by holding the pen and brush between his teeth. He has a varied portfolio, including winter landscapes, religious scenes and whimsical characters, and he is able to support himself today by holding art shows throughout the country.

Jim has turned some of his inspirational drawings into beautiful Christmas cards and calendars. Inside each of Jim's cards is a Bible verse, and printed on the back is the notice: "Mouth-painted by Jim Ritter. Jim is paralyzed from the neck down and draws with a pencil and brush held between his teeth."

How easy it is to justify giving up on our dreams with a ready excuse. "It's too difficult." "I'm not that smart." "I don't have time." Jim Ritter is living proof that no excuse is good enough.

Sharon Whitley

Consider This

All great achievements require time.

David Joseph Schwartz

Consider this:

Robert Frost, one of the greatest poets that America has produced, labored for twenty years without fame or success. He was thirty-nine years old before he sold a single volume of poetry. Today his poems have been published in some twenty-two languages and he won the Pulitzer Prize for poetry four times.

Albert Einstein, often said to be the smartest person who has ever lived, is quoted as saying, "I think and think for months and years. Ninety-nine times the conclusion is false. The hundredth time I am right."

By the end of World War II, prominent CBS newsman William Shirer had decided that he wanted to write professionally. During the next twelve years he was consumed with his writing. Unfortunately, his books rarely sold, and he often had difficulty feeding his family. Out of this period, however, came a manuscript that was 1,200 pages long. Everyone—his agent, his editor, his publisher, his friends—told him it would never sell because of its length. And when Shirer finally did get it published, it was priced at ten dollars, the most expensive book of its time. No one expected it to be of any interest except to scholars. But *The Rise and Fall of the Third Reich* made publishing history. Its first printing sold out completely on the first day. Even today it remains the all-time biggest seller in the history of the Book-of-the-Month Club.

When Luciano Pavarotti graduated from college, he was unsure of whether he should become a teacher or a professional singer. His father told him, "Luciano, if you try to sit in two chairs, you will fall between them. You must choose one chair." Pavarotti chose singing. It took seven more years of study and frustration before he made his first professional appearance, and it took another seven years before he reached the Metropolitan Opera. But he had chosen his chair and had become successful.

When Enrico Caruso, the great Italian tenor, took his first voice lesson, the instructor pronounced him hopeless. He said his voice sounded like wind whistling through a window.

Walt Disney was once fired by a newspaper editor for lack of imagination. Disney recalled his early days of failure: "When I was nearly twenty-one years old I went broke for the first time. I slept on cushions from an old sofa and ate cold beans out of a can."

Scottie Pippen, who won four NBA championship rings and two Olympic gold medals, received no athletic scholarship from any university and originally made his small college basketball team as the equipment manager.

Gregor Mendel, the Austrian botanist whose experiments with peas originated the modern science of genetics, never even succeeded in passing the examination to become a high school science teacher. He failed biology.

Failure is only the opportunity to begin again more intelligently.

Henry Ford

Henry Ford forgot to put a reverse gear in the first car he invented. He also didn't build a door wide enough to get the car out of the building he built it in. If you go to Greenfield Village, you can see where he cut a hole in the wall to get the car out.

Dr. Benjamin Bloom of the University of Chicago conducted a five-year study of leading artists, athletes and scholars based on anonymous interviews with the top twenty performers in various fields, as well as with their friends, families and teachers. He wanted to discover the common characteristics of these achievers that led to their tremendous successes. "We expected to find tales of great natural gifts," Bloom commented. "We didn't find that at all. Their mothers often said it was another child who had the greater talents." What they did find were accounts of extreme hard work and dedication: the swimmer who performed laps for two hours every morning before school and the pianist who practiced several hours a day for seventeen years. Bloom's research determined conclusively that drive, determination and hard work— not great talent—were what led these individuals to their extraordinary achievements.

Deferred joys purchased by sacrifice are always the sweetest.

Bishop Fulton Sheen

Arthur Rubenstein once astounded a young inquirer with the statement that he practiced piano eight hours a day, every day of his life. "But, sir!" exclaimed the young

man. "You are so good. Why do you practice so much?"
"I wish to become superb," replied the master pianist.

A study of elite violinists showed that the number of hours spent practicing was the only factor that separated potential music superstars from others who were merely good. Following the careers of violinists studying at the Music Academy of West Berlin, psychologists found that by the time the students were eighteen, the best musicians had already spent, on average, about 2,000 more hours in practice than their fellow students.

A visitor once told Michelangelo, "I can't see that you have made any progress since I was here the last time." Michelangelo answered, "Oh, yes, I have made much progress. Look carefully and you will see that I have retouched this part, and that I have polished that part. See, I have worked on this part, and have softened lines here."

"Yes," said the visitor, "but those are all trifles."

"That may be," replied Michelangelo, "but trifles make perfection and perfection is no trifle."

The greater the difficulty, the more glory in surmounting it.

Epicurus

One of the most beautiful speaking voices on stage and screen belongs to James Earl Jones. Did you know that Jones has long battled a severe stuttering problem? From age nine until his mid-teens he had to communicate with teachers and classmates by handwritten notes. A high school English teacher gave him the help he needed, but he still struggles with his problem to this day. Yet there is no finer speaking voice than his. He was recently listed among the ten actors with the most beautiful speaking voice.

Charles Darwin spent most of his adult life in pain, suffering from one mysterious ailment after another. Yet he made immeasurable contributions to the study of the origins of life.

Born prematurely and left in the care of his grandparents, Sir Isaac Newton was taken out of school early and became an inept farm boy. Now he is considered one of the greatest figures in the entire history of science.

Paul Galvin created Motorola out of the ashes of his own bankrupt company. In 1928 Galvin was able to piece together enough money to buy back a small division of a company he had owned that was on the auction block. From that division he built Motorola, a Fortune 500 company that has been highly successful.

Nothing is particularly hard if you divide it into small jobs.

Henry Ford

The *Guinness Book of World Records* records the true story of a man who ate an entire bicycle, tires and all! But he didn't eat it all at once. Over a period of seventeen days, from March 17 to April 2, 1977, Michel Lotito of Grenoble, France, melted the parts into small swallowable units and consumed every piece.

There is no such thing as a self-made man. You will reach your goals only with the help of others.

George Shinn

George MacDonald once noted that one draft horse can move two tons of weight. However, two draft horses in harness, working together, can move twenty-three tons of weight.

Jack Canfield and Mark Victor Hansen

The Miracle of Love

A weed is but an unloved flower.

Ella Wheeler Wilcox

David was ten years old when he came to my summer camp, and he arrived with a lot of "baggage." He'd grown up with an alcoholic, rageaholic, abusive father whom David had repeatedly seen beat up his mom. David had a twelve-year-old sister who was very quiet and very good at becoming invisible, as many kids learn to be when they grow up in such a home. David, on the other hand, became like a lightning rod for his parents' anger and rage. He was put down a lot and hit a lot. He'd been diagnosed with such labels as attention deficit disorder, learning disorder, behavior disorder and conduct disorder. He was constantly getting into fights at school despite being put on half a dozen different medications ranging from Ritalin to Prozac. What we saw when David arrived at camp was a boy who couldn't look people in the eye, who trudged around with slumped shoulders looking pale and angry. In short, he just looked beat up.

Not surprisingly, the first day of camp, at our opening

circle, David got into a fight. He got the worst of the ten-second altercation, with a slightly swollen lower lip to show for it. Once again he was beat up and separate, a reflection of how he felt inside. Those first couple of days, David was tough to reach—resistant, distant and disconnected even from the other kids. But slowly he began to trust us.

On the third day of our group processing sessions, we got through. David talked about his dad, the abuse, his fear and anger and sadness. He began to cry, and slowly the crying turned to sobbing, deep sobbing, as he released some of the deep hurt and sadness he'd been holding onto for years. After that session, David was different. Some color came back to his face. He smiled, made eye contact, played with the other kids more. He allowed the adult counselors to "hang" with him. He just came alive. It was so incredible to watch him come out from his protective shell and just be himself. He was our biggest miracle that week.

The afternoon before the last day, when the parents were to arrive to pick up their kids, David got into a fight. He hadn't shown that kind of behavior since the first day, although it's common for our campers to feel anxious the day before their parents come. Anxious because some of them are going back to unhealthy environments; anxious and sad because they will soon be leaving new friends they've become so close to. We separated the kids and they worked out their disagreement, and then I asked David to take a walk with me. As we walked, I told him how proud I was of him for all the work he'd done that week; how open and vulnerable he'd been; how he'd been willing to trust us and let us in; how much he'd changed.

At that moment, this beautiful butterfly came fluttering around us and landed on the path right in front of us, so we stopped for a moment to admire it. I told David that the butterfly's presence was perfect because in Native American folklore (which we had been talking about during the week), when a butterfly crosses your path, it symbolizes that you are about to undergo a big transformation (just as the caterpillar changes into the butterfly). And it was perfect because the butterfly was reinforcing what I'd been telling him about all the changes he had made this week. But David looked up at me with the old, discouraged look on his face and said, "What if the butterfly is not here for me? What if he's here for you!"

Whew! I was momentarily stunned and my mind started racing, trying to come up with some great reassuring answer. Before I could figure it out, the universe, as usual, came through. The butterfly suddenly flew up into the air, fluttered around us again, and then landed right on David's shirt, right over his heart! No words were spoken; no words were needed. But I'll never forget the look on that boy's face in that miraculous moment. It was one of pure joy and hope—hope that he could be different, hope that his life and future could be different. It was as if in that one moment, he internalized all the lessons he had learned that week. Lessons like: I can trust people; it's safe to let people in; there are people who will care about me and love and accept me for who I am.

Sometimes I worry about campers like David going back to homes that are not as healthy and supportive and loving as they deserve. But I have faith that those magical moments created by our group sessions, our loving counselors and that miraculous butterfly will create a place in their hearts that they can turn to in those tough times, when they need to remember just how lovable and awesome they truly are.

Tim Jordan, M.D.

Medically Impossible

I remember it was almost Christmas because carols softly played on the radio in the nurses' station. I walked into Jimmy's room. A small seven-year-old, he seemed dwarfed by the big, indifferent, mechanical hospital bed with its starchy white sheets.

He looked up at me through suspicious eyes, hidden in a face puffed up from the use of steroids to control his kidney condition. *"What are you gonna do to me now?"* they seemed to ask. *"What blood tests are you gonna order? Don't you know they hurt, Doc?"*

Jimmy had a disease called nephrotic syndrome, and it was not responding to any therapy we had tried. This was his sixth month with the illness, his second week in the hospital. I was feeling guilty—I had failed him. As I smiled at him my heart felt even heavier.

The shadow of defeat had dulled his eyes.

Oh no, I thought, *he's given up.* When a patient gives up, your chances of helping that patient lower dramatically.

"Jimmy, I want to try something."

He burrowed into the sheets. "It gonna hurt?"

"No, we'll use the intravenous line that's already in

your arm. No new needles." What I planned I had tried a few weeks earlier without success. I gave him intravenous Lasix, a drug that is supposed to "open up" the kidneys.

This time I planned a new twist, which the nephrologist said probably would not work but was worth a try. A half hour before I injected the Lasix I would inject albumin, a simple protein that would draw water from the bloated cells into the bloodstream. Then, when I gave the Lasix, the water flooding the bloodstream might flow into and open up the kidneys. The problem was, if it didn't, the "flooded" blood vessels could give Jimmy lung congestion until his body readjusted. I had discussed this with his parents. Desperate, they agreed to try.

So I gave albumin into his intravenous line. A half hour later I came back to give the Lasix. He was breathing harder and looked scared. I had an idea. I never believed in divine intervention, but Jimmy came from a very religious family.

"You pray a lot?" I asked.

"Yes, " he answered. "I pray every night. But I guess God don't hear me."

"He hears you," I replied, not knowing in all honesty if God did or didn't, but Jimmy needed reassurance. And belief. "Try praying as I give this medicine to you. Oh, and I want you to pretend you see your kidneys—remember all those pictures of them I showed you awhile back?"

"Yes."

"Well, I want you to picture them spilling all the extra water in your body into your bladder. You remember the picture of your bladder I showed you?" I figured I might as well try visualization. This was in the early 1970s. Some articles had been written about visualization and some evidence existed that it worked—in some cases, anyway.

"Yeah."

"Good. Start now. Concentrate on your kidneys." I placed my hands there and shut my eyes, concentrating—just to show him how, you understand. Then injected the Lasix.

Jimmy closed his eyes and concentrated, and mouthed a prayer.

What the heck. I also prayed, even though I knew it wouldn't work. I did not believe in divine intervention. When I died I would have a few choice questions for God about why he allowed certain terrible things to happen to certain children. One of my friends suggested that when I did die, God would probably send me the other way just to avoid me. But in for a penny, in for a pound.

"How long will it take to work?" the nurse asked as she adjusted the dripping intravenous line. I motioned for her to step from the room.

"In a person with normal kidneys, maybe twenty minutes—fifteen minutes tops," I replied. "With Jimmy, I'm hoping a half hour. But I have to tell you, it's a real long shot. Stay with him. If he has trouble and needs oxygen, call me. I'll be at the nurses' station writing all this down."

I sat down and opened Jimmy's cold, metal-jacketed chart, almost cursing the irony of the Christmas carol on the radio: "Oh Holy Night." Before I had scribbled one sentence, the nurse stuck out her head from Jimmy's room. "A half hour to work?" she asked.

"For normal kidneys."

"Otherwise fifteen minutes 'tops,' right, Doc?"

"That's what I said."

"Well, the floodgates have opened: He's urinating like crazy. Within just two minutes he asked for the urinal. I've got to go get another."

Two minutes? Impossible. I went to the room as fast as my cane would allow me to walk. Jimmy had already filled the plastic yellow urinal. The nurse rushed in with another two. He grabbed one and started filling that one, too. He grinned at me, the light back in his blue eyes.

I left the room, a numbness coursing through my mind and body. It couldn't be. If he diuresed—if his kidneys opened up—he was on the way to a cure. No, it just could not happen that fast. Impossible. Medically impossible. And yet . . .

Was it sheer pharmacology and physiology breaking the rules? Was it the visualization?

I could clearly hear a fragment of a carol on the radio. I felt goosebumps: "Fall on your knees, oh hear the angel voices . . ."

A paraphrase of the last line from *Miracle on 34th Street* came to me: "And then again, maybe *I* didn't do such a wonderful thing, after all."

John M. Briley Jr., M.D.

One Step at a Time

Running has always been a great love of mine. For fifteen years I ran five miles a day, four days a week. I had developed a very successful business as a sales representative, and my work required a great deal of travel. Living near Lake Ontario, I covered New York, western Pennsylvania and eastern Ohio. I drove an average of 35,000 miles a year to meet with customers. I was always active, always on the go.

A few years ago, I began to feel a minor irritation in my left eye. Finally, after many months, I decided to see a doctor. X rays revealed a small growth behind my eye. It didn't appear cancerous, but the surgeons recommended having it removed as soon as possible.

Because my travel was usually very light around Christmas, I scheduled surgery for December 19th. I was not looking forward to the surgery, but at least while recuperating I could stay home and enjoy the company of my wife, Barbara, and our three children: Denise, then nineteen; Barry, seventeen; and Chuck, twelve.

When I awoke after the operation, nothing seemed clear. Conversations made no sense. I remember experiencing everything as a series of short, dream-like situations. I felt as though I were lost in the hospital and nobody could help me. *Wake up, Jerry,* I told myself. *This dream is scary!* Actually, I hadn't been dreaming at all.

During the surgery, a blood vessel that removes blood from the brain had been severed. Although this was a routine procedure, it had devastating effects. My brain tissue began to swell. The next day, I suffered a stroke to the left-front temporal lobe, affecting my speech. I could no longer communicate and the look of terror on my face alerted my daughter to my fears.

My brain continued to swell, and that evening I suffered another stroke, affecting vision. I had lost the right-peripheral vision in both eyes. I was rushed into emergency surgery. The only option left to the doctors was to remove a small portion of my brain which was already damaged by the stroke, in order to make room for any additional swelling. When the doctors finished surgery, they told my wife, "We've done all we can, the rest is in God's hands." They explained to Barbara that I could be paralyzed, blind and unable to speak.

I was hospitalized for three months at St. Mary's Brain Injury Rehabilitation Unit in Rochester, New York. During that time, I was reintroduced to my wife and children, but had no idea who they were. When I returned home for a visit, I stood there shaking, asking my wife, where we were. I recognized nothing. Literally, everything had to be reintroduced to me.

After leaving St. Mary's, I attended their outpatient rehabilitation program for another year. With the wonderful support of the therapists, doctors, family and friends, I began to relearn all the basic tasks of everyday life. During this period, I often used to see a man with long hair and a beard and wearing red-and-white clothing. His arms were outstretched, and there was a glowing heart in the middle of his chest. I loved staring at this wonderful sight. At the time, I didn't know that this man was appearing in the part of my field of vision that was supposed to be blind.

At the school, I would always use the walking machine at break time. My body slowly started to feel the urge to run again. But because of my near blindness, I was discouraged from running. One day during my prayers, I broke into tears at the thought of never being able to run again. All of a sudden I felt a warm hand touch my leg, and I heard the words, "You can run again."

Sustained only by an unyielding faith in those words, I gradually retrained myself to run indoors on the walking machine. That was in February 1996. Little by little I did more and more until, in March, I started running outdoors. My family watched me so I wouldn't get hurt or lost. It was over a year since I had run outside, but my body was adjusting nicely. When I made it down to the lake, I yelled, "Hi, Lake Ontario! It's me, Jerry Sullivan!"

I worked my way back up to twenty miles a week. My friends took me to the St. Patrick's Day Five-Mile Run. What a thrill that was! I could run again, and it seemed life was coming back to me.

Driving was next in line. Although 50 percent blind, I learned to drive again. When I passed my driving test, my mother-in-law gave me a gift—a small religious sticker to place in my car. On the sticker was a picture of a man with long hair and a beard, dressed in red and white. There on his chest was a glowing heart. It was the same man I had seen so often during my recovery.

I don't know what to make of this coincidence. But I do know the extraordinary power of faith. If it can make a blind man run, it can truly work miracles in our lives.

Jerry Sullivan

A Mother's Search

"Would you please put this in the Wailing Wall for me?"

I carefully held the small paper that had a picture of Jerusalem's Western Wall on it. Below, in neatly printed ink, were the words: "To find my son Pieter."

"Of course. I'll be glad to do it," I told my friend Marti Nitrini, when she learned of my upcoming trip to Israel. "Can non-Jews put items in the Wailing Wall?"

Marti, a Holocaust survivor, assured me that they could. "But the women have to go on a separate side," she explained.

I first met Marti several years ago when I wrote a piece in the *San Diego Union-Tribune* about *The Diary of Anne Frank*. She had called me.

"I was in the same concentration camp as Anne Frank," she said quietly. Intrigued, I asked Marti many questions about her life. We decided to meet in person.

While we sat sipping tea in her Mission Valley condominium one morning, Marti poured out her tale of horror to me, with details she hardly told anyone before.

A native of Prague born in 1918, she and her two older brothers had a happy, privileged childhood. Her

Hungarian father and German mother owned small department stores that carried leather goods and custom jewelry. Her parents had wanted her to attend an all-girls school, so she went to a nearby cloister.

"It was a Roman Catholic school, and I was the only Jew out of 500," Marti said. "The nuns were so nice and wonderful. I never forgot it. And I still visit when I go to Prague."

Marti was married at a young age—fifteen—to a handsome man ten years her senior with whom she had fallen madly in love. Despite her parents' initial reluctance, they had a very happy marriage. Their baby boy, Pieter, was born in 1938.

Marti's happy world shattered one day in 1942 when her family received orders to assemble at a certain location, to be transported to "a special resort" for Jews.

"If you didn't show up, they'd come and shoot you," she remembers. "They assembled thousands and thousands of people. You could bring only what you could carry."

Marti and her husband and small son were sent to a Czech concentration camp called Theresienstadt. She and Pieter lived in a small room, about 300 square feet, with four other mothers and seven other children. Her husband was in another barracks. Later they were sent to Auschwitz, in Poland. Marti recalls having only one bowl of soup with potato peels and one tiny slice of bread to eat all day. All she had to wear during the cold winter was a cotton shirt and skirt.

"It was at Auschwitz that we started to find out . . . that we saw the chimneys and started to realize what was happening," she quietly recalls. "You couldn't believe it. A normal person couldn't believe that something like this was going on. But you saw the chimneys and smelled the sweet smell of burning meat."

When General George S. Patton's troops smashed Hamburg, 5,000 people were needed to clean up the rubble. "My husband came to me and said, 'Look, if you stay here, you will not survive. I'll keep Pieter with me.'"

Marti recalls having "to parade naked in front of SS men" to be "selected," then traveling in railroad cars for three days to Hamburg, where she was so hungry she would look in garbage cans for food.

"One day, I found a burnt pancake that someone had tossed out," she says. "That was my highlight, one burnt pancake. If you found a turnip to eat, it was like a million dollars. We used to eat burned wood and leaves."

Marti tried to run away but was caught and beaten, then forced to do hard labor. Then on April 1, 1945 (her birthday), she was moved to Bergen-Belsen, where there was no food, except for one daily slice of bread that the SS had poisoned, making everyone sick and weak. It was at Bergen-Belsen that Marti saw Anne Frank.

"She was lying on the bunk in a coma," Marti says. "I remember her dark hair and her big eyes. She was all alone there, lying in bed like a skeleton." Anne died not long after that.

On April 15, the British liberated Bergen-Belsen and Marti helped to move corpses that were lying all around so that the tanks could drive in. Of the 50,000 inmates who survived to see the liberation, 25,000 died within days of it.

Marti lost forty-three relatives in the Holocaust, including her parents and her husband. To this day, she has never known what became of her son, Pieter Reich, who would be fifty-nine.

She came to the United States in 1945 and remarried four times—divorced once and widowed thrice. She never had any more children. Not long ago, Marti was videotaped by Steven Spielberg's company for the Shoah Foundation, which documents the stories of Holocaust survivors so that no one ever forgets what happened.

A few years ago, Marti visited Israel to search for Pieter at the Hall of Names at the Yad Vashem Holocaust Memorial in Jerusalem. She found his name on a list, which noted that he was last seen in Bergen-Belsen. To this day, she still holds out hope that he is alive, and has made numerous efforts to find him.

When I visited Yad Vashem recently with a group from Solana Beach Presbyterian Church, I walked through The Children's Memorial Hall, which commemorates the 1.5 million Jewish children who perished in the Holocaust. In a quiet, darkened, mirrored room, five burning memorial candles were multiplied into an infinite number, symbolizing these children's souls. As sad, eerie music played, the names, ages and hometown of each child was read in a solemn voice. I thought of Marti's son, Pieter, who was only six when she last saw him. I could hear muffled sobs of people—of all faiths and nationalities—walking through the memorial.

Later, as I stood at the women's section of the Western Wall, I paused briefly and reread Marti's poignant plea for her son. *How could a mother bear to not know for certain what happened to her child?* I wondered. *How has Marti been able to endure this heartache all these years?*

Then I stepped up to the wall, folded her note as small as possible, and stuck it into a crevice. *This is the very least I can do for you, Marti,* I thought, as I said a prayer for her and Pieter. Since meeting Marti, I have admired her emotional strength and cheerful attitude despite the evil adversities that she has had to endure.

I recalled what Marti had said to me earlier. "You've got to go on living. One door closes and another opens, and you just keep on going."

Sharon Whitley

The Purpose

Life was coasting along for Jim Colbert. He had a good home, nice wife, three kids, a good job. And he had reached the fine age of twenty-eight, when maturity really starts to take its grip and settle in.

Then life took a sudden curve for Jim. Instead of coming back to his good home, he found himself plunging steeply downward, as if he were on tracks headed for the blackest cave he had ever known.

Soon after the day Jim found himself having trouble walking, the next thing he knew he was strapped into an iron lung, living at a hospital, confined in a coffin-like machine. The only thing that protruded was his head. For nine months, Jim was unable to move his body.

Doctors informed him he had polio. If he left the machine, his life would be over. He would no longer be able to breathe.

Jim was living his nightmare wide awake. He watched as his wife stood over him at the hospital and whispered that she had to leave him and take the kids with her.

"Go ahead," he told her firmly. "I'm worthless, anyhow."

That was his assessment. A worthless man with a worthless body. He forgot, however, that he didn't have a worthless brain.

When he was released from the hospital, he contacted the state department of rehabilitation and soon went back to school to study psychology. He had to accept that he would never walk again.

His life now came equipped without a wife, children or a good home. Instead, it came with a wheelchair, two disabled roommates and an apartment they shared in Los Angeles.

It was a time when Jim could have steeped in bitterness. His classes were tough and his two roommates were the partying kind. One also was in a wheelchair. The other had a fatal disease called cystic fibrosis. All three, however, quickly learned how to have a good time and do crazy things. Disabilities didn't stop them. They even went on desert camping trips.

Jim considered himself only a half-man, living in a wheelchair. His attitude began to change when women smiled back. Relief swept over him. Maybe that side of his life wasn't completely over. It wasn't.

Within a few years, Jim became a full-time psychologist. He helped set up foster care group homes. He worked with juvenile offenders. And in the end, he went into private practice, where he made quite a tidy living and carried some prestige in his community.

Years rolled by until one evening, he woke up in a sweat. He was getting older, and it suddenly struck him that he hadn't fulfilled his life's purpose. He didn't know what that purpose was, but he knew it wasn't just to live a life of affluence and prestige.

He began to shed his material life, his material goods, like a snake gets rid of old skin. But it was still unclear to him what he was supposed to do.

Friends and colleagues found the answer for him. Go to the county institution where foster children are temporarily kept, they pleaded, and read the files of the kids who don't get out of there.

He found that the kids who remained institutionalized, without any type of foster home, were children with severe medical needs. They were either dying or needed full-time care because of chronic illnesses.

The case that stopped him short was of a seventeen-year-old boy who sat in his wheelchair slamming his head all day long against a cement wall. He had never been provided a foster home. His life had been only the institution. No love. No warmth.

The next day Jim donated his home and opened one of the first foster care homes devoted to chronically and terminally ill children. Within four years he had opened four homes, wheeling and dealing with friends for low rents. He wheeled and dealed for board members. He wheeled and dealed for people to give their time and donations.

Forced to operate all the homes on a shoestring budget, he manages to pay his staff the highest wages in the industry—which still isn't much. Each home (which includes one for deaf children) has a philosophy of providing the most love possible for each child. Here's what has happened with some of his children:

Carlos, twelve, had cystic fibrosis. When he arrived at the home, he was angry and bitter. He hated the home. He hated the staff. But when he realized they weren't leaving, he began to show his own love and affection that had been locked away inside. Within a short time, he was the mascot of Samadana foster homes. The entire staff loved him. Before he died, he lost several of his friends to illness. He dreamed that he was standing on a cliff and his friends were waving at him. *Don't be afraid,* they told him. *You can breathe so much easier here. When you're ready, a white horse will come and carry you over to us.* He died believing that. He died feeling loved.

Tanya, seven, had cystic fibrosis and a zest for life that enthralled Jim and his staff. One thing she liked more than anything in the world was Barbie dolls, so her caregivers went out of their way to get her the biggest and best Barbies. Not one of Tanya's birthdays went by without a Barbie, and usually more than one. When she fell so ill and was hospitalized, Tim, who helps manage the homes, came up with a giant pink Barbie caravan with more dolls, just to give Tanya the edge to keep on living. Tanya is now reunited with her mother.

Alicia, fourteen, had two liver transplants and has been given a life estimate of forty-five years. Nothing stops Alicia. She lives her life to the fullest. When she graduated from junior high, she asked the staff to throw her a party with all her friends and to buy everyone lunch. The staff did. When she was awarded a trip to Washington, D.C., from a school program, they scraped up spending money for her. They love her spirit and joy in life. Most of all, they love her because she has a deep well filled with gratitude that she shares.

Despite his success, Jim still worries. He's aging now. There are still many children to be rescued. He wants to make sure his program will carry on and that there will be enough money and visionaries to continue and expand.

If it does, he will have found his true purpose for living.

Diana Chapman

Soccer Balls and Violins

We are members of a vast cosmic orchestra in which each living instrument is essential to the complementary and harmonious playing of the whole.

J. Allen Boone

It was early fall. I was enjoying my role as volunteer assistant soccer coach for a group of energetic ten-year-olds. My duties consisted primarily of maintaining some degree of control over this highly rambunctious lot, as my true knowledge of the game was limited.

One early morning at work, I was musing about the previous night's soccer practice. I was handed the chart of ten-year-old Bradley, who was to be my first ultrasound exam of the day. Bradley was a young man I remembered well, even though I had not seen him in a number of years. At the age of four, Bradley had been involved in an automobile accident that had left him paralyzed from the waist down.

In any children's hospital, tragic situations are unfortunately quite common, and certainly paraplegia is not unusual. However, on that particular morning, my mind was full of the images of ten-year-olds running, jumping and kicking, so I felt a bit depressed as I entered the room to see Bradley, knowing that he would never realize the joy of playing soccer.

I began Bradley's ultrasound exam and we started chatting about the inconsequentialities of life. Suddenly, his eyes lit up as he began telling me about his music: his violin, his piano and his flute. Bradley expressed how wonderful it was to be able to "make music." In fact, Bradley had been selected to participate in a regional competition with the Omaha Symphony. What joy and enthusiasm he radiated! Then, almost as if he felt embarrassed by his exuberance, he turned to me and asked, "Dr. Brown, do you play an instrument?"

"Why, no, I don't," I replied, feeling a bit embarrassed myself. I felt the need to go ahead and explain to Bradley that I had indeed tried to learn music, and there were numerous piano teachers and a few clarinet teachers out there who had indeed tried to teach me. But they all wound up telling my parents the same thing: "I'm sorry. Jim tries real hard. He just has no talent whatsoever."

"Oh," Bradley said. "I'm real sorry, too, Dr. Brown." He quite genuinely felt bad for me, and the crazy thing was, *I* also felt bad for me. So there we were in that instant, both feeling a bit of grief for my musical deficiencies. Then, for another instant, I experienced this inane urge to point out to Bradley that *he* was the one handicapped here. Or was he?

"Thank you, Bradley," I said, "but it's okay. God has given me gifts in other areas."

"I know, Dr. Brown. You're right, and I sure am glad you are a good doctor. But every day I feel so lucky and I am so thankful because there really is nothing like being able to make music!"

Bradley and I said our good-byes. His ultrasound exam had been normal and he was joyfully on his way to a musical function. I felt good and at peace. I had once again been reminded of the fallacy of two very common human tendencies. One is the tendency to make worldly things too great in importance (like running and jumping), and the other is the tendency to keep God too small.

James C. Brown, M.D.

A Father's Calling

On August 28, 1982, Carl and Joyce Lambert sat by their daughter Karen's bedside in shock and grief. The day before, Karen had been a bouncy, spirited sixteen-year-old, a good student and budding musician. Then, the call that every parent dreads: there had been an accident. Karen had been on her way home from a flute lesson when her car overturned on an onramp. She was thrown through the windshield and landed on the pavement, where she was hit by another car. As Carl and Joyce hovered over her in intensive care, Carl felt a strong sense of helplessness. His daughter was not expected to live, and there was nothing he could do to help.

Yet Karen did live. She had twelve hours of surgery to repair internal bleeding, multiple fractures, a crushed shoulder and elbow, and a torn and bleeding liver. She was in a coma with severe head injury, and was in shock. But Carl was a computer scientist, not a doctor. For eighty-one days there was nothing he and Joyce could do but wait and pray.

Then, on day eighty-two, Karen woke up.

It was their Karen, but it was almost as if she were an

infant again. She no longer knew how to swallow, talk, count, walk, or even think clearly.

Carl's sense of helplessness persisted, though he did all he could. Karen spent four more months in the hospital and the next six in therapy as an outpatient.

The Lamberts worked out a plan in which Joyce continued her full-time job for income and benefits while Carl stayed at home with their daughter.

When Karen arrived home in a wheelchair, her parents breathed a sigh of relief. Carl and Karen began the long process of rehabilitation. Therapists cost $60 to $120 an hour, but Carl himself was willing to put in as much time as was necessary—being a parent was his most important priority.

Everything was time-consuming and required the utmost patience—on both their parts. To teach Karen to speak again, Carl had her utter the word "hut" for five hours a day. He found this stretched the vocal chords and began to make speech possible.

As she improved, the two began playing card games to help Karen's concentration. Even small progress required playing for long stretches of time, sometimes up to eighteen hours a day. Karen was improving, but the pace was slow. The strain was becoming too much for both of them.

What was a father to do?

While in the shower one morning, it hit him. True, he wasn't a doctor. He wasn't even a professional therapist. But he *was* a computer scientist. And perhaps that was what could help Karen the most!

A computer would be the perfect aid to help Karen learn tasks such as counting, concept formation, pattern recognition and problem solving. A computer would never tire of repetition, could work at Karen's own speed, and would be on call twenty-four hours a day. It could even provide fun!

So Carl got to work. He called in occupational and speech therapists, doctors, psychologists and even a physical therapist. They proposed problems to be worked on; he designed computer programs offering games and stimulating activities to solve them. And that's how Karen learned the basic skills, and once again developed concentration and memory.

In fact, the software programs were so helpful, motivational and fun, that they were packaged as the Karen Lambert Foundation programs, and are now in use across the country.

Today, Karen Lambert is again a spunky young woman with a charming sense of humor. She's thirty-one, happily married, and enjoys taking college courses now and then.

You'd be hard pressed to find a prouder father than Carl. He's not only glad that Karen is finding a sense of independence, but that his days of feeling helpless are well behind him. He discovered that it's all well and good to be a doctor or a professional therapist. But sometimes, it's even better to be yourself.

Sharon Whitley

A Turning Point

In order to be a realist you must believe in miracles.

David Ben-Gurion

Seventy years ago I was quite a small little girl, the baby of the family, with an older brother and sister. My father was very ill at the time, and my mother took in sewing of any kind so we could live. She would sew far into the night with nothing but dim gas mantles and an old treadle sewing machine. She never complained even when the fire would be low and the food very scarce. She would sew until the early hours of morning.

Things were very bad that particular winter. Then a letter came from where her sewing machine was purchased, stating that they would have to pick up her machine the next day unless payments were brought up to date. I remember when she read the letter I became frightened; I could picture us starving to death and all sorts of things that could come to a child's mind. My mother did not appear to be worried, however, and seemed to be quite calm about the matter. I, on the other hand, cried myself to sleep, wondering what would become of our family. Mother said God would not fail her, that he never had. I couldn't see how God was going to help us keep this old sewing machine.

The day the men were to come for our only means of support, there was a knock at the kitchen door. I was frightened as a child would be, for I was sure it was those dreaded men. Instead, a nicely dressed man stood at our door with a darling baby in his arms.

He asked my mother if she was Mrs. Hill. When she said she was, he said, "I'm in trouble this morning and you have been recommended by the druggist and grocer down the street as an honest and wonderful woman. My wife was rushed to the hospital this morning, and since we have no relatives here, and I must open my dentist office, I have nowhere to leave my baby. Could you possibly take care of her for a few days?" He continued, "I will pay you in advance." With this he took out ten dollars and gave it to my mother.

Mother said, "Yes, yes, I will be glad to do so," and took the baby from his arms. When the man left, Mother turned to me with tears streaming down a face that looked as though a light was shining on it. She said, "I knew God would never let them take away my machine."

Adeline Perkins

A Match Made in Heaven

There is nothing the body suffers that the soul may not profit by.

George Merideth

I scrubbed and gowned while my OB-GYN colleague explained the situation to me. A first-time mother carrying twins had gone into labor three months before her due date; all attempts to stop the labor had failed. As I entered the delivery room I noticed the father tenderly supporting his wife while she prepared for the delivery.

The obstetrician looked up at me strangely, then handed me an object as the father looked on. It was a tiny arm. Within seconds out came Twin A, crying and noticeably premature. I quickly took the baby to the bassinet, gave him oxygen and assessed his status. He was working to breathe. I was certain that with this degree of prematurity he would suffer hyaline membrane (a lung disease affecting premature infants). I left Twin A with a nurse and returned to receive Twin B, also vigorously crying. The only obvious deficiency was the absence of his left arm.

The twins were taken to the neonatal nursery. Chest X rays revealed moderately severe premature lung disease, requiring high oxygen support. After the twins had been stabilized, I finally had a chance to talk with the parents, Mr. and Mrs. Arnold. We discussed premature lung disease and the potential complications, and how the first forty-eight hours were very critical in their care and prognosis. Then I addressed the issue of the absent left arm.

I explained that when an appendage of the baby *in utero* pokes through a developing membrane surrounding the baby, the membrane closes back again, amputating the limb or digit. The Arnolds' responses to these grave conditions were full of hope, and I was struck by their strength of character. They remained strong through the next several days, lovingly encouraging their twins, Mathew and Jonathan, as the babies suffered complications.

The twins responded well. It was a joy to see them finally go home without any residual effects from their premature birth, such as permanent lung disease or brain damage. The Arnolds continued their dedication to their children, immediately exploring different prosthetic options for Mathew. Mrs. Arnold phoned and researched many sources to find out when and how a prosthesis should be utilized with a growing child. She read voraciously. She made contacts all over the world, trying to find the most knowledgeable individuals to help Mathew. It was an honor to witness this mother's love, trying to solve this child's special challenge.

Two years later our family moved to the Midwest, but Mrs. Arnold still kept me up to date on Mathew's progress. About ten years later, while I was working as a pediatric radiologist at a children's hospital, I met the Sanders. They had just adopted a six-month-old infant from Korea. Baby Billy had a swollen elbow, the result of a tumor in the elbow joint of the right arm. A biopsy revealed a malignancy, and because of the extensive involvement of the joint and bone, amputation above the elbow was the only possibility for complete cure.

Once again I witnessed the love and fortitude of caring parents. Right away, Mrs. Sanders set out to find all about the prosthetic devices. I knew Mrs. Arnold had thoroughly investigated this problem. It was an easy connection to make. The two mothers communicated by phone and by letter, and I know their connection became a tremendous support for both families.

Later, I learned that young Mathew began to write Billy encouraging letters. Mathew had become an outstanding young man, both academically and athletically. He participated in all sports, and excelled in basketball and soccer. In his letters, Mathew offered Billy helpful tips on shoe tying and tree climbing, and ways to respond to public stares. As Billy got older, Mathew became a very important role model.

One summer when Billy was five years old and Mathew was fifteen, the Arnolds took a cross-country vacation, which brought them through our city. We held a three-family picnic in our backyard. It was touching to see young Billy meet Mathew, his longtime hero and role model. I saw Billy on the sideline, awestruck as he watched Mathew play basketball, and I could almost see the wheels turning in his head: "Wow, if he can do that with one arm . . ."

At the end of the day, we were all sitting around the picnic table and I was saying what a blessing it was for the families to have found each other, and for Billy to have come to know Mathew. It was clear to me that problems surrounded by love become blessings that reap more of the same.

As we were talking, everyone noticed that Billy's and Mathew's absent arms were side by side. Billy looked around at everybody and said, "Yep, I guess we're a match made in heaven."

Everyone laughed—with tears in our eyes.

James C. Brown, M.D.

Puppy Love

I've heard two things for nearly most of my life. One, that animals don't have any human emotion—even though I knew they possessed fear and pain. Two, that breeders who weren't happy with imperfect dogs had them destroyed. When I became an amateur breeder myself, I would learn these things on my own.

My family and I owned one remarkable Dalmatian, Kami, who had given us companionship, warmth, love and many sloppy-tongued kisses. We loved her so much, we decided we wanted some of her pups. So we matched her with a purebred named Bo.

We had no idea exactly what it would be like to have Dalmatian pups, but we were sure we could find homes for each and every one we didn't keep. There was excitement in the air the night of their births. Kami was so large and the babies were so busy inside her that their tiny feet and heads were bulging out of her skin.

We felt like we were playing a part in *101 Dalmatians* that night. The first one popped out. Then the second. We counted slowly throughout the night, ten . . . eleven . . . twelve. Twelve Dalmatian pups. We couldn't believe it.

The thrill of having Kami's pups was remarkable. I felt like a dad of twelve puplets. And fortunately in this case, there was no cruel character like in the movie. Or so we thought.

The pups roamed, tumbled, wrestled and snuggled with each other. We had to help Kami nurse the twelve pups because the largest shoved the smaller guys away. We blended milk with canned puppy food and put it out in pie tins. It was always a daring adventure trying to tip-toe through twelve yapping puppies who could easily be squished with one wrong step.

It was then when we noticed life's small dose of cruelty—trouble with two pups. They didn't respond to us like the others. They didn't charge me when I called out that it was chow time. They ran smack into barking pups. We soon learned that the two brother pups were deaf. It was recommended that the best option was to put them to sleep.

I pondered it for a few moments. While breeders would put them to sleep in a second, it just wasn't what I or anybody in my family wanted to do. I thought, *Why should two pups die just because they were born deaf?* I was rewarded for the decision at the next chow time. I stepped out into the feeding frenzy and only ten pups charged me. The eleventh looked at me and ran for the bushes. He stopped and looked back at me again.

I followed, wondering what he was doing. He'd seen me carry the pie tins filled with food. *What could he possibly be waiting for?* In a few seconds, I knew. Seeing me coming, he charged into the bushes. Seconds later, he reappeared, nudging his sleepy deaf brother from the brush. An overwhelming sense of loyalty and satisfaction swept over me. I learned then the puppy's sense of love, loyalty and caring. I learned then what an unselfish action the pup had taken.

The brother pups are now living happily together at a home where the family appreciates them immensely.

Last I heard, they brought their adopted family a double amount of love and happiness.

Mark Malott
as told to Diana Chapman

Giant in the Crowd

Since drama is made up of life, teaching drama gives one the opportunity to teach life. However, I don't think I ever taught my students as much as I was privileged to learn from them. One such student was the giant named Jimmy, who walked into my class in 1963.

Jimmy was one of the "special education" students who was being mainstreamed, and I felt privileged to have him. As it turned out, he was most definitely "special," as he was to educate us all.

Drama students are great fun; they are creative, spontaneous, outspoken and disarmingly honest. However, these very qualities sometimes get in the way of a thing called consistency. So it was that after two months, the only student who had completed every single assignment was Jimmy. I could only imagine how hard it was for him at times. He was fighting muscular coordination, as well as speech and vision problems, but he never shirked from any responsibility.

I constantly bragged about him being "excuse-free." One day I called on him, and he looked back at me, smiled and told me he was not ready to perform. I detected a slight twinkle in his eye. I asked him to stay after class for a moment.

"Jimmy, you were ready, weren't you?" I asked.

"Yes, sir," he replied.

"Why, Jim? You did the work, you deserve the credit."

He shuffled his feet, looked up, smiled and said, "Well, I didn't want the other kids to feel bad. I have more free time than they do, and I didn't want any of them to get discouraged."

As the year progressed, the class became more aware of the good fortune in having a genius in the art of humanity in their midst. I have asked this question to countless groups in seminars and the reply is always the same: When you see someone crying, you go up to them and usually say something. What is it you say? Everyone replies, "What's wrong?" Jimmy never said that. His question was always, "Can I help?"

One day, I asked him why he never asked the same question everybody else did.

"Well, Mr. Schlatter," he said, "I never thought much about it, but I guess I figure that it's not my business 'what's wrong.' But if I can help them fix what's wrong, that *is* my business."

We ended every year with a speech and drama banquet modeled after the Academy Awards. The students wanted to give Jim some special recognition for all he had meant to them.

I gave him a poem to read called *Myself* by Edgar Albert Guest, which I felt best reflected his unspoken but totally lived philosophy.

We had saved his moment to be near the end, and after he was introduced, he approached the front of the auditorium without his book. He wasn't going to read it; he had memorized it. He smiled and in a slow deliberate manner, touched our hearts as he read:

I have to live with myself and so I want to be fit for myself to know.

I want to be able as days go by to look myself straight in the eye.

I don't want to stand with the setting sun and think of things I have or haven't done.

I want to go out with my head erect.

I want to deserve all men's respect, I want to be able to like myself.

I don't want to look at myself and know that I'm a bluster, a bluff and an empty show.

I can never hide myself from me. I see what others may never see.

I know what others may never know.

I can never fool myself and so whatever happens, I want to be self-respecting and conscience-free.

First there was total silence, then thunderous applause. Two students went to the podium and hugged Jimmy, after which they gave him a trophy that was inscribed:

To Jimmy

> *Thank you for the*
> *Honor and Privilege*
> *of knowing you.*

Class of '64

But the story does not end there. In the audience was an eighth grade girl named Cathy Aquino. Over the summer, she wrote a speech about Jimmy entitled Giant in the Crowd. She delivered it in speech competitions throughout California and Arizona. More important than the awards she won was the fact that during the course of the year, three girls told her that her speech convinced them to go into the field of special education.

In 1992, I was invited to a reunion of that class. The students had made a special effort to make sure Jimmy was there.

One of the women who had graduated with that group was telling me of her daughter, who had been born with multiple birth defects, and the great plans she and her husband had for that girl's life.

"Your voice is filled with such courage and optimism, it inspires me," I said.

"What do you expect?" she replied, looking across the room in Jimmy's direction. "I went to school with a giant."

Jack Schlatter

7

ECLECTIC WISDOM

God asks no man whether he will accept life.
That is not the choice. You must take it.
The only question is how.

Henry Ward Beecher

The Best Time of My Life

Nothing is worth more than this day.

Goethe

It was June 15, and in two days I would be turning thirty. I was insecure about entering a new decade of my life and feared that my best years were now behind me.

My daily routine included going to the gym for a workout before going to work. Every morning I would see my friend Nicholas at the gym. He was seventy-nine years old and in terrific shape. As I greeted Nicholas on this particular day, he noticed I wasn't full of my usual vitality and asked if there was anything wrong. I told him I was feeling anxious about turning thirty. I wondered how I would look back on my life once I reached Nicholas's age, so I asked him, "What was the best time of your life?"

Without hesitation, Nicholas replied, "Well, Joe, this is my philosophical answer to your philosophical question:

"When I was a child in Austria and everything was taken care of for me and I was nurtured by my parents, that was the best time of my life.

"When I was going to school and learning the things I

know today, that was the best time of my life.

"When I got my first job and had responsibilities and got paid for my efforts, that was the best time of my life.

"When I met my wife and fell in love, that was the best time of my life.

"The Second World War came, and my wife and I had to flee Austria to save our lives. When we were together and safe on a ship bound for North America, that was the best time of my life.

"When we came to Canada and started a family, that was the best time of my life.

"When I was a young father, watching my children grow up, that was the best time of my life.

"And now, Joe, I am seventy-nine years old. I have my health, I feel good and I am in love with my wife just as I was when we first met. This is the best time of my life."

Joe Kemp

Josh and His Jag

About ten years ago a young and very successful executive named Josh was traveling down a Chicago neighborhood street. He was traveling a bit fast in his sleek, black, sixteen-cylinder Jaguar XKE, which was only two months old.

He watched for kids darting out from between parked cars and slowed down when he thought he saw something. As his car passed, no child darted out, but a brick sailed and—whump—smashed into the Jag's shiny side door.

SCREECH! Brakes slammed. Gears pounded into reverse, and tires madly spun the Jaguar back to the spot from where the brick was thrown. Josh jumped out of the car, grabbed the kid and pushed him up against a parked car. He shouted at the kid, "Just what was that about? Who do you think you are?" Building up a head of steam he continued, "That's my new Jag; that brick is going to cost you plenty. Why did you throw it?"

"Please . . . please, mister, I'm sorry. I didn't know what else to do," pleaded the youngster. "I threw the brick because no one else would stop."

Tears were dripping down the boy's chin as he pointed around the parked car. "It's my brother, mister," he said. "He fell out of his wheelchair and I can't lift him up." Sobbing, the boy asked the executive, "Would you please help him back into his wheelchair? He's too heavy for me."

Moved beyond words, the young executive tried desperately to swallow the rapidly swelling lump in his throat. He helped the youngster upright the wheelchair, and the two of them lifted his brother back into the chair.

It was a long, long walk back to the sleek, black, sixteen-cylinder Jaguar XKE—a long and slow walk. Now, Josh never did fix the side door of his Jaguar. It reminded him not to go through life so fast that someone has to throw a brick at him to get his attention.

Josh Ridker

Grass

I believe a leaf of grass is no less than the journey-work of the stars.

Walt Whitman

My mother was ninety-three when she died. She had all the tragedies of life without any of the compensations. She had lost our dad after only a few years of marriage and was left with two young boys during the Depression of 1929. She gave up her job as a trained nurse and governess to a millionaire's children in order to do housekeeping, which would allow her to keep the remains of our family together. Although her hands looked like a construction worker's, due to scrubbing clothes and floors, God was kind and gave her a life with minimal sickness.

After getting my brother and me through school, her only happiness was a TV I had bought her, an occasional visit from my brother, who lived in northern California, and Sunday mornings when I would take her to breakfast.

It was one of these mornings that followed a workweek where my life seemed a study in futility. The only beauty in my world was that there were at least twenty more hours until I had to start a new workweek.

It was a delightfully cool California summer morning. As I drove up to my mom's old house, she was already sitting on the rough front porch. Mom loved her little old house, which was perhaps the first permanent residence she had ever enjoyed. As I got out of the car and walked toward the porch, I could see her tired old face was radiant with love and the anticipation of the short ride to the neighborhood coffee shop and breakfast.

Her black shoes, as usual, were immaculately polished and as neat and clean as the black skirt and simple white blouse. The blouse was pinned closely around her neck with a blue swallow broach that had gold wire on the surface spelling "Mother." I remembered giving that cheap little piece of jewelry to her on a Mother's Day at least forty years ago. Mom never asked for much and apparently never got much either.

She never had much time to teach me about life or things of value, but if you took the time to watch how she treated and talked to people, there was a world of knowledge to be gained in values and living.

I sincerely tried to have Mom feel that these next few hours were as important to me as I knew they were to her. I'm sure I failed in her eyes as I did my own. I was too totally convinced of the ugliness of the world and the importance of my job and material gains.

I helped Mom into the car and as we drove off she said, as she did each Sunday, "My, my, Buddy, what a beautiful car." I looked upon it as an old model of two years ago with twelve more months of payments until I could get a new one.

Each time she spoke it was of joy and hope, and each time I replied I heard myself returning a courtesy answer, without genuine interest or encouragement. The breakfast finally ended and I was shamefully looking forward to dropping Mom off so I could get back to the dirty, materialistic, real world.

Mom had been quiet the past few minutes, perhaps in the realization that another Sunday visit was coming to an end and that only a few blocks remained until she would be home again with her aloneness.

I was looking at the street's need for patching and all the houses that were badly in need of paint when Mom suddenly said, as if she were seeing a sunset for the first time, "Oh, Buddy, look, look! Isn't it beautiful?" It was about 11 A.M., there wasn't any sunset. What, then, would be so beautiful on this dingy old neighborhood street? Out of courtesy I responded, "What, Mom? What is so beautiful?"

"The grass, Buddy, the grass. Look how beautiful the grass is!" *Beautiful grass?* As I turned to look at the grass I saw Mom's wrinkled old face, her thinning white hair, and her long hands with enlarged veins and knuckles that she had earned from eons of sacrifice and love. Her old dimming eyes were bright and shining, and her face was radiant as she pointed to lawn after lawn of plain green grass.

I have seen beautiful faces for quite a few years now, but none as beautiful as this dear lady's as she perceived the beauty in ordinary grass. How rich she was to have been blessed with seeing and finding beauty in the ordinary. How impoverished and unfortunate I was with my shallow sense of values. As my eyes left her face in shame, I, too, looked at the grass. It *was* beautiful!

I returned my gaze to my mother's face. She looked at me as if to say, "See, Buddy, you can see it, too. The grass is beautiful."

I didn't want to say a word. I was afraid the magic would pass, that I would lose this wonderful warm peace.

Suddenly I found myself opening the front door of my mother's home. "Well," she said, "thanks, Buddy, for this beautiful morning. I know you're very busy. What are you going to do with the rest of your day?"

I hoped my guilt wasn't showing, but that she could feel my gratitude for the lesson I had just learned. I took her in my arms and held her tightly as I whispered in her ear, "Mom, I'm going to rush right home and look at the grass."

John Doll

A Good Heart to Lean On

There was a time, when I was growing up, that I was embarrassed to be seen on the street with my father. He was severely crippled and very short, and when we would walk together, his hand on my arm for balance, people would stare, and I would inwardly squirm at the unwanted attention. If he ever noticed, or was bothered by it, he never let on. It was difficult to coordinate our steps—his halting, mine impatient—and because of that we didn't say much as we went along. But as we started out he always said, "You set the pace. I will try to adjust to you."

Our usual walk was to or from the subway, which was how he got to work. He almost never missed a day, and would make it into the office even if others could not. A matter of pride. He went to work sick, and despite nasty weather, which was the toughest on him. When there was snow or ice on the ground it was impossible for him to walk, even with help. At such times he would have my sisters or me pull him through the streets, he sitting on a child's sleigh, to the subway entrance. Once there he would cling to the handrail with both hands until he reached the lower steps that the warmer tunnel air kept ice-free. When he reached them he was okay, for in Manhattan the subway was the basement of his office building, and he would not have to go outside again until we met him in Brooklyn when he came home.

When I think of it now, I marvel at how much courage it must have taken for a grown man to subject himself to such indignity and stress. And at how he did it—without bitterness or complaint.

He never talked about himself as an object of pity, nor did he show any envy of the more fortunate or able. Although I think he was the object of prejudice (there is still, today, some prejudice toward the disabled), he was not prejudiced himself. He cared nothing about a person's religion, ethnicity or race—what he looked for in others was a "good heart," and if he found one the owner was good enough for him. Now that I am older, I have come to believe that is a good standard by which to judge people, even though I still don't know precisely what it is. I know the times I don't have one myself, though.

Unable to engage in many activities that healthy people take for granted, he still tried to participate in some way. Never able to play sports, he was still an avid and knowledgeable baseball fan, and often took me to Ebbets Field to see the Brooklyn Dodgers play. When a local sandlot baseball team found itself without a manager, he stepped in to keep it going. Deferred from military service in World War I, he served on our local draft board in World War II. Even though he could not dance, he liked to go to dances and parties, where he could have a good time just sitting and watching. On one memorable occasion, at a beach party, when a fight broke out, with everyone else punching and shoving (fueled, no doubt, by copious amounts of bathtub gin), he wasn't content to sit and watch, but he couldn't stand unaided on the soft sand. In frustration he began to shout, "I'll fight anyone who will sit down with me! I'll fight anyone who will sit down with me!"

Nobody did. But the next day people kidded him by saying it was the first time any fighter was urged to take a dive even before the bout began.

I now know he participated in some things, vicariously, through me, his only son. When I played ball (poorly), he "played," too. When I joined the Navy, he "joined," too. And when I came home on leave, he saw to it that I visited his office, where I was almost as uncomfortable at being shown off as I had been when I walked with him on the street, as a child. Introducing me to his coworkers, he was really saying, "This is my son, but it is also me, and I could have done this, too, if things had been different." Those words were never said aloud.

After what proved to be a full life, he died in 1961, from a disease that is cured routinely today. Confined to bed for the last few months of his life, he just drifted away. He was off on his final commute, unencumbered by his legs, for the first time in over sixty years.

I think of him often now, not just at Father's Day. I wonder if he sensed my reluctance to be seen with him during our walks, and if he did, I am sorry I never told him how sorry I was, how unworthy I was, how I regretted it. I think of him when I don't have a good heart, or when I complain about trifles, or when I am envious of another's good fortune. At such times I put my hand on his arm, to regain my balance, and say, "You set the pace. I'll try to adjust to you."

Augustus J. Bullock
Submitted by Ted Kruger

The Golden Rule

Do unto others as you would have others do unto you.

We have committed the Golden Rule to memory.
Now let us commit it to life.

Edwin Markham

Therefore, whatever you want men to do to you, do also to them, for this is the Law and the Prophets.

Matthew 7:12

And just as you want men to do to you, you also do to them likewise.

Luke 6:31

One should seek for others the happiness one desires for one's self.

Buddhist

What you do not want done to yourself, do not do to others.

Confucius

Let none of you treat his brother in a way he himself would not like to be treated.

Muslim

We should behave to our friends as we would wish our friends to behave to us.

Aristotle

The law imprinted on the hearts of all men is to love the members of society as themselves.

Roman

What is hateful to you, do not do to your neighbor. That is the whole Torah.

Rabbi Hillel

Do as you would be done by.

Persian

Deal with others as thou wouldst thyself be dealt by.

The Hindu *Mahabharata*

Do to others as I would they should do to me.

Plato

The Train Ride

It was 9:30. I was sure I would miss my train, the last one for the evening. Getting to the depot had been an ordeal in its own right. Now, struggling through a crowded hallway in Los Angeles' Union Station, I was battling slow-moving travelers, those who had managed to make it early enough to catch their trains and didn't feel the need to move quickly.

Turning the corner toward the platform, I saw another obstacle. The stairs were blocked by a man who struggled with too many suitcases for one person to carry, especially if that person was handicapped, which this person was. His left arm hung uselessly by his side, and he had only partial use of his right arm. One of his legs was twisted inward. I watched him move each piece of luggage up one step, then return for the next. When he had successfully transferred all of the items up to the same step, he would repeat the process. He was on step number five, of about twenty.

He barked at a porter who offered assistance with the luggage, and glared at a fellow passenger who tried to help with a bag. Any effort on my part wouldn't make a difference. While I appreciated his desire for independence, I had no intention of letting him delay me from my train. I had just experienced a particularly unpleasant week and returning home was the most important thing in the world to me. So when I saw my chance, I stepped over his bags, made it to the top of the stairs, and boarded the train.

Though I had planned to stretch out and relax, I was soon reminded of the adage, "Plans are useful, but don't get attached to them." Occupying the seats across the aisle from me were two little girls. They were very excited, very active and very, very loud. One look at their exhausted father and I knew my two brief hours of quiet introspection were about to be replaced with 120 lengthy minutes of chattering and giggling. When I thought it couldn't get worse, it did. The man from the stairway limped into the car, grunted at me to move my feet, and plopped himself down beside me.

Upon closer inspection, I realized his ailment affected not just his limbs but his face, which was twisted in a permanent scowl. He was the kind of figure little children would laugh at or run from if he got too close. His patience with the girls across the aisle was shorter than mine. After two minutes he growled at them, "Keep it down!"

My new travel companion was less than delightful. He took every opportunity to complain to the conductors about the temperature, the lighting, the slow service at the ticket counter, the noisy little girls (who hadn't said a word since his chastisement), the stale peanuts he bought in the café car, and, oh yes, the little paper cups that didn't give him enough water to swallow his pills. All this, and we had not been moving for more than fifteen minutes.

I'm normally a pretty nice guy, but the milk of human kindness was souring in my veins. I focused on my misfortune of having to sit next to this man whose heart seemed to be as twisted as his body. As I sat there feeling sorry for myself, my conscience decided to make an uninvited appearance. *Perhaps,* I thought, *if I reach out with a simple kind word, I could be the catalyst to change his demeanor—maybe even his life.*

I was tired, irritable and in no mood to leave my comfortable cocoon of silence and self-pity. So I fought that voice that told me to do the right thing, to be a friend to a stranger, and to help someone in need. The more I fought it, the louder it got. Though I had never met this man, I knew he was in pain and needed to talk to someone. As I sat pondering my dilemma, a person with much less self-interest took action.

It was a sweet voice, unmistakably innocent. "Hey mister, what's the matter with you?" One of the girls across the aisle had stepped up in a way I had been unable to do. Her question was not new to the man, who responded, as he probably had hundreds of times throughout his life, that he had a disease that made his muscles not work right. Unsatisfied with the answer, she shook her head. "That's not what I mean. Why are you so mad at everybody?"

The man sat for a moment before uttering a choked response. "I guess I'm just mad at life. It hasn't treated me very well."

The little girl looked puzzled. "Maybe life would treat you better if you treated it better. I mean, I know you're sick, but I bet you still have lots of stuff that could make you happy."

The man turned toward the girl, and though I lost sight of his face, I knew he was not looking at her angrily. "You're awfully young to think you know so much about life."

It was her turn to pause. "I guess I learned a lot of things like that when my mommy went to heaven." She sat back in her seat and looked away from the man. She didn't want to talk anymore. That was okay. She had said enough.

The rest of the trip was quiet, as the girl eventually drifted off to sleep and the man seemed less eager to complain about things. I'll never know what long-term effects the conversation had on him, but I was touched in a way I'll not soon forget. Lately, I've been seeing my problems as a bit less traumatic, smiling at people a lot more, and appreciating the many gifts I have. And do you know something? Life seems to be treating me a little better every day.

David Murcott

True Forgiveness

Character before wealth.

Amos Lawrence

Forty-three years seems like a long time to remember the name of a mere acquaintance. I have duly forgotten the name of an old lady who was a customer on my paper route when I was a twelve-year-old boy in Marinette, Wisconsin back in 1954. Yet it seems like just yesterday that she taught me a lesson in forgiveness that I can only hope to pass on to someone else someday.

On a mindless Saturday afternoon, a friend and I were throwing rocks onto the roof of the old lady's house from a secluded spot in her backyard. The object of our play was to observe how the rocks changed to missiles as they rolled to the roof's edge and shot out into the yard like comets falling from the sky.

I found myself a perfectly smooth rock and sent it for a ride. The stone was too smooth, however, so it slipped from my hand as I let it go and headed straight for a small window on the old lady's back porch. At the sound of fractured glass, we took off from the old lady's yard faster than any of our missiles flew off her roof.

I was too scared about getting caught that first night to be concerned about the old lady with the broken porch window. However, a few days later, when I was sure that I hadn't been discovered, I started to feel guilty for her misfortune. She still greeted me with a smile each day when I gave her the paper, but I was no longer able to act comfortable in her presence.

I made up my mind that I would save my paper delivery money, and in three weeks I had the seven dollars that I calculated would cover the cost of her window. I put the money in an envelope with a note explaining that I was sorry for breaking her window and hoped that the seven dollars would cover the cost for repairing it.

I waited until it was dark, snuck up to the old lady's house, and put the envelope of retribution through the letter slot in her door. My soul felt redeemed and I couldn't wait for the freedom of, once again, looking straight into the old lady's eyes.

The next day, I handed the old lady her paper and was able to return the warm smile that I was receiving from her. She thanked me for the paper and said, "Here, I have something for you." It was a bag of cookies. I thanked her and proceeded to eat the cookies as I continued my route.

After several cookies, I felt an envelope and pulled it out of the bag. When I opened the envelope, I was stunned. Inside was the seven dollars and a short note that said, "I'm proud of you."

Jerry Harpt

Have a New Look and a New Name —
But the Message Remains the Same!

The

Chicken Soup for the Soul

Companion!

(Formerly *THE CHICKEN SOUP FOR THE SOUL NEWSLETTER*)

Chicken Soup for the Soul™ COMPANIO

The **CHICKEN SOUP FOR THE SOUL COMPANION** is a wondrous collection of h
warming stories, cheerful anecdotes, inspirational messages and just plain old-fashion
fun and humor. It's **Chicken Soup** a very special way, and it can be yours six times a
— just for saying "yes" today.

The very first issue of the **CHICKEN SOUP FOR THE SOUL COMPANION** is sche
to arrive just in time for some extra holiday cheer. Be one of the first to delight in its
felt inspiration. Share the stories of others whose lives have been touched in some w
Chicken Soup for the Soul.

Subscribe today to this BRAND NEW, DELIGHTFUL AND DEFINITELY ONE-OF-A-KIN
PUBLICATION. You won't find it in stores or on newsstands. This new and delicious
of soup is only available through subscription.

Send no money now . . . just return this card so you're guaranteed to receive the ver
First Edition . . . it might even turn into a **Chicken Soup Collector's Item**.

Act Today . . . AND LOOK FORWARD TO CHICKEN WISDOM AN
INSPIRATION ALL YEAR LONG!

☐ *ABSOLUTELY!* Sign me up today, send me my *First Edition* copy of the **Chicke
Soup for the Soul Companion* as soon as it's ready and don't bill me until then!

(Please check one option)

☐ 1-Year Subscription, 6 issues, **Special Introductory Offer only $18** (reg. price $
☐ 2-Year Subscription, 12 issues, **Special Introductory Offer only $34** (reg. price $

(PLEASE PRINT)

Name _____

Address _____

City _____ State _____ Zip _____

Telephone ( ) _____ (in case we have a question about your

Remember, you won't even receive a bill until after you receive your very first issue. Even then, yo
under no obligation. If the publication is not all you've hoped for just return your bill marked "Can
and you won't receive any more issues.

*Formerly titled **The Chicken Soup for the Soul Newsletter**. If you've already signed up for the newsletter, there is no n
respond again. You will automatically receive the first issue of the **"Companion"** in its place.

Spelling Bee

Rather fail by honor than succeed by fraud.

Sophocles

In the fourth round of a national spelling bee in Washington, eleven-year-old Rosalie Elliot, a champion from South Carolina, was asked to spell the word avowal. Her soft Southern accent made it difficult for judges to determine if she had used an *a* or an *e* as the next to last letter of the word. They deliberated for several minutes and also listened to tape recording playbacks, but still they couldn't determine which letter had been pronounced. Finally the chief judge, John Lloyd, put the question to the only person who knew the answer. He asked Rosalie, "Was the letter an *a* or an *e*?"

Rosalie, surrounded by whispering young spellers, knew by now the correct spelling of the word. But without hesitation, she replied that she had misspelled the word and had used an *e*.

As she walked from the stage, the entire audience stood and applauded her honesty and integrity, including dozens of newspaper reporters covering the event. While

Rosalie had not won the contest, she had definitely emerged a winner that day.

God's Little Devotional Book for Students
Honor Books

Grandpa's Little Girl

Tell me a story
I would sweetly say,
as Grandpa sat in his favorite chair.

He scooped me up with his carpenter hands
placing me on his lap,
and though I'd heard it many times before,
he told it again.

Walk with me Grandpa
I'd excitedly plea,
while slipping my hand into his.

He wrapped his big callused hand around mine,
and though we'd walked the path before,
out through the garden we went.

Watch me Grandpa
I'd joyfully say,
as I danced in circles around him.

He stopped his work,
and though he'd seen my dance before,
he clapped and whistled along with me.

Advise me Grandpa
I seriously asked,
as I sat at his feet.

He looked at me carefully,
and though he'd given advice before,
he shared his wisdom with me.

Say it one more time Grandpa,
I said with hope,
as I gazed into his dimming eyes.

He mustered all the strength he had left,
and though I'd heard it many times before,
he replied, "I love you, honey."

Remember me Grandpa,
I said in tears,
as I stood by his bed.

His weathered hand stretched to take mine,
and though we'd never been here before,
we knew it was good-bye.

Darlene Harrison

Lessons You Learned

For every petal you pluck from a daisy,
You're granted one measure of love.
For every rainbow you find with two ends,
I wish you two stars from above.

For every tear you brush from a cheek,
I promise you kindness will follow.
Wherever you walk, under rainbows or stars,
Over daisies, or down lonely hollows.

For every child you play with and talk to,
I grant you one heart full of laughter.
For every smile you place on a face,
I promise you peace ever after.

If you think "I" am giving you priceless gifts,
Look close at yourself and your deeds.
The gifts you earned were the lessons you learned
While answering other folks' needs.

Marlene Gerba

More Chicken Soup?

Many of the stories and poems you have read in this book were submitted by readers like you who had read earlier *Chicken Soup for the Soul* books. We are planning to publish five or six *Chicken Soup for the Soul* books every year. We invite you to contribute a story to one of these future volumes.

Stories may be up to 1,200 words and must uplift or inspire. You may submit an original piece or something you clip out of the local newspaper, a magazine, a church bulletin or a company newsletter. It could also be your favorite quotation you've put on your refrigerator door or a personal experience that has touched you deeply.

In addition to future *Servings of Chicken Soup for the Soul*, some of the future books we have planned are *A 2nd Helping of Chicken Soup for the Woman's Soul, Christian Soul* and *Teenage Soul* as well as *Chicken Soup for the . . . Teacher's Soul, Jewish Soul, Pet Lover's Soul, Kid's Soul, Country Soul, Laughing Soul, Grieving Soul, Unsinkable Soul, Divorced Soul* and *Loving Couple's Soul.*

Just send a copy of your stories and other pieces, indicating which edition they are for, to the following address:

Chicken Soup for the *(Specify Which Edition)* **Soul**
P.O. Box 30880 • Santa Barbara, CA 93130
phone: 805-563-2935 • fax: 805-563-2945
To e-mail or visit our Web site:
http://www.chickensoup.com

We will be sure that both you and the author are credited for your submission.

For information about speaking engagements, other books, audiotapes, workshops and training programs, please contact any of the authors directly.

Soup Kitchens for the Soul

One of the most exciting developments with *Chicken Soup for the Soul* was the impact it had on readers who are welfare recipients, homeless or incarcerated in state prisons.

As a result we established The Soup Kitchens for the Soul Project, which donates *Chicken Soup for the Soul* books to individuals and organizations that cannot afford to purchase them. We have already donated over 15,000 copies of *Chicken Soup for the Soul* books to men and women in prisons, halfway houses, homeless shelters, battered women shelters, literacy programs, inner-city schools, AIDS hospices, hospitals, churches and other organizations that serve adults and teenagers in need.

Many of these books are provided by the publisher and the authors, but an equal number have been donated by readers like you. We welcome and invite your participation in this project in the following ways. For every $12.95 you contribute, we will send two copies of *Chicken Soup for the Soul* to programs that support people in need. We also invite you to submit the names of worthy programs that you think should receive copies of the books.

The program is administered by the Foundation for Self-Esteem in Culver City, California. Please make your check payable to The Foundation for Self-Esteem and send it to:

Soup Kitchens for the Soul
The Foundation for Self-Esteem
6035 Bristol Parkway • Culver City, CA 90230
or call 310-568-1505 and make your contribution
by credit card

We will acknowledge receipt of your contribution and let you know where the books you paid for were sent.

The GOALS Program

With each *Chicken Soup for the Soul* book that we publish, we designate one or more charities to receive a portion of the profits that are generated. Charities that we have supported in the past include the American Red Cross, Literacy Volunteers of America, the National Arbor Day Foundation, the Union Rescue Mission, the Breast Cancer Research Foundation, the American Association of University Women Education Foundation, Habitat for Humanity, Save the Children, Feed the Children, Covenant House and the Yellow Ribbon Project.

We will be donating 25¢ per book (for the first million books sold) to the Foundation for Self-Esteem, a 501(c)(3) non-profit education corporation, to pay for the free distribution of the GOALS Motivation Program to non-profit educational institutions, homeless shelters and welfare programs to benefit at-risk adults and teenagers.

The GOALS Motivation Program is a multi-media self-esteem development and life skills program developed by Jack Canfield. To date, GOALS has successfully served over 300,000 participants. By following the program's self-sufficiency concepts, many of them have been converted from tax users to taxpayers.

GOALS teaches the secrets of success used by self-made millionaires, Olympic athletes and world leaders to individuals who need extra help in overcoming life's many barriers, and who may otherwise get trapped in a cyclical pattern of negative behavior.

The program has a successful track record of helping underserved groups and at-risk individuals through Welfare-to-Work and JOBS/GAIN programs, prevention programs, housing projects, homeless shelters, prisons, mentoring programs, community colleges and adult schools.

The following are comments from GOALS participants:

Someone such as myself (who has eight prison num-
bers and many other incarcerations) really needed this
in my life. . . . I've been existing, going with the motions
of the environment around me . . . I just took the first
session and already I'm beginning to work on me.

Brenda W.

When I first came to GOALS, I wasn't working.
Since GOALS I have worked, making enough money
not only to survive without any assistance from the
government, but to be financially comfortable. GOALS
was the answer for me to get up and believe in myself.
After years of failing, it's hard to believe you can do it. I
am very happy and excited about life. It's been this way
since I was in GOALS (two years ago), and it hasn't
stopped.

Kellie G.

You may contact this organization at:

Foundation for Self-Esteem
6035 Bristol Parkway
Culver City, CA 90230
310-568-1505

Who Is Jack Canfield?

Jack Canfield is one of America's leading experts in the development of human potential and personal effectiveness. He is both a dynamic, entertaining speaker and a highly sought-after trainer. Jack has a wonderful ability to inform and inspire audiences toward increased levels of self-esteem and peak performance.

He is the author and narrator of several bestselling audio- and videocassette programs, including *Self-Esteem and Peak Performance, How to Build High Self-Esteem, Self-Esteem in the Classroom* and *Chicken Soup for the Soul—Live.* He is regularly seen on television shows such as *Good Morning America, 20/20* and *NBC Nightly News.* Jack has coauthored numerous books, including the *Chicken Soup for the Soul* series, *Dare to Win* and *The Aladdin Factor* (all with Mark Victor Hansen), *100 Ways to Build Self-Concept in the Classroom* (with Harold C. Wells) and *Heart at Work* (with Jacqueline Miller).

Jack is a regularly featured speaker for professional associations, school districts, government agencies, churches, hospitals, sales organizations and corporations. His clients have included the American Dental Association, the American Management Association, AT&T, Campbell Soup, Clairol, Domino's Pizza, GE, ITT, Hartford Insurance, Johnson & Johnson, the Million Dollar Roundtable, NCR, New England Telephone, Re/Max, Scott Paper, TRW and Virgin Records. Jack is also on the faculty of Income Builders International, a school for entrepreneurs.

Jack conducts an annual eight-day Training of Trainers program in the areas of self-esteem and peak performance. It attracts educators, counselors, parenting trainers, corporate trainers, professional speakers, ministers and others interested in developing their speaking and seminar-leading skills.

For further information about Jack's books, tapes and training programs, or to schedule him for a presentation, please contact:

The Canfield Training Group
P.O. Box 30880 • Santa Barbara, CA 93130
phone: 805-563-2935 • fax: 805-563-2945
To e-mail or visit our Web site:
http://www.chickensoup.com

Who Is Mark Victor Hansen?

Mark Victor Hansen is a professional speaker who, in the last twenty years, has made over four-thousand presentations to more than 2 million people in thirty-two countries. His presentations cover sales excellence and strategies; personal empowerment and development; and how to triple your income and double your time off.

Mark has spent a lifetime dedicated to his mission of making a profound and positive difference in people's lives. Throughout his career, he has inspired hundreds of thousands of people to create a more powerful and purposeful future for themselves while stimulating the sale of billions of dollars worth of goods and services.

Mark is a prolific writer and has authored *Future Diary, How to Achieve Total Prosperity* and *The Miracle of Tithing.* He is coauthor of the *Chicken Soup for the Soul* series, *Dare to Win* and *The Aladdin Factor* (all with Jack Canfield) and *The Master Motivator* (with Joe Batten).

Mark has also produced a complete library of personal empowerment audio- and videocassette programs that have enabled his listeners to recognize and use their innate abilities in their business and personal lives. His message has made him a popular television and radio personality, with appearances on ABC, NBC, CBS, HBO, PBS and CNN. He has also appeared on the cover of numerous magazines, including *Success, Entrepreneur* and *Changes.*

Mark is a big man with a heart and spirit to match—an inspiration to all who seek to better themselves.

For further information about Mark write:

P.O. Box 7665
Newport Beach, CA 92658
phone: 714-759-9304 or 800-433-2314
fax: 714-722-6912
Web site: http://www.chickensoup.com

Contributors

Many of the stories in this book were taken from books we have read. These sources are acknowledged in the Permissions section. If you would like to contact them for information on their books, tapes and seminars, you can reach them at the addresses and phone numbers provided below.

Many of the stories were also contributed by readers like yourself, who responded to our request for stories. We have also included information about them.

Bonita L. Anticola is a home economics teacher in Angola, New York. She is married, the mother of three, and when not busy with work, home, etc., she can be found sewing quilts. (Gayle passed away on August 31, 1997. Her family gave the red wagon to her in Gayle's memory.) Bonita can be reached at 9865 Hardpan Rd., Angola, NY 14006.

Marsha Arons is a writer and lecturer in Skokie, Illinois. She is thrilled to be associated with the *Chicken Soup* series, and her stories appear in *Woman's Soul* and *Mother's Soul*. She also contributes to national magazines such as *Good Housekeeping, Reader's Digest* and *Redbook*. She has authored a book for young adults and is currently at work on a collection of short stories dealing with mother-daughter relationships. You can contact her via e-mail for speaking or other assignments at RA8737@aol.com.

Kathleen Beaulieu is a divorced mom of two grown children, Eric and Amanda. She worked for eleven years with her former husband, running and organizing his contracting business. She specializes in organizing businesses and troubleshooting problem areas, including leadership issues and customer relations.

Dee Berry is a hobbyist writer and member in good standing of Frank's Writing Workshop. She wishes to thank "the gang" and her husband, Neal, for their honest and kind critiquing. She is a devoted gardener who often finds inspiration among her lavender and roses, or when hip-deep in compost.

Annette Paxman Bowen's work has appeared in magazines around the world. She is the author of two young-adult novels, *Get a Life, Jennifer Parker!* and *Live and Learn, Jennifer Parker*, as well as a nonfiction book, *Donuts, Letters and Midnight Phone Calls* (Desert Book Company, Salt Lake City, UT 800-453-4532).

John Briley is an "in the trenches" pediatrician who is also a writer and Irish-style storyteller. His proudest accomplishment, other than his children, is helping to establish an infant development (child enrichment) program on Maui where he lives with his wife, who somehow puts up with him!

James C. Brown is the husband of Justine and the father of Ryan and Sally. He is a physician involved in the care of children and a faculty member at Creighton University School of Medicine in Omaha, where he enjoys teaching. Dr. Brown is an author, bronze sculptor and coach. With his wife, Justine, he raises and trains Belgian draft horses. He can be reached at Creighton University Medical Center, Department of Radiology, 601 N. 30th St., Omaha, NE 68131, or by calling 402-449-4753.

April Burk will chronicle her mothering experiences until her unsuspecting subject is old enough to tell her to get a life of her own. April's essays have appeared in *Mother to Mother, Pandemonium* and numerous magazines. She lives with her husband, Sam, and their daughter, Kayla, at 410 E. Park St., Archer, FL 32618.

William Canty's cartoons have appeared in many national magazines including *Saturday Evening Post, Better Homes & Gardens, Woman's World, National Review* and *Medical Economics*. His syndicated feature *All About Town*, runs in forty newspapers.

Dave Carpenter has been a full-time, freelance cartoonist and humorous illustrator since 1981. His cartoons have appeared in *Barron's, The Wall Street Journal, Forbes, Better Homes & Gardens, Good Housekeeping, Woman's World, First, The Saturday Evening Post* and numerous other publications. Dave can be reached at P.O. Box 520, Emmetsburg, IA 50536 or call 712-852-3725.

Diana Chapman has been a journalist for fourteen years, having worked at the *San Diego Union, The Los Angeles Copley Newspapers* and *The Los Angeles Times*. She specializes in human interest stories and is currently working on a book involving health issues, since she was diagnosed with multiple sclerosis in 1992. She has been married for nine years and has one son, Herbert "Ryan" Hart. She can be reached at P.O. Box 414, San Pedro, CA 90733 or call 310-548-1192.

Patricia Chasse has read many of the *Chicken Soup for the Soul* books. She was inspired by her daughter to write of the experiences she had following the death of her son. She has also been instrumental in establishing a chapter of Compassionate Friends Support Group in Millinocket, Maine, for bereaved parents. It has helped her and many parents survive the loss of a child.

Barbara Chesser, Ph.D., is a former professor and administrator at six different universities, author of four books, coauthor of six books, editor of numerous others and author of numerous research and popular articles in publications such as *Reader's Digest*. Teaching, research and writing assignments have taken Dr. Chesser to the Philippines, Greece, Turkey and Africa. She is currently president of a product development company that services a number of affiliated companies in the United States and in more than sixty countries worldwide. She can be reached at P.O. Box 7332, Waco, TX 76714, or by faxing 254-776-6331.

Samuel P. Clark has found truth in both tragedy and humor and ultimately understands that sharing is fundamental to his growth. He is the associate director of a social services agency, a city commissioner and a crisis intervention trainer. He lives with his wife, April, and daughter, Kayla, at 410 E. Park St., Archer, FL 32618.

Karen Cogan is a published author of over 125 inspirational stories and articles. In addition, she has authored three inspirational romance novels that can be previewed and ordered online through http://www.epub.com.

Cheryl L. Costello-Forshey is a freelance writer/songwriter and poet who offers her original poetry for any occasion as well as memorials, and a unique gift idea through her business, *Photographic Verse*. For more information, send a SASE to Photographic Verse, 36240 S. 16th Rd., Barnesville, OH 43713 or call 740-757-9217.

Wayne Cotton experienced a successful twenty-eight-year career as a life insurance agent. He now serves as a consultant and productivity coach to the insurance industry. Wayne has addressed over 800 industry audiences in 16 countries worldwide. Contact Wayne at 203-4445 Calgary Trail, Edmonton, Alberta, Canada T6H 5R7, or by calling 403-434-7615.

Mary Beth Danielson is an award-winning essayist (that sounds like she won a blue ribbon for bringing the cleanest cow to the county fair). She writes a weekly newspaper column that explores and exploits the drama of being a fortysomething Midwesterner. Do you have a publication that could use a new voice? Contact her at 139 Tera Lee Ct., Racine, WI 53402.

Dianne Demarcke resides near the small town of Lorette, Manitoba, Canada and has been a portrait photographer for over twenty years. She enjoys life on her five-acre property and loves to travel, dance, read and write.

Albert DiBartolomeo is the author of two novels, *The Vespers Tapes* (*Blood Confessions* in softcover) and *Fool's Gold*. He has published a number of short stories, memoirs and commentary pieces in publications such as *Italian Americana, Reader's Digest* and the *Philadelphia Inquirer*. He lives in Philadelphia, where he teaches at Drexel University.

Tyree Dillingham is currently a student at San Diego State University, with a double major in political science and international business. Tyree is always keeping herself busy with one or two jobs and is always first to participate in any community service activities. She can be reached at 2012 Linden Grove Way, Carmichael, CA 95608, or by calling 916-485-1767.

Kathleen Dixon likes to think of herself as a Christian adventurer. She raised her four children in rural Northern California on mostly minimum-wage jobs. In spite of the hard times, she says, "Life is supposed to be fun and exciting; if it's not, you're doing it wrong. Trust in God."

John Doll and his wife, Lanie, are presently living in the middle of a twenty-five-acre orange and avocado grove. Before his retirement in 1987, he did international marketing for one of Times Mirror's corporations. He is a freelance writer with a number of short stories published. His forte is nostalgia and memories. Originally he wrote special material for Lawrence Welk. He can be reached at 2377 Grand Ave., Fillmore, CA 93015 or call 805-524-3821.

Dorothy DuNard, a 1939 graduate of the University of Missouri Journalism School, was ad manager of The Bon Marche in Yakima, Washington, and of Parks Department Store in Columbia, Missouri, and ad representative for the Columbia *Daily Tribune*. A freelance writer, she has five children, six grandchildren and three great-grandchildren.

Melissa Eastham enjoys writing and reading great children's books and teaching second grade at N.W. Harllee Elementary School in Dallas, Texas. She is married to her high school sweetheart, Collyn, and they have a wonderfully talented three-year-old son, Colton. She hopes to one day publish some of her children's stories, but is content in the meantime with her small-town life in Red Oak, Texas. She can be reached at 972-576-3413 or via e-mail at MEastham.aol.com.

Ben Fanton is a freelance writer whose articles have appeared in *Reader's Digest, TV Guide, Nations Business* and roughly 200 other national publications. He often works in partnership with his wife, Barrie, a photographer.

John F. Flanagan Jr., has employed his leadership capabilities in multi-faceted careers in business, academia, government and military. He had fought a war, held operational P&L responsibilities, worked for the White House, taught in universities, counseled governments and has run for Congress. He now shares his experiences through his writings, interviews, and lectures in order to protect the foundations of America. His e-mail is JFFLAN@aol.com.

Brenda Gallardo was born in Kansas but grew up in Livermore, California. She lives there currently with her husband, Anastacio, daughter, Kimberly, and sons Joey and Justin. She balances her life between being a mother and a full-time secretary at a local middle school. In any spare time she may have, she enjoys reading, gardening and writing short stories. You can reach her at 510-449-1915.

Oliver Gaspirtz is a professional cartoonist and occasional writer. To order a copy of his latest book *A Treasury of Police Humor*, send a check or money order for $12.95 (plus $3.00 for S&H) to: Lincoln-Herndon Press, 818 South Dirksen Parkway, Springfield, IL 62703 or call 217-522-2732.

Nancy Sullivan Geng is a homemaker, mother and freelance writer. Her mailing address is Box 299, Hopkins, MN 55343.

Marlene T. Gerba has written occasional verse for over thirty years and recently completed her first manuscript entitled *Dancing With My Shadow*, yet it is not published yet. She is a gardener and floral designer and resides with her husband, four cats and a dog. She can be reached at 5101 S.E. Wilma Circle, Mailwaukie, OR 97222 or 503-654-2201.

Eva Harding, award-winning poet, is a member of the Poetry Society of Virginia and of The National League of American Pen Women. Her second book of poetry is in progress. She also writes short stories, both serious and humorous. She is listed in national and international editions of *Who's Who.* She can be reached at 312 Yale Drive, Alexandria, VA 22314.

Michael D. Hargrove is an author, trainer and professional speaker. He has conducted seminars and workshops for thousands of attendees on communication skills, state management skills, sales and management skills, team building and more. He can be reached through Bottom Line Underwriters, Inc., P.O. Box 1218, Lake Oswego, OR 97035, or by calling 888-697-8223. Visit him online at www.blueinc.com.

Jerry Harpt has served the public school system and counselor for thirty-two years. He has a regular newspaper column entitled *Challenging Our Limits* which deals with interpersonal motivation. He is currently working on his first book. He can be reached at N-3231 River Dr., Wallace, MI or call 906-863-8862.

Darlene Harrison is an inspirational writer and author of two books *Shared Journey* and *North of the Sky.* They are collections of her poems. She credits her inspiration and talent to the God of the Universe. She lives with her beloved cat, Bingo, in San Dimas, CA.

Jonny Hawkins is a nationally known cartoonist whose work has appeared in *The Saturday Evening Post, National Enquirer, Barron's* and over 175 other publications. His syndicated comic feature *Hi and Jinx* runs in many U.S. newspapers.

Margaret (Meg) Hill writes articles, short stories and young-adult books. Recent titles are *Coping with Family Expectations* (Rosen, 1990) and *So What Do I Do About Me?* (Teacher Ideas Press, Libraries Unlimited, Englewood, Colorado, 1993). Kirk is the pen name she uses when writing from the viewpoint of a teenage boy.

Tim Jordan, M.D., is a Behavioral Pediatrician, national speaker, author, husband, father, teacher, coach and owner/founder of self-esteem building summer camps. Tim aspires to be a national spokesperson for children and families. He has inspired parents, professionals and corporations with his warm, energetic, experiential presentations on parenting and work-family balance. You can reach Tim at 314-530-183 or e-mail Anne2U@aol.com.

Colleen Keefe and Shauna Dickey are now actively involved in awareness seminars for fellow students. Colleen is the president of Students Against Drunk Driving (SADD) and Shauna is the vice president. Both students are heading to college and speak to groups about the importance of being an organ donor. Any ideas or comments will be gratefully accepted. Contact them by writing to 18 Winter Street, Natick, MA 01760, or calling 508-655-5141.

Joe Kemp is pursuing a master's degree in human behavior studies. After spending twelve years as a city police officer, Joe has changed his career direction to continually strive to reach his full potential. He can be reached at 258 Wales Cres., Oakville, Ontario, Canada, L6L 3X7.

David Kettler is a full-time business owner, house-husband, father of three sons, charity volunteer, athlete, golfer and amateur poet. David resides in Southern California. He can be reached at 4811 Van Buren Blvd., Riverside, CA 92503, or by calling 909-359-4516.

Joe Kohl has been an internationally published magazine cartoonist and illustrator for over twenty-five years. His cartoons and designs also appear on numerous greeting cards, tee-shirts, mugs and books. Joe has several of his own cartoon books out. He can be reached via e-mail at joekohl@aol.com or visit his website at http://www.newl.com/jkohl.

Paula (Bachleda) Koskey has spent a few extremely long days— but far too many quick days—with her wonderful children, Jesse, HopeAnn and Luke. A speaker and freelance writer, she maintains her balance by eating chocolate, walking, listening to James Taylor and believing in miracles. Paula can be reached at 1173 Cambridge, Berkley, MI 48072.

Louise Ladd became a writer so she could go to work in her bathrobe if she wanted to. Her seventeen novels for young adults include *The Double Diamond Dude Ranch* series (Tor Books, 1998). For adults, she coedited *Sandy Dennis: A Personal Memoir* (Papier-Mache Press, 1997). Her first suspense novel is due out in 1999.

Mike Lipstock is a seventy-three-year-old optician who started writing after he retired. His work has appeared in close to one hundred magazines and four anthologies. He is listed in the *Directory of American Poets and Fiction Writers*.

Kevin Lumsdon is managing editor for *Hospitals & Health Networks*, a magazine for health care executives.

Mark Malott lives in Newport Beach, California, and works for Southland Corporation as a consultant. He grew up in the San Fernando Valley and went to Granada Hills High School. He graduated from George Fox University in Newberg, Oregon, with a bachelor's degree in business administration. He can be reached at 123 34th St., Apt. B, Newport Beach, CA 92663, or by calling 714-642-0247.

Deborah Roberto McDonald has a poem published in a book printed by the National Library of Poetry as well as a story in her local newspaper. She is the mother of two sons and has been in the international transportation business for over twenty years. She is a member of Lions Club International and participates in other community-based activities. Deborah plans to begin research for a book about adults who have lost a parent during childhood and the paths they take because of that loss. Writing is her hobby, and she likes to write about people and things that have touched her heart and soul.

Sherry Miller is a wife, mother and actress who genuinely enjoys reaching out to others. Years in drama ministry, a B.A. in Theatre Arts and stage experience have led to her current endeavor, Enlightening Theatrics. Her goal is to inspire students and their audiences in the areas of acceptance, love, ethics, trust and self-esteem. Sherry, available as a consultant and teacher, can be reached at 2907 Wellesley Ct., Fullerton, CA 92831.

Randy Loyd Mills has taught special education classes in Winnipeg, Manitoba, Salt Lake City, Utah, and North Bend, Washington. She is currently semi-retired so that she can enjoy a new facet of teaching—raising her two children, Kelsey and Cory. She can be reached at 2800 Brown Rd., Ferndale, WA 98248, or via e-mail at millsgang4@juno.com.

Beth Mullally is a newspaper columnist and reporter whose work in journalism has earned her twenty major writing awards in thirteen years. She is also a regular contributor to *Reader's Digest* and author of the book *The Best of Beth,* a collection of her nationwide readers' favorite columns and essays. She can be reached c/o *The Times Herald-Record,* 40 Mulberry St., Middletown, NY 10940, or by calling 914-343-2181 ext. 1450.

Christine Pisera Naman is a writer, mother, teacher and homemaker. She can be reached at 155 Glenwood Dr., Monroeville, PA, or by calling 412-374-0685.

Carol O'Connor, L.I.C.S.W., is a nationally known speaker on stress management and communications. She is also the author of *Remember When,* a book that provides a humorous look at change. Her expertise on issues related to grief and loss come from her work as a former hospice social work therapist. Carol can be reached at 43 Norgate Rd., Attleboro, MA 02703, or by calling 508-226-9537.

Terry O'Neal is a mother, grandmother and a Christian businesswoman. She is vice president of a corporation and works full time with her husband at their Fresno car dealership. Her passions are friendships and writing. She can be reached at 408 N. Blackstone, Fresno, CA 93701, by calling 209-485-6300, or via e-mail at hal@lightspeed.net.

Rulon Openshaw, a writer, lives in Los Angeles, the city where he was born, raised and shot. Despite a fondness for tropical climates, he continues to reside in L.A. because it is the center of the movie industry and has excellent Mexican restaurants. His e-mail address in RulonO@aol.com.

Rochelle Pennington is a freelance writer currently finishing her first book, *A Turning.* As a stay-at-home mother and wife, she is actively involved in Christian education and volunteer care for the terminally ill through Hospice Hope. She can be reached at N1911 Double D Road, Campbellsport, WI 53010, or by calling 414-533-5880.

Adeline Perkins is eighty years old and has four daughters and seven grandchildren. She cooked for twenty-six years at St. George Hospital and bought stamps by the hundreds for cards to shut-ins. She made phone calls to the ill, for the community chest and gave elder care for twenty years. Her mother was her inspiration.

Roy Popkin is a retired Red Cross Disaster Relief expert with a distinguished career in emergency management. As a writer, he has written books, magazine articles and numerous publications for The Red Cross and government agencies. He is now a writer-editor at the Environmental Protection Agency and a freelance consultant. He can be reached at 2111 Hanover St., Silver Spring, MD 20910.

Penny Porter is a mother of six and a grandmother of seven. She is a former teacher and school administrator. An award-winning writer, Penny is one of the most successful freelancers ever to hit *Reader's Digest*. Her fifteenth and sixteenth stories will appear in September and November. Penny has been published in a wide range of national magazines and is the author of three books. Her inspiration is rooted in the love of family and human values, which children of today need so desperately.

Duke Raymond is a freelance writer and has been published in several newspapers and magazines, as well as a columnist for a regional newsletter. He is also a writer/producer of several cable access video productions addressing oral and written family histories. He facilitates writing groups in the genre of nostalgia. You can reach him at 861 Liberty Bell Dr., Beaverton, OR 97006 or call 503-645-7912.

Dan Rosandich's cartoons appeared in *Mother's Soul* and *Christian Soul*. He is also under contract with One On One Computer Training in Addison, Illinois, drawing cover illustrations for their twenty-six training manuals. Under contract with the World Fencing Data Center, he draws the *Pete and Jake* cartoon for *World Fence News*, chronicling the adventures of two bumbling fence company workers. Dan will fax samples to anyone interested in illustrations for T-shirts, company newsletters, magazines and books. Call and fax him at 906-482-6234.

Carmen Richardson Rutlen decided it was time to dream loud. Writing is her dream. She is working on her first book, *Dancing Naked . . . In Fuzzy Red Slippers*. She can be reached at Richard Rutlen Advertising, 236 N. Santa Cruz Ave., Ste. 206, Los Gatos, CA 95030 or by calling 408-354-4272.

Terry Savoie is a retired U.S. Air Force cmsgt. He served for twenty-five years and in seven foreign countries. He is an entertaining public speaker who regularly speaks to active-duty people and high school students. Terry is presently an aerospace science instructor with JROTC at Central High School in San Angelo, Texas. He can be reached at 1428 S. Van Buren, San Angelo, TX, or by calling 915-658-1808.

Jack Schlatter is a well-known speaker, writer and recording personality. A frequent contributor to *Chicken Soup for the Soul*, who can be heard and seen on the audio and video version of the inspired series and stars in the best-selling *Gifts by the Side of the Road* by Career Track. Jack's listed in *Who's Who*

Among Teachers in America and his talks are filled with humor, wisdom and inspiration. He can be contacted at Show Path Productions, P.O. Box 3126, Grand Junction, CO 81502.

Priscilla Stenger is proud of her four daughters and five grandchildren. Besides enjoying time with family, she volunteers as parish retreat coordinator at church. She enjoys participating in small faith-sharing groups. Priscilla feels drawn to writing about experiences that have touched her life, such as her story "Department Store Angel."

Angela Sturgill is a third-year pre-med student at the University of Colorado in Boulder. She plans to get her master's degree in Deaf Education before entering medical school. She enjoys hiking, dancing, going to the movies and spending time with her cats. Angela is currently single and waiting for that special someone. She can be reached at 665 Manhattan Dr. #202, by calling 303-494-2822, or via e-mail at sturgill@ucsub.colorado.edu.

Gerald J. Sullivan says that reading people's personal stories has always touched him. He has one hope that he can touch others. As a very busy man, he never suspected what would happen to him. As sad as his situation appears, it has created beauty within him that is difficult to explain.

Gwen Belson Taylor is an Australian poetry writer who has published two volumes of poetry, *Who Loves the Sun* and *The Stars Look Down*. She was a primary school teacher for twenty-five years. "Blessed Are the Pure in Heart" was written about her first great-grandson. She can be reached at 40 Moolabar Street, Morning Side, Brisbane, Queensland, Australia.

Bob Thomas is the owner of Kristi's Gallery in Swansboro, North Carolina. After thirteen years as an executive recruiter, he decided to pursue a less stressful lifestyle and move to the North Carolina coast. His gallery represents over 180 artists and craftspeople from across the United States. Since his move to the coast, he has discovered a love of writing and publishes his own in-house monthly newsletter, mainly for his own entertainment! He can be reached at P.O. Box 2066, Swansboro, NC 28584, or by calling 910-326-7222.

S. Turkaly is an amateur writer who also enjoys archaeology and paleontology.

Susan Union is a freelance writer who regularly contributes to magazines and newspapers. She is completing her first novel, a mystery. She holds a degree in finance and with her husband owns a real estate company in San Diego. Susan participates in competitive horse showing and snow skiing. She can be reached at P.O. Box 9561, Rancho Santa Fe, CA 92067, or via e-mail at unionwest@aol.com.

Henry Matthew Ward is a Realtor and home builder in Murfreesboro, Tennessee. His hobbies are playing the trumpet in civic bands and writing poetry and short stories. He can be reached at 615-890-2178, or via e-mail at MATTWARD@aol.com.

David L. Weatherford, Ph.D., is a child psychologist who has published a book and numerous articles on child development, developmental disabilities and parenting. David himself is an ex-child who did his childhood tenure under the tutelage of Bill and Jackie Weatherford, his parents, in Hopkinsville, Kentucky. In gratitude for helping him survive the foolishness of his youth (he is currently working through adult foolishness on his own), David says to his parents, "Many have inspired my writing, but you have inspired my living." Write to David at 1658 Doubletree Lane, Nashville, TN 37217.

Marion Bond West has written for *Guideposts* for twenty-five years and is a contributing editor. The author of six books, including *The Nevertheless Principle,* she is also an inspirational speaker on subjects such as When Women Hurt and Living Fear-Free. She can be reached at 1330 DeAndra Dr., Watkinsville, GA 30677, or by calling 706-353-6523.

Sharon Whitley, a freelance writer/editor, is a former special education teacher. Her work has appeared in *Reader's Digest* (eighteen international editions), *Los Angeles Times Magazine, A 4th Course of Chicken Soup for the Soul* and *Chicken Soup for the Teenage Soul.* She can be reached at 5666 Meredith Ave., San Diego, CA 92120 or call 609-583-7346.

Gwyn Williams is director of music for the Hazel Green United Methodist Church near Huntsville, Alabama, where she resides with her husband and two children. The writing and telling of true, inspirational stories have long been hobbies and the source of great joy for her.

Jacqueline Zabresky has been a Registered Nurse for twenty years and is currently a third-year law student. She has shared her experience, insights and knowledge in writing and speaking engagements with health care professionals and the general public. Jacqueline looks forward to receiving your comments and inquiries at P.O. Box 298, Dallas, Pennsylvania 18612, or by calling 717-675-4396.

Permissions *(continued from page iv)*

Rufus. Reprinted by permission of Carmen Richardson Rutlen. ©1997 Carmen Richardson Rutlen.

One Wing and a Prayer and *Scarecrow.* Reprinted by permission of Penny Porter. ©1997 Penny Porter.

Nonny. Reprinted by permission of Eva Unga. ©1997 Eva Unga. Excerpted from *Woman's World Magazine.*

The Light Was On, The Beloved, Karen, Do You Know Him? The Crooked Smile, Rodeo Joe, Soccer Balls and Violins and *A Match Made in Heaven.* Reprinted by permission of James C. Brown, M.D. ©1997 James C. Brown, M.D.

Best Friends Forever. Reprinted by permission of Louise Ladd. ©1997 Louise Ladd.

The Giving Trees. Reprinted by permission of Kathleen Dixon. ©1997 Kathleen Dixon.

An Elf's Tale. Reprinted by permission of Tyree Dillingham. ©1997 Tyree Dillingham.

Ben and Virginia. Reprinted by permission of Gwyn Williams. ©1997 Gwyn Williams.

Don't Hope, Friend . . . Decide! Reprinted by permission of Michael Hargrove. ©1997 Michael Hargrove.

Love That Lasts. Reprinted by permission of Annette Paxman Bowen. ©1997 Annette Paxman Bowen.

The Decade Diary: A Love Story. Reprinted by permission of Henry Matthew Ward. ©1997 Henry Matthew Ward.

Could You Have Loved as Much? By Bob Considine, March 1959. Reprinted with permission from *Guideposts* Magazine. ©1959, *Guideposts* Magazine, Carmel, NY 10512.

A Gift-Wrapped Memory. Reprinted by permission of Dorothy DuNard. ©1979 Dorothy DuNard. First appeared in *Unity* Magazine.

A Tribute to Gramps. Reprinted by permission of Dana O'Connor and Melissa Levin. ©1997 Dana O'Connor and Melissa Levin.

The Canarsie Rose. Reprinted by permission of Mike Lipstock. ©1997 Mike Lipstock.

The Pitcher. Reprinted by permission of Beth Mullally. ©1993 Beth Mullally. First appeared in the Times Herald-Record, 1993.

Hall of Fame Dad. Reprinted by permission of Ben Fanton and the 1995 *Reader's Digest.* ©1995 Ben Fanton.

The Puzzle. Reprinted by permission of Jerry Gale. ©1997 Jerry Gale.

My Dad's Hands. Reprinted by permission of David Kettler. ©1997 David Kettler.

One Small Stone, Unforgotten, The Thing About Goldfish and *The Funeral.* Reprinted by permission of Marsha Arons. ©1997 Marsha Arons.

Sending Kids Off to School. Reprinted by permission of Susan Union. ©1997 Susan Union.

Let's Go Bug Hunting More Often. Reprinted by permission of Barbara Chesser, Ph.D. ©1997 Barbara Chesser, Ph.D.

A Mother's Day Review. Reprinted by permission of Paula (Bachleda) Koskey. ©1997 Paula (Bachleda) Koskey.

What I Want. Edgar Guest. Public Domain.

My Dad. Reprinted by permission of Brenda Gallardo. ©1997 Brenda Gallardo.

Father's Day. Reprinted by permission of Sherry Miller. ©1997 Sherry Miller.

A Lesson from My Son. Reprinted by permission of Kathleen Beaulieu. ©1997 Kathleen Beaulieu.

Blessed Are the Pure in Heart. Reprinted by permission of Gwen Belson Taylor. ©1997 Gwen Belson Taylor.

Slender Thread. Reprinted by permission of Karen Cogan. ©1997 Karen Cogan.

Neither Have I. Reprinted by permission of Rochelle M. Pennington. ©1997 Rochelle M. Pennington.

The Day We Became Brothers. First printed in the June 1997 *Reader's Digest.* Reprinted by permission of Ellen Levine Literary Agency. Copyright ©1996 by Albert DiBartolomeo.

Drop Earrings. Reprinted by permission of Nancy Sullivan Geng. Published in *Focus on the Family.* ©1996 Nancy Sullivan Geng.

A Genius For Loving. By Mary Ann Bird, January 1985. Reprinted with permission from *Guideposts* Magazine. ©1985, *Guideposts* Magazine, Carmel, NY 10512.

Thank You for Changing My Life. Reprinted by permission of Randy Loyd Mills. ©1997 Randy Loyd Mills.

When Children Learn. Reprinted by permission of David L. Weatherford. ©1996 David L. Weatherford.

Academic Excellence Begins with a '51 Studebaker. Reprinted by permission of Terry A. Savoie. ©1996 Terry A. Savoie.

The Second Mile. Reprinted by permission of John F. Flanagan Jr. Published in *The American Legion.* ©1995 John F. Flanagan Jr.

Do You Disciple? Reprinted by permission of Christine Pisera Naman. ©1997 Christine Pisera Naman.

It's a House . . . It's a Cow . . . It's Ms. Burk! Reprinted by permission of April Burk. ©1994 April Burk. First appeared in *Mom's Network News.*

What Color Are You? Reprinted by permission of Melissa D. Strong Eastham. ©1997 Melissa D. Strong Eastham.

Tommy's Shoes. Reprinted by permission of Samuel P. Clark. ©1993 Samuel P. Clark. First appeared in *In My Shoes.*

Broken Days. Reprinted by permission of Mary Beth Danielson. ©1997 Mary Beth Danielson.

Every Loss Is a Mini-Death. Reprinted by permission of Carol O'Connor. ©1997 Carol O'Connor.

Keeping the Connection. Reprinted by permission of Patricia Chasse. ©1997 Patricia Chasse.

Love Letters. Reprinted by permission of Kevin Lumsdon. ©1997 Kevin Lumsdon.

Crying's Okay. Reprinted by permission of Kirk Hill. ©1997 Kirk Hill.

A Blanket for a Friend. Reprinted by permission of Shauna Dickey and Colleen Keefe. ©1997 Shauna Dickey and Colleen Keefe.

When No Words Seem Appropriate. Permission granted by Ann Landers and Creators Syndicate.

The Rose with No Thorns. Reprinted by permission of Eva Harding. ©1997 Eva Harding.

The Butterfly Gift. Reprinted by permission of Wayne Cotton. ©1997 Wayne Cotton.

Action Hero. Reprinted by permission of Rulon Openshaw. ©1997 Rulon Openshaw.

Who Was That Masked Man? Reprinted by permission of Robert R. Thomas. ©1997 Robert R. Thomas.

In a Cathedral of Fence Posts and Harleys. Reprinted by permission of Reverend Neil Parker. ©1997 Reverend Neil Parker. Reprinted from *United Church Observer.*

Jackie Robinson and Me. By Harold "Pee Wee" Reese, September 1997. Reprinted with permission from *Guideposts* Magazine. ©1997, *Guideposts* Magazine, Carmel, NY 10512.

Department Store Angel. Reprinted by permission of Priscilla Stenger. ©1997 Priscilla Stenger.

"Hey Nurse . . . Thanks." Used with permission from Jacqueline Zabresky, R.N.: *Hey Nurse . . . Thanks, Nursing 93* 23 (8):49, ©Springhouse Corporation.

The Little Black Box. Reprinted by permission of Deborah Roberto McDonald. ©1997 Deborah Roberto McDonald.

Dinner Out. Reprinted by permission of Duke Raymond. ©1997 Duke Raymond.

Sudden Inspiration

For the first time ever, you can enjoy a batch of new "short" stories—each one no more than two pages long. This delectable gem is chock-full of insightful cartoons, inspirations and uplifting messages. #4215—$8.95

The very best short stories from *Chicken Soup for the Soul, A 2nd Helping* and *A 3rd Serving* are right at your fingertips. This single-serving volume is filled with morsels of wisdom, teaspoons of love and sweet pinches of heartwarming goodness. #4142—$8.95

This personal journal provides you with a unique place to create your own magic. Neatly lined blank pages are interspersed with words of encouragement giving you a special place to record your day's activities, plans, goals and dreams. #4843, hardcover—$12.95

Available in bookstores everywhere or call **1-800-441-5569** for Visa or MasterCard orders. Prices do not include shipping and handling. Your response code is **CCS**.

New from the *Chicken Soup for the Soul*® Series

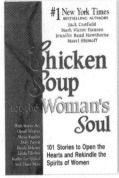
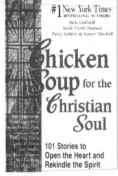
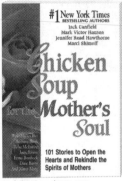

Books to Nurture Your Body & Soul!

PUPPIES FOR SALE and Other Inspirational Tales

A "Litter" of Stories & Anecdotes That Hug the Heart & Snuggle the Soul

DAN CLARK

One of the best-loved storytellers from the

#1 New York Times Bestseller
Chicken Soup for the Soul

with
Michael Gale

This anthology of entertaining and emotionally uplifting stories is written and compiled by Dan Clark, one of the most popular primary contributing authors to the *New York Times* bestselling *Chicken Soup for the Soul* series. The eponymous story from which the author has taken the title *Puppies for Sale and Other Inspirational Tales* is one of the most beloved stories from the original *Chicken Soup for the Soul* book. Starting with this story's powerful message of understanding, Clark follows it with nearly 300 unforgettable tales that lift readers up and pull at their heartstrings. These short but powerful messages will fill readers with joy and love, whether they read one story each day or the entire book in one sitting.

1-55874-452-5, 365 pp., 5½ x 8½, trade paper..$12.95
1-55874-469-X, 365 pp., 5½ x 8½, hardcover...$24.00

Available in bookstores everywhere or call 1-800-441-5569 for Visa or MasterCard orders. Prices do not include shipping and handling. Your response code is **CCS**.

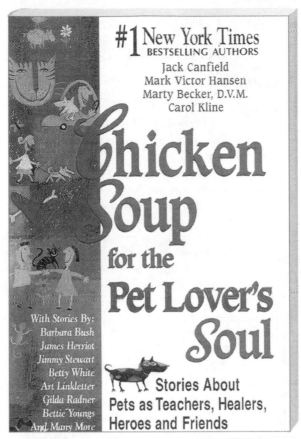

Chicken Soup for the Pet Lover's Soul®

Jack Canfield, Mark Victor Hansen, Martin Becker, D.V.M. & Carol Kline

Like the bestselling *Chicken Soup for the Soul* books, animals bring out the goodness, humanity and optimism in people and speak directly to our souls. This joyous, inspiring and entertaining collection relates the unique bonds between animals and the people whose lives they've changed. Packed with celebrity pet-lore—this book relates the unconditional love, loyalty, courage and companionship that only animals possess.

Code 5718, paperback, $12.95 • Code 5726, hardcover $24.00
Code 5742, one 70-minute CD, $11.95
Code 5734, one 90-minute audiocassette, $9.95

Available at bookstores everywhere or call 1-800-441-5569 for Visa or MasterCard orders. Prices do not include shipping and handling. Your response code is **CCS**.

Books from *Chicken Soup for the Soul*® Contributing Author
Bettie Youngs, Ph.D.

Taste-Berry Tales
Stories to Lift the Spirit, Fill the Heart and Feed the Soul

In a time when many of us have stopped believing in the goodness of humanity, we need to remind ourselves that though there is dissonance in the world, there is even more peace, kindness and love. Youngs inspires readers with 25 poignant short stories of real-life people who make a difference in the lives of others. These individuals, by their example, show us how to use the events of daily life to improve the world we live in and the lives of others with whom we share it. The *Richardella-dulcisica*, better known as the taste-berry, causes the taste buds to experience all food, even distasteful food, as sweet and delicious.

Code 5475, $11.95 • Code 5483, hardcover, $24.00

Values from the Heartland

Readers will discover the deeper side of integrity, commitment, honor, self-discipline, connection and character in this beautiful collection of poignant stories. It inspires us to remember that what is enriching and lasting in life is often the result of long-term investments in the people we love and care about. • Code 3359, $11.95

Code 3340, hardcover, $22.00

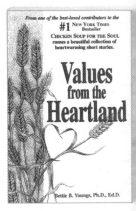

Gifts of the Heart

Youngs inspires readers with 27 real-life parables. These actual life lessons are genuine, potent and precious, and show the process of the heart at work. All show the path to greater tolerance, acceptance, patience, grace, kindness and forgiveness.

Code 4193, $11.95

Code 4509, hardcover, $24.00